THE MAN WHO CRIED GENOCIDE

William L. Patterson in 1940's.

The Man Who Cried Genocide

An Autobiography

by William L. Patterson

INTERNATIONAL PUBLISHERS

New York

Library of Congress Catalog Card Number: 78-148516

SBN 7178-0305-8 (cloth); 7178-0306-6 (paperback)

Printed in the United States of America

Contents

Receiving award from Ben Gold, President of the International Fur &
Leather Workers Union, 1952—"In recognition of your devotion to the
cause of Constitutional rights and for outstanding contributions in the
struggle against genocide."

Foreword

IN THESE pages I look back over nearly eight decades of my life, in an attempt to record one Black man's journey through the jungles of bigotry in this land. I am not unaware of my own relative good fortune—I did get enough formal education to acquire a law degree, and I have found fulfillment in family, friends, associates and in work. Nevertheless, I have never been able to escape or forget the pervasive racism that poisons the air. Son of a slave mother who had made her hazardous and heroic way from the South of her bondage to the West Coast, I could no more evade the clash with racism than a fish could live out of water.

My color and my family's poverty made the attainment of a law degree an arduous task—interrupted by a variety of jobs, including several voyages abroad as a seaman. Later, practicing law in the teeming streets of Harlem, I got the full impact of the brutal treatment perpetrated upon the Black people— and its ravages. I found I could not in good conscience continue in the practice of law for personal profit, and before long I had embarked on another educational process—one that was to prepare me to serve in the crucial civil rights and political struggles of our time.

As it happened, it was in the historic campaign to save two white men, Sacco and Vanzetti, that I first joined actively with the progressive men and women who were participating in the struggle. My closest associates, it turned out, were Communists, and I began to sense that the conscience of man has no color. My cumulative indignation at racial injustice was augmented by this spectacle of class injustice. How implacably the Commonwealth of Massachusetts wreaked its vengeance against a poor shoemaker and a fish peddler—because they dared to be radicals! Ignoring the outraged cries of millions of decent people throughout the world, ignoring the lack of evidence to prove their case, the state and the prosecutors put two Italian workers to death. And the world marvelled at the courage and dignity with which they met their fate.

It began to dawn on me that the schools I had attended were not in the slightest concerned about the basic causes of injustice or racial persecution. Indeed, they dealt in euphemisms and misinformation. A great majority of journalists, officials, politicians, authors—sharing the comforts and immunities of the ruling class—were apologists locked into the conspiracy to obscure the truth about the persecution of Black men, their history, their contributions to America. Few writers understood the destructive impact of racism on both the Black and the white people of our country, threatening its very survival.

With the help of my new progressive and Communist friends, I began to explore the roots of society's most rampant diseases—racism and exploitation. They lay deep in the imperative for continuing profit and power among those who controlled our economy, our legal system, our government. As time went on, it became crystal-clear to me that the horrors of color persecution and poverty could only be fully grappled with in a struggle against the economic and social forces that had spawned them. In my special concern with the oppression of Black men and women, I felt it was essential to achieve unity between Black and white workers—nothing was more certain than that the powers that be were concerned with preventing that unity at all costs.

If, in these pages, I direct my sharpest barbs against racism, it is because I could not get away from it—it was my constant and unwanted companion. How could I possibly speak dispassionately of the crimes committed in its name? But the military-industrial-governmental complex lays heavy burdens on other minority peoples as well as on white workers, turning them, periodically or chronically into jobless, homeless expatriates in a land of plenty. To me, the only hope lay in socialism—the only system that had shown itself capable of ending the terrible contradictions of a profit society. When I saw that the Communist Party was taking the lead in the struggle for the rights of minorities and of labor, exposing the role of imperialism in conquest and war, I found that my constant concern with the racist issue became an integral part of the broader struggle for human rights everywhere.

If Uncle Sam has made my color the dominating factor in my personal story and the central theme of this book, I have been far from a stranger to all the other struggles for justice of this half-century. The number of years one man has lived, his intellectual growth, his political dedication are, however, not alone decisive—fierce, persistent and relentless battle by all who want freedom and love justice must be waged unremittingly. The cumulative damage sustained by the bodies and minds of people too long abused must be mitigated, must be exposed. New and insidious forms of lynching, of genocide creep in through the back door even when some small degree of progress has been achieved and token opportunities won.

In defending the victims of oppression and legal lynching during the 30's and 40's, the organizations with which I was identified became deeply involved in a long procession of campaigns—some of them of world-wide impact. The Scottsboro Boys, Willie McGee, the Martinsville Seven, uncounted "little Scottsboro cases" absorbed our energies as we worked to get the facts before the public, to develop the mass action without which legal justice was a will-o'-the-wisp. Cases like these, under the aegis of either the International Defense or later, the Civil Rights Congress, which I headed, occupied my life during these years.

We had lived through the depression of '29, with its evictions, rent strikes, Hoovervilles, hunger marches—in all of
which I and my Party took an active part—organizing, teaching, writing, publishing, speaking. Through these crowded
days, through the months and years of inquisitions and jailings
and abuse, I continued to study the science of Marxism-
Leninism both here and in the Soviet Union and to deepen my
understanding of the class struggle.

The period ushered in by the defeat of Hitler and his racist
myths of blond Aryan supremacy marked one of the great
turning points of history. Millions of people in Europe and
Asia gained their political freedom; the victory of the Allies
(with the immeasurable contribution in lives and treasure from
the Soviet Union) seemed to prepare the way for a better era.
The United Nations was established with its aim " to reaffirm
faith in fundamental rights, in the dignity and worth of the
human person, in the equal rights of men and women."

The trial of the German war criminals had been held; for the
first time in history the instigators of an aggressive war were
placed in the dock as criminals. The Black soldiers who had
helped smash the Hitler war machine and the Blacks at home
felt there was some hope that the myths of white superiority
were on their way out. A good part of the content of Justice
Jackson's opening address to the UN about the Nazi war
criminals could apply equally to the racists in our own
country.

But the Black soldiers were soon disillusioned; even while
still in uniform, they were lynched when they demanded
recognition and respect for their constitutional rights. Black
workers were the first to be fired, and their protests were stifled
by the stark terror incited by the tycoons who controlled big
business and the media of propaganda. And no administrative
branch of the government, the judiciary nor the legislature ever
made any serious effort to defend the victims.

The civil rights fights of the post World War II era were in
many cases linked with these protest struggles and with the
efforts made by various defense organizations and groups to

protect the lives of Black men, women and youth victimized by
false accusations of rape and other crimes. No Black man could
expect even a semblance of legal justice in or out of the South
(nor could union organizers nor civil rights workers). One of
the tactics of our struggle was confirmed beyond all doubt—
legal defense was almost useless in itself, since officers of the
law were so often implicated in the indiscriminate murder of
Black men in the South. It was proved beyond doubt that mass
indignation and protest action had to be mobilized in over-
whelming degree to make any dent at all in the solid front of
blind bigotry. Such demonstrations do not guarantee a people's justice, but without them the hope is slim indeed.

These methods were, of course, the forerunners of today's
sit-ins, strikes, protest marches, peace rallies. Few organizations would now plan a campaign that did not include mass
protests in various forms. The social forces engaged in the
fiercely fought civil rights battles of the 40's and 50's still
confront each other. At stake in many a legal battle there still is
the liberation of the Black man, his very survival, as harsh
sentences, prohibitive bail, naked murder are meted out to the
militants.

The cry of genocide is raised once again, as it was in 1951 by
the Civil Rights Congress, under whose aegis Paul Robeson
led a delegation to present the petition, *We Charge Genocide:
The Crime of Government Against the Negro People* to the
Secretariat of the UN in New York, while I did the same to the
UN General Assembly then meeting in Paris. The petition was
a detailed documentation of hundreds of cases of murder,
bombing, torture of Black nationals in the United States. It
dealt unsparingly with "mass murder on the score of race that
had been sanctified by law" and it stated "never have so many
individuals been so ruthlessly destroyed amid so many tributes
to the sacredness of the individual."

We live in a land into whose development the blood and
sweat of millions of Black men have, for centuries, been
poured. As slaves, these men made cotton king, felled forests,
built railroads and cities. Now their children must spend their

lives in slums and ghettos. They have never been permitted to
enjoy the feeling of belonging to the nation their fathers helped
to build and mold. Americans by birth and historical development, they will accept nothing less than equality for all.

Crispus Attucks, a Black freeman, was one of the first to die
for liberty. Black slaves and freemen fought under George
Washington and Lafayette throughout the Revolutionary War.
"Give us this day," their children say, "the equality of rights
we have won on blood-drenched battlefields, fighting for those
who now rule this country. Give us this day the inalienable
rights denied us as human beings and the civil rights denied us
as citizens."

In 1976 this country will celebrate the 200th anniversary of
its independence. Will we celebrate it as one nation or as a
nation with the majority of Blacks still psychologically and
economically enslaved, and the great majority of whites dehumanized by their own prolonged acceptance and participation
in this monstrous wrong?

Unless there is equality of opportunity and rights for all, the
"law and order" of ruling class America becomes tyranny; the
protest actions of those who are denied their rights are called
"lawlessness," and their suppression becomes the order of the
day. The constitutional basis for a legal struggle for redress of
grievances is destroyed, and the ghettos into which the exploited, oppressed Black and other minorities have been herd-
ed become occupied territory on which every known degradation can be grafted.

An ideological struggle is being waged throughout the world
for the minds of men; the fight against racism becomes an
integral part of the fight for peace and freedom throughout the
world. The socialist sector of the world has proven how
ignorance and poverty can be overcome for the millions, and
devotes its energies to trying to build a society in which there
will be an end to war and racism and exploitation.

Today, as liberation struggles multiply throughout the
world, we still live in the shadow of the atomic bomb; Vietnam,
one of the cruelest wars in the history of the United States,

robs our people of resources needed desperately to heal the sick, educate our children, house our homeless—while it engages in the genocidal destruction of the Indochinese peoples. The issues have been more sharply drawn; we see on all hands the collapse of public and private services and the pollution of our continent. We see our country's plots to thwart peoples' revolutions wherever they raise their heads, to make the whole earth subject to its domination. But the enemy is not invincible. The youth of the land and the oppressed more and more reject the false and murderous standards foisted upon them; the socialist states act as a powerful counterbalance to imperialist depradations.

But it was never more imperative that we direct our energies through organized political channels. Millions of our fellow-Americans are still entrapped in the web of white supremacy, as well as in the illusion that the United States fights wars only in defense of democracy. The majority of such people can still be won for the fight against racism and imperialism—especially if they are made to realize that their own interests are more and more jeopardized by unemployment, inflation, suppression of dissent as a result of these policies.

May the record of my experiences in this battle add some useful first-hand evidence from one man who was deeply involved. The government and its institutions still belong of right to the people, as Abraham Lincoln said. But they must take it over. If I have dwelt largely upon my identity as a Black man profoundly concerned with the agony of my race, it is because I know that a decisive part of the rebellion against tyranny will emanate from the most oppressed. Born out of struggle, they have an affinity with all who fight for the liberation of mankind.

So I hope I have brought you some news of the battle as it was waged for a half century—in preparation for the greater struggles which are as inevitable as the dawn.

—THE AUTHOR

New York, November 1970.

Mary Galt Patterson, my Mother, and James Edward Patterson, my Father.

CHAPTER 1

The Family From Which I Came

MY MOTHER often talked to us about her childhood on the Virginia plantation where she was born as a slave in 1850 and had lived until she was ten. It was in cotton lands not far from Norfolk—she knew that because her grandfather, who often drove to the "big city," was seldom gone for long. Her father, William Galt, was a slave who belonged to the owner of an adjacent plantation, and as a child she saw very little of him. As coachman for his master—who was also his father—he drove back and forth on visits to the Turner plantation, where he met and later married my grandmother, Elizabeth Mary Turner.

The big house was set back from the magnolia-lined plantation road leading to the main highway to Norfolk. But my mother lived in the slave quarters, which were quite some distance back from the manor house. Here, separated from her mother and grandmother, she lived with older slave women who were part of the crew that served the master's immediate household.

My grandmother was personal maid to the white wife of her father and master; my great-grandmother was head of the house slaves and also her owner's slave woman (at that time the word "mistress" was not used in this sense). My mother had learned of her grandmother's role from gossip among the field hands, but it was beyond her to question the morality of this situation. Morality played no part in the relationships between white slaveowners and their slave women—the masters' morals were class morals in judging the slave system or their own personal relations with slaves.

According to the gossip, my great-grandmother first came to the notice of the big house through her ability as a cook. In line with the general mistreatment of field hands—rags for clothing, shacks for living quarters, cheap and primitive medication—they were never well fed. When my mother's grandmother was living among the field slaves, she got the slaves who slaughtered and cut up the hogs and cattle to bring her the entrails, hooves, heads and other "throwaway" parts, along with similar leftovers from chicken killings. Somehow she had acquired great skill in the use of herbs for cooking as well as for healing. She converted the leftovers into such tasty dishes that she soon gained a reputation as the best cook on the plantation. Before long she was ordered into the big house to cook for the master's family. She was an attractive woman and, as the story goes, the master found more than her cooking to his taste. Eventually she gave birth to three of his children.

The field hands, according to my mother, said that Cap'n Turner's wife knew of the relationship—it would have been something in the nature of a miracle had she not known. But there was little or nothing she could do about it and, after all, the slave mother and her children were no economic threat to her.

Stable family relations were, obviously, almost impossible among slaves, and this enforced instability was conveniently put down as being inherently characteristic of Black people. The lie was useful and incredibly persistent—it became a substantial part of the myth of white superiority.

Slave conditions such as these dominated my mother's life until the tensions that were to explode into the Civil War began to build up toward a climax. Slave uprisings were launched with increasing frequency and, following their example, the

Abolitionists strengthened and sharpened their activities, and John Brown launched his ill-starred attempt to seize Harpers Ferry, in October 1858.

Despite his slaveowner's morality, great-grandfather Turner revealed a sense of responsibility toward his families—both Black and white. He recognized the danger of war to his children, as did his friend Galt, and he believed in the right of a master to free his slaves. Before the war broke out, he managed to move his families away from the land that was destined to be drenched in blood. He sent his white family north to Bridgeport, Connecticut; the Black west to California. My grandfather Galt sent his son along with them.

My great-grandmother, then an old woman, stayed behind with the father of her children—they must have been deeply attached to one another. My grandmother was given the responsibility of settling her white relatives in New England. The trust reposed in her was not an uncommon thing. Her master obviously had great faith in his dark-skinned daughter's ability to take care of duties like these.

Those who were sent on the Westward trek went by way of Panama and from there across the Isthmus. The trip down the Atlantic Coast may have been more or less routine but crossing the Isthmus along a narrow, single-track line must have been much more difficult. At Colon on the Pacific side, the freed men and women took a ship to San Francisco—a long and hazardous trip.

It is likely that the Black Galts and Turners were sent to California by way of Panama to avoid the overland trek through Indian territory as well as to escape the fugitive slave hunters who plied their lucrative trade beyond the Eastern seaboard.

Here was a small group of Black men, women and young people just out of slavery traveling thousands of miles to find what was to them dearer than life—freedom. The courage and ingenuity of these Black Americans was profoundly impressive, as was that of the thousands of Afro-Americans who helped build the "Underground Railroad" before the Civil War and managed to escape to northern cities and Canada.

My mother, Mary Galt, was about five-feet-three in height. Her complexion was brownish yellow; her hair wavy, with streaks of gray as she grew older. Strong and energetic, she was a fighter when she knew what the fight was about. She was ten when her grandfather sent his liberated Black children west.

Originally there were four children in our immediate family. My sister Alberta was the child of my mother's marriage to Charles Postles, who came west from North Carolina. He died shortly after Alberta was born, and my mother subsequently married James Edward Patterson.

My father was born in the British West Indies, in Kingston, capital of the island of St. Vincent. His mother, he told us, was a Carib Indian; his father, a full-blooded African. Actually he knew little enough about either of his parents, at times referring to his mother as a kind of witch doctor. He said she was called Lady Estridge—probably the name of the British family for whom she worked. So far as he knew, his parents were never married; he often spoke bitterly of bastardy as if he were painfully affected by the thought of it.

At an early age my father left his birthplace. There was nothing for him in St. Vincent; the poverty of the mass of the people drove him to seek his fortune on the seven seas. He became an able-bodied seaman. Soon however he left the deck for a place in the galley, became a good cook, then a chef. In later years he was the first black steward ever hired by the Pacific Mail Steamship Company.

As I knew him, father was a dark-skinned man, not more than five-feet-five-inches tall; he could not have weighed more than 135 pounds. His face was ascetic and kindly and did not reveal the intense devotion he gave to his religious beliefs— nor the terrible temper that was aroused when he was crossed.

My father found his fortune on the Pacific Coast despite his color. As steward on a Chinese clipper, he was able to participate in the lucrative racket of smuggling Chinese into

San Francisco. (This was after Congress passed the Chinese Exclusion Act, later signed by President Chester A. Arthur, in 1882.)

With the money he had made from smuggling, my father bought a house on Mason Street in San Francisco. It was about then that he met and married my mother, a widow in her late thirties. My brothers and I were born in what was called "the smuggler's house." Although the San Francisco earthquake and fire destroyed the official birth records, I believe my correct birth date is August 27, 1891.

When I was about five years old, my father became a Seventh Day Adventist. I do not know how or why this came about. He was not a citizen of the United States. He was a Black man in what must have seemed a white man's world. Whether he sought a security beyond money; whether he found something in the Adventist practices and ideas of the hereafter with which he could identify, I have no idea.

I recall a story he often told about having been swept overboard in the Indian Ocean and having been carried back on board his ship by another huge wave. He attributed this miracle to God's mercy. Perhaps the superstitions entertained by so many seafaring men had some effect upon him. At any rate, God was now elevated to the place that Queen Victoria had occupied in my father's mind, and the life of our family underwent a drastic change.

The house on Mason Street was sold; all we possessed of worldly goods was turned into cash, and, along with these gifts, my father dedicated his life to the church. The uprooted family was moved across the bay to Oakland, on Myrtle Street near 23rd. My father became an Adventist missionary and went off to the island of Tahiti, with the family left to survive as best it could. Thereafter his missionary work carried him away for years at a time. My father quite naturally wanted his family to follow the road he had chosen; if they could not follow, he could not turn back. He took the Bible literally, studying it night and day. I was too young to understand him then, and even now I cannot criticize him. Undoubtedly, he found identity, atonement for his "sins" and hope for a place of refuge after death.

I can only regard him as a "loner," made so by the dehumanizing racism of this society. I don't recall his having Black friends, nor did any of his white Adventist acquaintances ever come to the house. Thus our social life was extremely limited, no doubt because of my father's inflexible position—he wanted nothing to come between him and his God.

And yet my father was in some ways a remarkable man. He had little formal education but his command of both Spanish and English was considerable, and he also spoke French and German.

If I never learned to love him, I didn't hate him either. The severity with which he beat us when he thought we had failed to observe some religious tenet was frightening. Indeed, in one of these outbursts, he permanently injured my sister because she had failed to say a prayer while the family was participating in one of his religious observances. I once saw my father whip my brother until the blood ran down his side, because he caught him mocking some religious rite.

These cruel punishments made an indelible impression upon my thinking and upon my attitude toward religion. Actually I had no knowledge of what my father did on his missionary treks. In his lifework of "soul saving" he may have been a very compassionate and exemplary man for all I know. But I found nothing in his work or his relations with our family with which I could identify. The hardship and suffering inflicted on my mother throughout their life together could not fail to affect me. Sometimes I saw him as a lost soul, "punchy" from the beating he was administering to himself.

I don't remember too much about life in California in those early days. I do know that Negroes, along with other nonwhites, Mexican Americans, Indians and Chinese met every kind of discrimination. I also know that my grandfather, William Galt, took an active part in the struggles initiated and

led by Black men to secure citizenship rights for themselves
and for Mexican Americans and Indians. A few years after he
arrived in California, grandfather Galt organized a regiment of
Negro volunteers known as the California Zouaves. Undoubtedly my grandfather feared the efforts of confederate
sympathizers to take California, a free state, out of the Union
and was determined to do anything to help prevent such a
monstrous catastrophe. Governor Frederick P. Low of California honored him for his work in his regiment at a banquet in
Sacramento, the capital, presenting him with a huge pewter
platter and pitcher on which were inscribed the names of the
governor and my grandfather. The set fell to our branch of the
family and remained a cherished heirloom until we were
forced to pawn it.

William Galt took part in other great liberation battles,
prepared anti-racist conferences and conventions, helped
fight civil rights cases through the state and federal courts in
valiant efforts to make the Emancipation Proclamation and
post-Civil War constitutional amendments instruments for
freedom. It was of great political importance that California
come into the Union as a free state, and Negroes, both escaped
slaves and freed Black men, participated in that fight. There
was a victory but not a complete one. The democracy preached
to Black men, Mexican Americans and Indians did not come
with statehood, and few white Americans who fought for
statehood were concerned with a fight for democracy for all the
people.

My formal schooling began in Oakland. My kindergarten
days were spent at a little place run by a kindly white woman;
about 20 girls and boys, of whom four were Black, attended.
The first time I remember feeling a color difference, however,
was at grammar school. It was at the Durant Grammar School
that I first heard the word "nigger." The eastern side of the
schoolyard was flanked by a large warehouse, the wall of
which was used for playing handball. I was a good handball
player and always rushed into the yard at recess to get a court,

since there were not enough of them to meet the demand. On one occasion, when I got to the court first, I had no ball. One of the older white boys who had his ball claimed that the ball determined priority. He cursed me as a "nigger" who was trying to change the rules. I yielded to the superior fighting forces of the white boys who sided with my opponent but later carried the matter to the principal, Mr. Dunbar, a stately-looking man with a long white beard.

The old man hemmed and hawed, using his ubiquitous swagger stick as though he were brushing off his trousers. Finally he declared that he knew of no ruling that gave the courts to the first comer with a ball. But he argued that since I had given up the court, the matter should be dropped. I said I hadn't given up the court—it had been taken from me. Mr. Dunbar was obviously reluctant to make a decision against the white lad. It wasn't only the loss of the court that I resented—it was the name-calling. I felt that the boy should at least be reprimanded and made to apologize. . . .

What kind of people were these? A deep resentment arose in me; this and subsequent incidents made me feel I was the object of color prejudice. I did not see fully then that the educational system was designed to develop in Black youth a feeling of inferiority, and in white youth the conviction that the world was theirs, a white world.

It was about this time that my father returned from one of his missionary trips and decided to move the family again, this time at the behest of his church leaders. He was to take the family to a Seventh Day Adventist Sanatorium, located near St. Helena in Napa County. Father had written a vegetarian cookbook for the Adventists, and they were going to introduce its recipes for about two years at the St. Helena Sanatorium.

We lived in a small house in a large vineyard located in the hills about two miles away from the sanatorium main buildings. About four miles away from our house was a one-room school which my brother Walter and I were to attend. Our four-room house, surrounded by the rolling hills that shaped

Napa Valley's many valleys, was in a beautiful, isolated spot. I am certain that my mother was hoping that we had settled down at last, but father attended an Adventist camp meeting and conference in San Jose in 1905 and returned to tell us he was off again to the South Sea Islands.

Mother seemed stunned by the announcement. My brother Walter had by that time disappeared. He had come to hate my father and, while the old man was away in San Jose, Walter packed and left. He could not stand dad's pious goings-on nor accept a penance that seemed likely to last forever. Walter left to avoid a fight with father that might well have ended in the death or serious injury of one or the other or both.

There was nothing to be done about my father's departure. Perhaps mother could have appealed to the church authorities against a decision that was to wreck a family. But father saw the matter as God's will. The family prepared to move back to Oakland. I remained with my mother; she got in touch with her sister, Anne Moody, who helped us find a vacant house on Grove Street between 22nd and 23rd.

I shall never forget our stay in that community. A large and beautiful Catholic church stood nearby; its size and seeming majesty impressed me deeply. Its doors were often open during the day, and the sound of the organ music floated out to the street. But, of course, I never dared go in—it was a white church. White churches of nearly all denominations were then jimcrow, which fact set me to wondering how God would divide his heaven. I concluded that if this were the manner in which God instructed his children on earth, I wanted no part of his eternal abode.

While living in the Grove Street house, we suffered one of the several evictions we had experienced after leaving San Francisco. Having no state or federal aid, mother was always on the desperate edge of survival; the task of raising a family on the pinchpenny wage a domestic could earn was a superhuman one. The house we lived in was small and the rent was excessive. When there was an increase, we could not raise it.

At this time a new traction company ran a feeder line along 22nd Street to the San Francisco Bay ferry, plying from West Oakland to San Francisco. The station for our neighborhood would be a block away from our house; naturally, the landlord was determined to cash in on the improved situation. When mother told him she couldn't pay the increase, he said he was sorry but she would have to move. The due day came and we had found neither the rent nor a place to go. The sheriff and his men drove up and put our furniture out onto the street.

The eviction of a family from what they have learned to call home must always be a tragedy. Neighbors, unless they are hostile, generally regard it the same way. There were no Negroes in that area but our white neighbors did come to express their sympathy. There was no reason here for them to take sides along racial grounds. And besides, landlords had few friends in a working-class community. I remember some of the white boys volunteered to help put the furniture into the "new" house, which was only two doors away. As a matter of fact, I believe we were really well liked by our neighbors. Here life came in conflict with my growing belief that all whites were prejudiced. I was perplexed.

The house we moved into had stood vacant for as long as we could remember—it was said that rats from the stable adjoining it made it unlivable. That was why my mother had bypassed it, but now she had no alternative. The sharpest memories I retain about our new home are about the rats. They were an ever present menace, but mother declared war on them at once. With indomitable courage and energy, she got rid of them and the pervasive odor they emitted.

Only much later did I come to appreciate fully the great inner strength that helped my mother to carry on. She possessed an everlasting hope for something better. All poor mothers, regardless of their color or creed, have some of this unbounded spiritual strength, but the mothers of the Black poor are forced to draw upon it more constantly. When I reviewed my relations with my mother during childhood, I could see how the conditions of her life had created barriers between us so deep

and wide that we could not bridge them. She could not
understand this new, *free* world, its racial hatreds nor the terror
and violence accompanying them. My mother could only
respond to the hardships that poverty forced on her by increasing her sacrifices and her labors. I could not talk to her about
freedom and what it meant to me. So I had to ponder alone on
the educational system which concealed or distorted reality.

So there I was, living alone with my mother with whom I
could hope for little rapprochement, despite our mutual love.
It was many years before I was to see my brother Walter. My
sister Alberta lived with a family named Morton in San
Francisco and came home only for visits. Alberta got some
schooling at the Mortons and eventually she became a mas-
seuse.

In spite of the handicaps of poverty, I worked my way into
the upper grades at Durant and finally graduated and moved on
to Oakland High School. It was within walking distance of the
house from which mother had cleared the rats. I already had
some thoughts about flight once I got a formal education. At
that time I wanted to be a mining engineer.

As I grew older I began to question more seriously the course
my father had followed. I could not learn to respect the point
of view which accepted and endured hell on earth for himself
and his family in exchange for an abode in heaven. Somewhat
later, friends introduced me to the writings of Robert G.
Ingersoll—not only one of the best known agnostics but a man
who challenged racism and fought for the rational concepts of
the French Revolution. I can still recapture some of the
intellectual delight derived from reading the essays and lec-
tures of this man who was scored by the established order as an
infidel. The more I read, the more I thought about what my
father had done, and the greater grew my abhorrence of his
entire course.

I had begun to earn money in a small way after school hours
by peddling the Oakland *Tribune,* then owned by Joseph R.
Knowland, father of William F. Knowland who later became a
U.S. Senator of unsavory, rightist reputation. I continued

selling papers through grammar school and into high-school days, earning pocket money which my mother could not provide and contributing something to the family budget.

Just before I graduated from grammar school, I began to suffer from an eye ailment that forced me to stay out of school for more than a year. During that period I went to the nearby Emeryville race track and got a job exercising horses. It paid better than selling papers and was far more interesting. One of the people I met there was Andy Thomas, a first-rate Black jockey. His contract was later sold to a Russian nobleman and he became one of the great "race riders" of the Tsarist Empire.

I learned a lot on the race track—some things I will never forget. This was the sport of kings. The rich whites who sat in the grandstands and clubhouse could bet thousands of dollars and not worry about losing. The owners and trainers were white; the stable "boys"—some in their fifties or older—the exercise boys, swippers and ground men were almost always Black. Those of us who worked in the stables had to worry about every nickel and dime. My pay for the week was two dollars and fifty cents.

After I went back to high school, I ran elevators after school hours and Saturdays. Later, during summer vacations, or when my eyes were giving me trouble, I stayed out of school for weeks at a time. More than once I shipped on the local freighters as a dishwasher, fourth cook or third cook.

About this time my mother met a wealthy white woman whose name was Mrs. Georgia Martin. She owned a beautiful small cottage in the hills in Sausalito in Marin County. She asked my mother to come and cook for her and her daughter at Sylvan Dell, as the cottage was called. My mother agreed. It was a stay-in job and I went along. I transferred to a new school, Mt. Tamalpais High, where we were all housed in a shack.

The school sat in the valley at the foot of Mt. Tamalpais, in the midst of unsurpassed natural beauty. The climate was ideal and the environment was conducive to educational achievement. This is where I was introduced to progressive thinking through my contact with two members of the staff who were my close friends for many years. One was the head of the manual training department who seemed to recognize my sensitivity and often talked to me about a form of society in which skin color would play no part. At that early stage of my life, he gave me a copy of Karl Marx's *Capital.* I tried to read and understand it but it was quite incomprehensible to me and I put it aside until later years.

The other teacher who became a lifelong friend and contributed to my intellectual development was Miss Elizabeth Keyser, who taught history. When I unburdened myself to her about the prejudice I encountered on the athletic field, she told me this was part of life's struggles and that one had to keep one's chin up and fight back. Her sympathy and solicitude buoyed up my morale in the face of the hostility of small groups of white boys. But while she could console me, she herself was completely unaware of the social source of racist behavior or how to fight it.

I now know that my friendship with these two individuals contributed to my ability to understand and critically evaluate my social environment. I came to know that there were and had been great white revolutionaries and dedicated progressive leaders among white people.

I graduated from Tamalpais High School in 1911 at the age of twenty. Up to this time I had lived with my mother and shared her privations and expenses. I now moved to San Francisco and lived by myself in a furnished room. I applied for admission and was accepted as a special student at the University of California. Despite my dreams of being a mining engineer, I took the usual introductory courses in the humanities.

When my eyes began to trouble me again, I left college and got a third cook's job on a Pacific Mail steamship running to Panama. On one of my trips I arrived two days after the Canal opened, in 1914—just in time to take part in the celebrations marking the completion of the project.

The American builders of the Canal had made Panama one

big ghetto. This marked American imperialism's first notable export of racism. I remember a location called Cocoanut Grove where they had even built a string of brothels for white employees only. The majority of the women were "colored."

When I got back to California, my eyes had improved. Since I had put aside a few dollars, I returned to the University. While there, I joined with six young Negro men, representing both town and campus, to form a group we called "The Blood Brothers." There was no political motivation—we simply pledged eternal friendship and proclaimed that if one of us got rich, he was to help the others. "The Blood Brothers" remained angry young men; I was the social rebel among them.

In the West our concepts of how to conduct the fight for equality were still primitive. Even in the East, where Dr. W. E. B. Du Bois had challenged Booker T. Washington's "separate but equal" theory, Negro struggles were developing on a more or less individual basis. Throughout the country and particularly in the West, Negroes were still marginal workers and had little influence on the country's political and industrial development. We had no understanding of how the apparatus of government was used to keep Negro and white divided, nor how it devised and spread the myths of white superiority.

In 1917 my college education came to a temporary halt because of a combination of factors. In the first place, I discovered I could not pay tuition for an engineering course and earn my living at the same time. There were no scholarships available to me. I also objected to the compulsory military training at Berkeley, for which I had neither time nor inclination. For that I was kicked out. Of the young Negroes on the West Coast, so far as I know, I was the only one to come out against World War I, and I did so on the erroneous basis that it was a white man's war.

I was reinstated in the University shortly afterward but I had not completed all the required subjects when I was again dropped because of my irregular attendance. I had to make a new start. Engineering was out of the question. I decided to study law.

I Study Law,
On And Off The Campus

I ENROLLED at the Hastings College of Law of the University of California in San Francisco in 1915, and my activities for the next four years were centered in and around that institution. I had asked my friend Leonard Richardson, who was studying law in Boalt Hall at the University in Berkeley, whether his law books would be available to me. They were.

I had saved a few dollars while working on the boats, but I also had to get a job. When I came across an ad saying that the Taylor Hotel needed a night clerk and elevator operator from eight in the evening to eight in the morning, it sounded like the perfect job for me. I could sleep or study at the switchboard; the hotel would be in easy walking distance of the City Hall building where classes were held. Classes began at 9 a.m. and ended in the early afternoon.

I lost no time in going to see Mr. Taylor, owner and manager of the five-story hotel, and I told him frankly of my plans to go on with college. He impressed me as being a man of strong character who would deal straightforwardly with me. He told me he thought the schedule would be trying—but he apparently liked my spirit and I got the job. I was given a small basement room adjoining the maid's kitchen. There was a shower handy and I had cooking and laundry privileges. I was to have every other Saturday night off.

Although I had to study at night and, for the most part, could sleep only between the hours of 3 and 8 a.m., I had a place of my own and was more or less independent. I missed my mother since I could see her only at long intervals, but I did write her regularly and she was happy over my relatively good fortune.

One day, as I walked to the hotel from the university, I was attracted by a copy of the *Crisis,* on display in the window of a bookstore. This was the official organ of the National Association for the Advancement of Colored People, and what particularly struck me was the headline "Close Ranks." It turned out to be the title of an editorial written by W. E. B. Du Bois, the magazine's editor. His injunction that colored people should support the U.S. war effort did not correspond with my own thoughts on the subject. But I wanted to examine the arguments in support of the opposite viewpoint. Walking into that store was like walking into a new life. Emanuel Levine, a short, stocky man of about 30, with a shock of black hair and a muscular body that made me think of a wrestler, greeted me cordially.

It was not surprising that a discontented Black law student should find pleasure in a place where he could engage in friendly and informative discussions. At school they were teaching me to accommodate to the racist society in which I lived, while in the bookstore I began to learn some fundamentals about the nature of that society and how to go about changing it.

I became acquainted with the *Masses,* a militant magazine that published lively social criticism of the entire American scene. I was introduced to Marxist literature and books; I read the *Messenger,* a magazine published in New York by two young Black radicals—A. Philip Randolph and Chandler Owen. I was stirred by its analyses of the source of Black oppression and the attempt to identify it with the international revolution against working-class oppression and colonialism. This was an enriching and exhilarating experience. For the first time I was being made aware that the study of society and

the movement to change it constituted a science that had to be grasped if Black America was ever to attain equal rights.

One day, Levine called me into his little cubby-hole of an office in back of the store and introduced me to Anita Whitney, an extraordinary person. She was at that time in her thirties but she seemed very young to me. A brief conversation revealed her keen, probing mind and her concern with the Black freedom struggle. Besides, she was lovely, gracious and very much alive. She was to become an outstanding Communist leader.

Anita Whitney, I was to learn, belonged to one of the oldest pioneer families in the United States. One of her ancestors, Thomas Dudley, succeeded John Winthrop as Governor of Massachusetts in 1634; an uncle, Stephen Johnson Field, was an Associate Justice of the U.S. Supreme Court for more than 34 years.

After my first constraint wore off, I listened attentively when she mentioned Tom Mooney and a committee set up in his defense. Was I involved in the defense? she asked. I had to tell her I had no knowledge of the case. "Well, you ought to be working with them," she replied. She evidently took it for granted that my interests lay in progressive social and political causes. She explained the case, making its importance so clear that when I left the store I went quickly to the office of the Mooney Defense Committee to learn more and see if I could do anything to help.

Tom Mooney, a labor organizer for the American Federation of Labor, had just led a hard-fought streetcar workers' strike. On July 22, 1916, a bomb exploded at the Preparedness Day Parade on Market Street; nine people were killed and 40 wounded. Tom Mooney was arrested, charged with the crime and subsequently tried, convicted and sentenced to death. Another labor leader, Warren K. Billings, was convicted as Mooney's accomplice.

After I read the stories in the press and analyzed the testimony of the witnesses and the "evidence" marshalled against Tom Mooney, I had serious doubts as to his guilt. The defense committee's literature confirmed my conviction that he was innocent. For days after I left the defense office I asked myself, "Well, what are you going to do about it?"

The question demanded an answer that was hard for a Black man to make at that time. Everything in me demanded that I support this man's defense. I discussed the case with some of my closest friends. John Derrick, editor and publisher of a Negro paper in Oakland, was sharpest in his reaction. I had written several pieces for the paper. He became extremely agitated when he learned I was thinking of involving myself in the case. So did my other friends.

"Are you crazy?" Derrick stormed. "They're going to hang this man." "Why?" I asked. "He's done nothing illegal."

"Oh, yes, he has, he tried to organize the streetcar workers. The men who run this city will get him."

"For what, John—organizing? That's his work. I am studying law and they haven't produced a case that will stand up in court."

"These are far-reaching social questions," he said, "and you should not be concerned with them right now."

I stood aghast. When *was* I to get interested in such matters? Before I could reply, Derrick came up close to me. "Pat," he said, "Mooney has refused to organize Negroes."

Greatly surprised, I asked what proof he had. "Well, you don't see any Negroes working on the streetcars, do you? If he weren't discriminating, wouldn't there be Negroes working?" I accepted this statement, although I did know that the employers did the hiring and that Mooney did not as yet have a union.

At this period, I had been growing increasingly subjective: I was more Negro than American—or even human. Whatever affected the Negro people and their immediate interests deeply affected me. This outlook began to control my reaction to all social problems. I broke my contact with the Mooney Defense Committee. When I tried to explain to Levine and Anita Whitney why I had done so, nothing they said then could make me change.

There was about Anita an air of confidence in the ultimate triumph of her cause. As a socialist, she based her convictions on historical forces. Temporary setbacks did not disturb her. She was not indignant at my inability to join her in the defense of Mooney. Indeed, it was not long after this that she invited me to speak at a Socialist Party meeting in Oakland. I readily accepted the opportunity to set forth my idea on Negroes' struggles and their relationship to social and political issues.

Anita's work with the NAACP had involved her in another struggle in relation to World War I. In 1917, when the United States entered the war "to make the world safe for democracy," there was nothing faintly resembling democracy in the armed forces. A week after war had been declared, the War Department slammed the door in the face of Negro volunteers. No Black men could serve in the Marines, the Coast Guard or the Air Force, and the Navy accepted them only as messmen.

Woodrow Wilson's government maintained a rigid racist position in all its relations with Black citizens, officially backing the enforced bigotry in the civil and military establishments. Wilson issued an order to demote and segregate most Negro federal employees in Washington.

As the war intensified and the draft began to function, two million Negroes registered, of whom 31 per cent were accepted. Most of them were shunted into jimcrow stevedore and other service (dirty work) battalions. Meantime, at home Negro soldiers were the recipients of "keep-the-Nigger-in-his-place" treatment in the Southern states, where training camps refused them every social service and subjected them to insults, beatings and murder.

In Houston, Texas, some of the Negro troops hit back at their attackers. Seventeen whites were killed. The Negro troops were disarmed and 64 members of the 24th Infantry were courtmartialed. Thirteen were sentenced to death; 41 imprisoned for life. It was the largest mass legal lynching in U.S. history.

I was given a peculiar inside view of the racist mind in uniform through a friendship I had developed with Colonel

Charles Young, then the highest ranking Black officer in the army. He was one of the first four Negroes to graduate from West Point; he had served as a cavalry officer under "Black Jack" Pershing in battles against the Apaches and other Indian tribes in the Southwest as well as against Pancho Villa. When the army began to expand for World War I, he was in line to be promoted to major general.

But the idea of a Negro general was intolerable to the army brass. He was useful in the murder of Indians, but the war in Europe was another thing. Army doctors suddenly found that Young was suffering from a variety of physical ailments and ordered him into Letterman Hospital, at the Presidio in San Francisco—obviously with a medical retirement in mind.

For weeks I paid regular visits to the hospital, and Colonel Young and I became fast friends. He told me many stories about the bitter insults he had been forced to endure during his military career; how the cadets at West Point had done every-thing in their power to drive him out of the academy; how he had had to take slurs from white officers and even white buck privates. His loyalty to a military establishment which had strewn his path with insults, to a War Department that had refused him his well-earned promotion, was beyond me. Completely lacking any understanding of the structure of society, his miseducation had permitted him to hunt down and murder Indians and to perform with equal efficiency against Villa.

Nevertheless, Young's fight for promotion had become a national cause among Negroes and a few progressive whites. Individuals, organizations, the Negro press—all were aroused by the issue. The NAACP was active in his support. (There were no Negro senior line officers in Europe.)

Anita Whitney organized a meeting in Oakland, under NAACP auspices, with Young as principal speaker. He made a brilliant speech, recounting some of his experiences in the Army and explaining why he thought the Negro people should give full backing to the government in its war effort. Despite the inhuman treatment he had received from the army, he held the cause of the American people as paramount; winning the war came first. That was why he was fighting to be sent to the battlefront.

In spite of all efforts, Young failed to win promotion. The War Department forced a medical discharge upon him. In a farewell protest gesture, this "sick" Black cavalry officer rode a horse from Ohio to Washington, D.C. He left the army sick at heart and died shortly thereafter.

The mistreatment my friend received strengthened my conviction that the war was a white man's war, and I was prepared to say so. I did just that at a picnic sponsored by the Negro Elks—the jimcrow wing of the BPOE. It was on my Saturday off, and I went with my close friend, Larkin Day. At our table we had been discussing the nature of the war. I condemned it, contending that the interests of the Negro people were not involved. The debate became heated, and I jumped up on the table in order to reach a larger audience and to make my voice heard above the laughter and noise at other tables. I declared the war was a "white man's war" and that Negroes should play no part in it.

Two young Negro sailors who were on the picnic grounds heard me and immediately reported my remarks to the military police. I was arrested and turned over to the Oakland city authorities and held incommunicado for five days. Then the NAACP found out where I was, and their attorney, Oscar Hudson, at the request of Anita Whitney, as well as that of my sister and Walter Brown, a family friend, appeared in my defense. After a short hearing, I was released.

It happened that at the hotel where I worked I had made the acquaintance of a young Irish woman, Rose Murphy. She would often stop in the lobby to talk with me about my studies, or come downstairs late in the evening to chat. She told me of the oppression of the Irish people by the British kings and queens (how different from the picture of the queen as the most beneficent woman "God had created," according to my father).

From this Irish revolutionary I learned that whites oppressed other whites all over the world. Oppression was not determined solely or even chiefly by skin color. One had to look beyond color to reach the core of the matter. I had enjoyed these talks, but now I almost had to pay dearly for them. At the trial I was charged with associating with Irish and East Indian revolutionaries. (Rose Murphy was friendly with the latter.) Luckily, the charges could not be proven. The government was not ready to frame me, but from then on it could never be my government.

At about that time Anita Whitney brought a speaker to California who was a lieutenant of Emmeline Pankhurst—a great leader and the organizer of the Women's Social and Political Union which led the fight for women's rights in England. The meeting was Socialist-sponsored and Anita asked me if I would appear on the program. I was honored. I told the gathering about the oppression and exploitation of the Negro, with the implication that I believed all whites were party to the crimes committed against black people.

Immediately after the meeting, the gracious young visitor from England called me aside: "You spoke well," she said, "but do you mind if I tell you frankly that I could not follow your logic or accept your conclusions. Not all whites are against all Blacks—not in England, not in America. Not all of them have power, and some are too occupied with their own problems to see yours or have concern for them. But that is different from hostility. The oppressor wants us, Black and white, to be hostile to each other. The root of the matter, as I see it, is *class* oppression. What is easier when people are different—especially in color—than to turn one against another on the ground that color difference makes for biological and intellectual differences. . . . If you want your convictions to have value, to bear fruit and move people to action, that's the thought you must bring to them with force and clarity."

The ideas she expressed were to remain with me for many years, as I came to learn that class, caste and color were all involved in the triple exploitation of the Black man in the United States.

Shortly after this, a group of prominent Negroes on the coast organized a meeting and brought James Weldon Johnson to speak on behalf of the government. Johnson was a light-skinned Black man of almost legendary repute—he had been a lawyer, a school principal, a poet and a lyricist for Broadway musicals. A friend of presidents, he had served as U.S. Consul at Puerto Cabello, Venezuela, in 1906, and later in Nicaragua. When he was invited to the Bay Area, he was national field secretary of the NAACP—altogether a gentleman of brilliance and distinction.

The meeting was held at the Civic Auditorium in Oakland, then a brand-new building, beautifully located on the shore of Lake Merritt. I was surprised and flattered when the sponsors sent a delegation asking me to act as chairman. I believe the invitation was in honor of my having been appointed chairman of the NAACP's legal advisory committee, although I was not yet out of college. I'm sure that Anita Whitney had influenced the appointment.

Knowing that my views would differ from those of the guest speaker did not alter my respect for him. In preparing my introduction, I took Wendell Phillips' essay on Toussaint L'Overture as a guide, in which he pictured Toussaint as a soldier statesman of extraordinary ability and then went on to tell of his many other talents—at that time almost unknown to Black people. I paid tribute to James Weldon Johnson in much the same manner, omitting the reference to Toussaint as a soldier.

Then Johnson spoke and proceeded to proclaim the merits of Woodrow Wilson and the virtues of the war. The NAACP leadership had come to the conclusion that Black men could benefit through participation in the war. All this took place not only before the large assembly of Negro people, but also in the presence of the Mayor of Oakland and a large number of dignitaries—who naturally supported Johnson's position.

My discussion with Johnson afterwards was very unsatisfactory to me. He advised me to stay in the West and "grow up with the country." Johnson was a politician and creative artist, unlike the army-bred Colonel Young, but Johnson, too, made country and government synonymous terms. He believed that love of country demanded support of its government.

My disagreement with two of my distinguished Negro contemporaries reflected my own sharp inner conflicts and also my confusion. Concern for the future of Negro freedom remained my dominating thought, on the principle that no one outside our own ranks could feel such concern to the full.

Nevertheless, in any school one finds some kindred souls. Two Jewish students in the law school and I naturally gravitated toward one another. In our discussions they advanced an argument to which I had no reply:

"Well, it's true, Pat, that when we come out of school we're going to have difficulties in getting placed, but not the difficulties you will meet. If you are refused accommodation in a hotel or restaurant, you go back to your own community and find there is no one who can do anything practical about it. When we are refused, our fathers often can build a hotel or restaurant with comparable but better accommodations. This doesn't resolve the problem but it sometimes helps."

In other words, they felt there was an economic road out of their problem which was not available to me. Their view had some truth for Jews in *their* economic stratum but what of the "Jews without money"?

As a matter of fact, when we were graduated from law school these two were inducted very readily into the San Francisco legal fraternity. One of them, Lorenz James Krueger, went into the legal department of a large corporation. The other, Peter Solomon Sommer, went into a Jewish law firm with an established practice. On the other hand, I was in a rather precarious situation, working in the office of a Negro lawyer whose practice was extremely varied and extremely insecure.

And I must mention Helen S. Smith, the lone woman student at Hastings law school. She fought back against the attitudes of male chauvinism displayed by both faculty and students. We often talked about the uncouth way in which she was made to

feel unwelcome. She and I were both curiosities in the
school—she the only female, I the only Black—both victims of
social sicknesses in our society.

Just before my graduation, a revealing incident took place.
The practice was for established law firms to solicit from the
university's seniors the names of those who could gain knowledge and practical experience as law clerks. This involved a
sort of on-the-job training, permitting the student to find his
footing in advance of his graduation and also maintaining a
link between the school and business. The office of Samuel
Shortridge—soon to be U.S. Senator from California—asked
our school for a candidate and the dean, British-born Edward
Robeson Taylor, sent for me. He may not have taken the racial
implications seriously or perhaps he may have been uncon-
scious of them.

When I came into Mr. Shortridge's palatial suite, the office
manager seemed extremely surprised. When I said I had been
sent in response to the application they had made for a law
clerk, he seemed still more astonished and told me that this
was a matter he could not handle himself. I would have to see
"the Senator."

After I had been kept waiting in the antechamber for some
time, I was told that Samuel Shortridge was ready to receive
me. I went down the hall past a number of offices to get to the
Big Man's headquarters. Without looking up, he invited me to
have a seat. I sat there a few minutes while he went over the
papers before him. He looked up and his face showed no
surprise whatever.

"Mr. Patterson," he said, "you are the young man who has
been sent from Hastings?" "Yes." He studied me, then asked,
"Just why are you studying law?" I answered, "Why shouldn't
I?" "From what group do you expect to draw a clientele?" I
said, "From San Franciscans." "How many Negroes are there
in San Francisco?" he asked. I replied that I wasn't certain but
that I didn't expect that only Negroes would patronize me if I
were a good lawyer. He went on, "How do you think my

clients would receive you?" I said, "I don't know." He said, "Well, it is my opinion that they would find it difficult to adjust themselves to talking business and personal matters with a Negro. I think the adjustment would be too difficult for them."

Finally, after some perfunctory discussion of my future, which he seemed to feel was a dubious one, he told me he could not use me.

The interview made a tremendous impact on me. I began to wonder whether it wouldn't be necessary for me to leave the United States. Here was a man who expected to represent all the people of his state in the Senate of the United States, yet found it impossible to employ the son of one of his constituents. Was his a realistic appraisal, mine an idealistic one?

I returned to the school to report my experience. In my talk with Dean Taylor he showed deep sympathy for my distress. He said he had never anticipated such an incident and then began to discuss the necessity for preparing myself for similar encounters that he was afraid would be forthcoming. He told me not to be daunted by these obstacles, to find in them a challenge which should be met and overcome. He was, of course, completely ignorant of the nature of the racist society and had no criticism of the position taken by Shortridge.

Shortly after my disappointment at Shortridge's office, I was told by friends that a newly arrived Negro lawyer had established an office in San Francisco. The man was J. McCant Stewart, Jr. He had come from Seattle, where he had not been financially successful. He undoubtedly hoped that things would be better in San Francisco with its larger Negro population.

Stewart's father was a prominent American lawyer who, in 1906, had been sent by President Theodore Roosevelt to Brownsville, Texas, at the time of the "Brownsville Riot," in which Negro soldiers of a jimcrow cavalry regiment, no longer able to endure the insults and opprobrium of the townspeople near their encampment, had finally shot up the town.

I went to see Mr. Stewart, and after a talk we agreed that I should come into his office after classes as a law clerk. I did that for a number of months and began to get some feeling about the practice of law. Mr. Stewart was not making money; as a matter of fact, his practice was not sufficient to meet the demands of his household. Just before I was to be graduated, in 1919, I returned to the office one afternoon to find it filled with policemen and others. J. McCant Stewart, my boss, had committed suicide. He had left a wife and daughter—and many debts. I wound up the estate.

During my clerkship, he had told me a good bit about his father. He said that shortly after the trial in Brownsville, in which some hundred soldiers of the Negro regiment had been found guilty—20 of them were to be hanged and others were sentenced to long prison terms—his father, in despair of successfully fighting prejudice in the United States, had gone to Liberia, where he had served on the Supreme Court. At the time his son had killed himself, he was fiscal agent for Liberia in England.

Several months before graduation, I had discussed with the younger Stewart the possibility of my going to Liberia. I had induced him to write a letter introducing me to his father. Even before I had my diploma, I had decided to leave the United States and try to find a place among those who were seeking to build a new life in Africa. The death of Mr. Stewart added further strength to this decision. I was 27, and I didn't want to lose any more time.

CHAPTER 3

In Search Of An Identity

THE HASTINGS COLLEGE graduation took place in the Greek
Theater at the University of California at Berkeley. My mother
and my sister were present along with my cousin Jennie Reed,
other members of the family, and friends. Their eyes glowed,
their faces were filled with joy and pride.

I tried to imagine the thoughts that were passing through my
mother's mind. Mother shared with other Black mothers the
dream of freeing her children by putting them through college.
I could then only dimly appreciate the tears and sweat she had
given to realize the goal. She had put in back-breaking years
working in rich white folks' kitchens in pursuit of her
dream—now so near to becoming a reality. Only the California
bar examination stood between her son and a legal career. Son
of a slave-born mother, he would become a brilliant lawyer. He
had been graduated from one of the foremost law schools in
the country. What was to stop him?

Alas, I flunked the California bar examinations! These are
given to determine whether a graduate should be certified to
practice in the state and whether his character is all it should
be—can he be trusted?

It is true that Negroes *had* passed the California tests, among
them Walter Gordon, who had been a well-known football
player on the University of California team and later was
governor of the Virgin Islands and a judge on a federal district

court bench. There was also a close friend of mine, Leonard Richardson, former baseball player on the UC varsity. And there were others, countable on the fingers of one hand. They were respectable men; none of them had ever been arrested and tried for condemning World War I as a white man's war; none had told Negro lads they would gain nothing by serving in such a war. There was no evidence that any one of them would fight the system that branded the black man inferior. Nor had any spoken from a Socialist Party platform at the invitation of the radical Anita Whitney or made a gesture in defense of Tom Mooney—then awaiting execution in the death house at San Quentin.

Obviously, then, they had more than just their unquestioned ability going for them; they were the kind of young men whom the politically powerful and wealthy trusted and needed. I cannot say that they were sincerely pro-war, but the people who held open the door to affluence and prestige were for the war and these young Negroes did not challenge them.

I talked to some of these friends about my plan to go abroad and they scoffed at the idea. They knew that my militancy and my arrest had influenced the examiners, but they told me that if I cooled off a little, I'd be sure to pass a later examination.

"You are well liked among the Negroes in this area," they said, and they painted rosy dreams of how I could become a leader among my people on the Coast, where such leaders were few. They even argued that the West needed me, but I had grave doubts about that. The West was not then in the main stream of political action and there was no foundation on which to build the kind of political struggle I felt had to be waged to win equality.

I never knew how my mother felt about my failing the bar; she never commented on it. But I think her heart bled. My sister was of the "try, try again" school; she had become a Christian Scientist—a church full of Cinderella myths. As for me, the action of the examiners helped me to make up my mind to leave the West and the country.

I had made contacts with people in Liberia. Africa, I believed, needed young men who were hostile to colonialism and the oppressors of Black people. I began to make preparations to depart, with no intention of ever returning.

On a sunny summer day in July 1919, I found myself crossing the Bay from the beautiful hillside town of Sausalito on my way to San Francisco. I sat under a radiant sun, gazing first at Mount Tamalpais, the sleeping beauty, then at Alcatraz Island and at San Francisco. The Bay and its environs were beautiful. The Berkeley hills were off to the left, with the houses and other buildings etched against the blue sky. To my right was the Golden Gate, the doorway to far horizons holding who knew what for me. Everywhere I looked there was almost unsurpassable beauty. But the prison on Alcatraz was an omen.

Richard Griffen, a steward on the ferryboat, came to sit beside me. Our friendship went back to my days at Tamalpais High School. We'd played many a game of billiards and pool together when I was "hustling a buck" to meet expenses.

"Pat," he said, "I hear you're going away." Without waiting for an answer, he went on, "What for? Where to, Man? Do you know what you're doing?"

"I know I can't stay here," I replied. "I don't see us making it out here. At least, I don't see myself making it. I want to go to Africa."

He looked at me with some puzzlement, then shook hands warmly and wished me luck before going off to his duties. He waved to me as I walked off the ferry after it had pulled into the slip in San Francisco. Did I know what I was doing? I wondered. All I was really certain of was that I had made a decision. I was going to Africa.

I went down to the main office of the Pacific Mail Steamship Line on the Embarcadero. I hoped to find a freighter going to Europe on which I could get a job. I was lucky. In a short time the *S.S. Barracuda* would be leaving for the east coast of England with a cargo for either Hull or Grimsby—both located at the mouth of the Humber River. A third cook and messboy were needed and I signed on. The "old lady" was due to leave in a relatively short time and to steam down the Pacific west coast, through the Canal at Panama and out across the Atlantic. I tried to get Leland Hawkins, a boon companion, to go along with me as the messboy that was needed. But he had sent to Washington, D.C. for his high school credentials and had been accepted at Hastings. He saw himself as more or less secure in my old job at the Taylor Hotel. He preferred to go on and complete his law studies and try his hand at the practice of law in California.

I was turned down by another friend, Frank Fields. We had talked together often and he seemed to agree with the theories I expressed. But the project I now suggested was something different. He had a Civil Service job as a post-office clerk and thought he saw chances to move up the ladder. A bird in the hand was worth more than one in some far-off African bush.

So I was going alone. I could scarcely contain myself. It was not the thought that I would find greener pastures but rather that I would find a freer political and social atmosphere, in which the struggle for economic security would be more endurable and, above all, a spot where I would find respect for human beings.

My sister was now all for my taking the venture. She had great faith in me and was deeply sympathetic with my desire to get away—she seemed to have a keener insight into my inner unrest than anyone else.

My mother reacted as perhaps all mothers do. I was the only one of her sons whose whereabouts she knew and she did not want to let me go. My brother Walter had disappeared and none of us even knew whether he was still alive.

It was late August 1919 when I left San Francisco—the beautiful, magnificent Bay area, with its bitter and its sweet memories. My mother, sister and friends saw me off; my friends had gotten together a purse, which to my surprise, contained nearly $120.

Mother cried as we kissed goodbye. I never saw her again.
Nor did I see California again until 1941.

On entering the ship's galley to report for work, I found that
the chef and second cook were brothers named John and
Edward Patterson. They were as surprised as I to find that I too
was a Patterson. I told them my father was from the island of
St. Vincent and that his name was James Edward Patterson.
They too laid claim to St. Vincent as their birthplace and
asserted that they were relatives of my father. In any case, I
immediately felt at home with "the family" as we steamed
through the Golden Gate and turned southward into the broad
Pacific Ocean.

Our first stop was at Acapulco—not a large city, as viewed
from the ship's rail. But I knew that as a Mexican city it must
be free of racial hatred, except for that which may have been
brought there by the Yankees. Shore leave was granted, and
when I set foot on the soil of Mexico I did what I had done
only once before. I knelt and kissed the ground. For me it was
like free soil; no man on board that ship had greater rights
ashore than I. Skin color was not a measure of human worth
here, I had left the standards that dominated life in the United
States.

We continued down the west coast uneventfully and reached
the Pacific entrance to the Panama Canal in several days. Then
we entered the Canal at Balboa and began the ascent to the
Atlantic side of the Isthmus. Now again I was back in a
jimcrow atmosphere. The racist mores of the rulers of the
United States governed all human relations on the Isthmus.
The transformation had been accomplished in a thoroughgo-
ing manner, including both class and color forms of exploitation.

As it happened, my father was in Panama City. Was it, I
mused, to teach the Panamanians, most of whom came from
the British West Indies, how to accept the cruel and certainly
un-Christian racism of the American colonial robbers and
conquistadores? He had completed a course in dentistry begun

in the United States and had opened a dental office. It was this, and not his missionary activities, that afforded him a living.

I made what was more or less a duty call. Yet I was glad to see him. He was terribly emaciated and looked like a very sick man. I did not know then that he was dying from tuberculosis of the stomach.

I could not but be impressed with his capabilities. The unlettered boy who had started out from Kingston as a sailor was now a dentist. Soon after he returned to Kingston, where he died a stranger and alone, forgotten by the church to which he had given his life and all else he possessed.

After talking with him for an hour, I embraced him. He knelt down to pray for my welfare. There was no greater understanding between us now than there had been in my childhood. But I admired him. He was a man. He was, according to his lights, a good man, even though his kind of thinking was alien to me.

Our ship steamed up the Atlantic Coast and put in at Norfolk, Virginia, from which, more than half a century before, my grandparents and their children had put out for California. I would like to have seen the plantation from which they came, but there was no time for sightseeing.

In Norfolk, a couple of men in the crew jumped ship, and two chaps were taken on to replace them. One of the newcomers, a tall, slender Southern white lad, though thoroughly indoctrinated with all the prejudices of his upbringing, made a few friendly overtures to me. After the work of the day, Charley and I often met on deck and talked about one thing or another—mostly Negro-white relations and what lay ahead. Our discussions ran the gamut of human experience, including sex, marriage, economics (so far as we understood it) and social matters of various kinds. Negro-white relations as they existed did not make sense to us, but neither of us could offer a solution.

The *Barracuda* did not stop again until it put in at Ponta Delgada in the Azores to take on water, food and other supplies. My Southern friend tried to get me to go ashore with him and "have a good time" but I declined. He offered to pay

the expenses, but I still refused. I had never been in a house of
prostitution and I did not want to start now.

In the late summer of 1919, we finally landed at Grimsby, on
England's east coast. I immediately jumped ship. With what
money I had, I took off by train for London. I was greatly
impressed with the beauty of the English countryside. Everything seemed so orderly; the truck garden plots were all so
carefully hedged off. The scene was beautiful.

The train finally pulled into London and I found myself in
the very heart of the British capital. I felt lost in the hustle and
bustle of the great city, like a schoolboy thrown out in the great
wide world. This, in truth, was what I was. I had passed the
quarter-century mark, but I had so much to learn about the
world.

I planned to try to find the elder McCant Stewart, who had
been sent to London to try to negotiate a loan from the
government or from banks, for the further development of
Liberia. I wanted to discuss with him ways and means of
getting to Africa, to learn what he thought of the possibility of
my finding something to do in Liberia. Each time I tried to see
him I was told he was not in.

In the meanwhile I started to look for lodgings. The papers
were full of advertisements for rooms and I selected one at
random from the *Daily Herald.* When I rang the bell of the
rooming house, a seemingly respectable landlady opened the
door. She looked hard at me and abruptly asked, "Are you a
'nigger'?" "I am an American Negro," I answered. "Oh," she
said. "Come in, come in!"

The hall bedroom on the third floor was small and clean and
the bathroom was close by. The price seemed reasonable. Then
she said, "Of course, we serve tea and toast for breakfast." I
paid for a week in advance and then decided to ask her what
she meant by her first question to me. "I thought you were an
Indian," she said. "We don't care for them, you know." I didn't
know, but I was not yet ready to debate the question. I was
flabbergasted—this was a form of prejudice worthy of further
consideration.

In my quest for a room, I had become acquainted with the London *Daily Herald,* organ of the British Labour Party. I was attracted by its editorial policy and its approach to events, including comments on the war just concluded and the Civil War in Russia. I decided I would like to talk to Robert Lansbury, whose byline was prominent in the paper. He was its editor and publisher, as well as being one of the leading figures of the British Labour Party. I went boldly to the paper, asked for Mr. Lansbury and had no trouble getting into his offices. The dingy offices on Fleet Street were in what Americans would call a loft building. I found Mr. Lansbury in a sort of cubbyhole, behind a desk piled high with papers and surrounded by newsmen. He quickly dismissed everybody and we started to talk.

He was anxious to find out about conditions in the United States, especially those faced by the Negro. Finally he invited me to do an article on the Negro's problems for the *Herald.* When I told him of the limitations of my experience, he still insisted. So I wrote an article, which was published while I was still in London, describing the development of the struggles of the Negro in the United States as I saw them. I drew heavily on my reading of the *Messenger* and the *Crisis.*

In our talks, Lansbury probed into my reasons for wanting to go to Africa. When I explained, he said, "Well, you're running away from struggle. You tell me that you want to fight for human rights and dignity, yet you are trying to get away from the main fight. Why don't you return to the States? Your country is going to be a great center of struggle for human rights and liberty. What will the position of the Negro be as the struggle develops?" I had no answer to his questions.

He asked what I thought about the events taking place in Russia. Aside from what I had read in the *Messenger* and the *Masses* and remembered from talks with Anita Whitney, I knew very little and I did not attempt to hide my ignorance. He looked at me speculatively, and then he proceeded to outline what he considered the world significance of the Russian Revolution. I recalled then that Anita had tried to awaken my

interest in the revolutionary events in Russia but I was
obsessed with the Negro issue.

Lansbury soon turned the conversation to my proposed
flight from America. His remarks had a sharp impact and I
mulled them over for hours after leaving his office. He saw the
Black man's struggle as an integral part of world crisis. His
remarks were still in my mind when, on the following day, I
made my final effort to meet McCant Stewart. This time I was
able to meet and talk with the father of the man who had been
my first employer in the legal field.

McCant Stewart was a small man, about five-feet-five. He
was brown-skinned and beginning to go bald. His voice was
brusque and gave no hint of welcome. He did not smile nor did
he extend his hand as he said, "What can I do for you?" He did,
however, invite me to sit down. I gave him the letter from his
son and told him of his son's death, without mentioning that it
was suicide. He read the letter without visible emotion—I
didn't even know if he had prior knowledge of his son's death.
He asked me no questions but simply looked me over as I
talked about my wish to get to Liberia and my desire to work
there in the interests of its government and people.

Then he spoke. He discussed the likelihood of my finding
employment in the African state. He said that Liberia didn't
need lawyers from the United States. What it needed were
artisans, men with some idea of commerce, engineering, industry, men who could help enlarge an extremely weak, almost
purely agricultural economy. He told me bluntly that I would
find little or nothing to do in Liberia; he did not see what I
could contribute. He seemed so brusque and severe that I
began to suspect that the letter had mentioned my arrest at
Shellmound Park and that Stewart felt he was dealing with a
trouble-making radical. It is, of course, possible that he merely
thought me naive.

In what was clearly a conclusion to our talk, he said he
thought a person with my outlook, who declared he desired to
strive for freedom and to further the struggle of Black people,

would find a place in the United States. But he did not inquire as to the situation at home; he did not mention his experience in the Brownsville trial where he had defended Negro soldiers—and I was glad he didn't. In saying he thought I ought to return to the United States, he put the matter in more forthright language than George Lansbury had used. But, after all, the two men lived in different worlds. I thought of the enslaver's role played by the Firestone Rubber Company in Liberia, and Stewart's attitude seemed to be that of a Firestone watchdog.

The similarity of the conclusions reached by men with such different motivations made me take a new look at my own thinking. I began to consider going back to the States. I saw my homeland more clearly from a newspaper office in London than I had been able to see it from a San Francisco classroom.

I wondered if the *Barracuda* was still at Grimsby. I did not think the dockers had finished unloading her. Would she offer passage back across the Atlantic? I took a train for Grimsby. I found the *Barracuda* still docked and went aboard. The first mate asked where I had been and took me to the captain. After some harsh words from the skipper, I got back my old job in the galley. The Pattersons and Charley, the Southerner, seemed glad to have me back. They were all eager to know where I had been and I said I had gone to see London. Actually, in the preceding few days I had visited the city's historic landmarks; walked along the Embankment from Westminster Abbey, stopped to view the Houses of Parliament and gazed at Big Ben in the clock tower. I also visited the Tower of London, the Inns of Court just past Fleet Street and I went to Hyde Park to hear politicians, demagogues, charlatans and just plain cranks expounding their ideas.

A fortnight later, the *Barracuda* steamed out of the Humber River and turned its prow toward theUnited States. I was on my way "home". I began to see it as a home for which I had some responsibility. We did not stop at the Azores but went straight across the Atlantic to Norfolk. The captain did not

penalize me for having jumped ship, so I had a couple of
hundred dollars in my pocket. I said good-bye to Charley and
my West Indian "cousins" and was on my way. I thought
about going back to San Francisco but decided against it. I was
not without a tinge of embarrassment at having left for Africa,
landed in London, and returned to the United States on the
same boat.

I bought a ticket for Seattle, but first I wanted to look at New
York. I wanted to see the largest city in the country. Besides, I
believed I had a brother there. My sister had written that he
turned up recently in New York City. I got a job on one of the
small coastwise steamers running from Newport News to New
York. On the trip I met a number of young black men, mainly
students working their way through Howard University by
taking vacation-time jobs on coastwise ships. One of them told
me he thought he could find a nice place to room in New York.
He described the neighborhood as "Strivers' Row." He warned
me about the dangers of New York, kidded me about steering
clear of the girls and advised me to take good care of my
money.

The New York skyline was amazing! The towering buildings
were like the castles of giants. They seemed to come right
down to the water's edge. I had something of the feeling of awe
I had when I first saw the giant redwood trees in California.

We tied up at one of the city docks and I stepped onto the
streets of New York. Fearful of the intricacies of subway travel,
I took a taxi to Harlem and went at once to the house the young
man had told me about. It was on a beautiful tree-lined street,
139th between Seventh and Eighth Avenues. I almost had to
show my law degree before I got the room at ten dollars a week.

I was now living among the upper classes. Harlem was at
that time being taken over by the Negro people as they moved
uptown from Hell's Kitchen. Blacks were seeking better conditions, as escape from the terrible downtown slum. Class
stratification was becoming noticeable. Some Negroes were
already trying to find a way to share in the exploitation of their

Black brothers. Speculation in dwelling houses was on a grand scale.

Strivers' Row was designed by Leland Stanford White for white middle-class occupancy a generation or two before. The houses were being taken over by Negro doctors, lawyers, social climbers—all seeking not only to better their living conditions but also to establish themselves in a prestigious location. It was one of the economic phases of what was sometimes called "the Negro Renaissance." Harlem, the new Negro community, was offering a market in which super-exploitation was the order of the day. Negro merchants were trying to find a place near the top; others were trying to gain a foothold on the political ladder. The black literati were stirring. Countee Cullen, Langston Hughes, the artist Aaron Douglas, and a host of poets, writers and musicians were emerging.

After I had settled the housing problem, two other tasks confronted me—I had to have a job and I wanted to find my brother. I had almost three hundred dollars and a train ticket to Seattle. But that amount would not last long in New York City. I needed work at once, so I went down to the docks and got a job as a longshoreman. There was irony in my living in Strivers' Row and at the same time going to work on the docks every day. I had been coming home with my overalls wrapped in a bundle, but I was found out anyway. My landlady said it wouldn't do. The doctor from whom I rented my room wanted his tenants to do "respectable" work. The joke was on me.

While I still lived there, I had met two young women who also roomed in the house—one was Eslanda Cardoza Goode (later Mrs. Paul Robeson); the other was Minnie Summer. Both were in their twenties. Eslanda was a medical technician at a city hospital. Five-feet-five, slender, her eyes were lively and searching. She was deeply concerned with social problems and at the same time acutely aware of the racial issue.

Minnie was taller and slimmer than Eslanda, always stylishly dressed, as befitted a young modiste just coming into prominence. Her outlook was middle class, and she was political only to the extent that she worried about what would happen to Negroes in general and herself in particular.

I was attracted to both young women, impressed with theirsophistication and urbane manners. I had never before met women like them.

And it was during this period, in 1920, that I met Paul Robeson. He was studying law at Columbia University, and often came to visit Eslanda. We soon became very good friends. My housing situation amused him but in truth it was no laughing matter. Since I could not afford to give up my job, I had to move from Strivers' Row. I had no desire to live up to its atmosphere anyway. Eslanda, Minnie and I had become fast friends and I did not believe my moving would break that friendship. So I proceeded to get a room-and-a-half apartment on 7th Avenue, between 132nd and 133rd Streets, and paid less for accommodations. I went to live among people who were not ashamed of workers or of being workers.

It was about this time that I found my brother Walter. The search had led me into a number of gambling joints—Harlem was saturated with them. They opened late in the afternoon or early in the evening and I had met people who said they knew a Patterson but didn't know where he lived. Then, one evening, I went into a place at the southeast corner of 134th Street and 7th Avenue, and I saw a man who looked, I thought, like me. He was sitting in on a big poker game, wore an eyeshade and didn't look up at the kibitzers around the table. Several times I heard him called "Pat." Finally I went over and said: "I think you're my brother. What's your name?" "What's yours?" he shot back, I said, "William Patterson." He said, "I'm Walter," rose, looked at me sharply, and proceeded to cash in his chips.

He said he would take me to his home; it turned out that he lived at 164 West 132nd St.—just half a block from where I was living. But that wasn't where he took me. It seemed he lived apart from his wife, Belle Fountain, and their little daughter Muriel. He wanted me to meet them first of all and took me to their apartment a little further uptown.

Muriel, a beautiful little brown child, was just three years old, and I fell in love with her at once. Her mother was a handsome woman, quite tall and quite fair. She and Walter were on speaking terms, but they could not get along when they lived together. I got to know her and Muriel well.

My brother had left San Francisco by sea in 1906 right after the earthquake and fire. After he quit the sea, he had gone to Vermont to live and had become that state's lightweight boxing champion. He then went to Montreal, where he opened a gambling house and prospered for a time; then he had come to New York.

I was glad to be in touch with him, glad to know he was alive. A few days thereafter I moved to the house where he was living. By coincidence, the housekeeper, May Holland, was keeping company with Dr. Oscar Brown, a pharmacist whom I had known in California as a boy. There was a warm reunion.

It was not long after this that I married Minnie Summer and made my first steps in the direction of a law career in Harlem.

The marital journey on which Minnie Summer and I had embarked proved to be of short duration. In the blissful atmosphere of courtship, lovers are so intent upon the attraction that has drawn them together that they overlook many complex and important life problems. Even if the attraction is based on sexual compatibility, on a common social circle, common interests in careers, and in the arts, it takes some time to realize that these do not embrace the total of the marital relationship. This is difficult to encompass under any circumstances but the problems are compounded for a poor Black couple beginning married life in a ghetto in jimcrow United States. If growth and development in mutual understanding and shared interest do not come about, physical attraction can lose its charm; affection wanes; togetherness can even become a torture—and love seeks the nearest exit.

For Black couples, marriage often means that both mates must work full time, and a tug o' war develops as to who does what about shopping and other household tasks; small but vexing conflicts create unresolved problems. I don't think either of us wanted the separation but despite our efforts to avoid it, we were soon heading in that direction.

We lived on 7th Avenue, between 133rd and 134th streets, in a three-room, second-floor flat. It was a two-family house; the landlord lived above us. Our combined income was not large enough to keep the household going. Besides, it soon became apparent that our outlooks were profoundly different—Minnie was a-political and I was a radical. For me, it was difficult enough to battle office problems, to endure the slurs and frustrations reserved for Black folks along the streets, the demanding work of appearances in prejudiced courts— without having to face continual wrangling at home.

By now it had become clear to me that the stage on which I, as a Black man, had to play my part was to be a political one. In the drama of this struggle, the Black man was never to be cast as the leading figure until he began to write the script. At home, it was money—not community problems—that had become the main issue. My wife and I were repelled by the conditions that dominated ghetto life: inordinately high rents, jacked-up prices for second-class foodstuffs (too often these had grown stale on store shelves in white neighborhoods before being dumped on the Harlem market). All around us we felt the presence of numbers runners, whores, neglected children, muggers and petty thieves.

We longed to escape the tragedy and degradation of this life. The growth of crime and vice was in almost geometrical proportion to increased unemployment and the worsening economic situation.

If neither of us clearly understood the sources of the evils about us, I found that Minnie was little concerned about the causes and the social pressures that created the sordid condi- tions. In this she differed greatly from Paul and Essie, who watched us grappling with our problem with deep concern. As for me, my life as a lawyer was interwoven with the woes of Blacks who were either fleeing or in trouble with the law. I saw no avenue for escape for them, and my inability as a lawyer to offer a solution disturbed me greatly. For the Black masses, the law and the courts seemed a treadmill—and I asked myself why I still was without a basic understanding of the problems that plagued us on all sides.

Minnie believed that money would solve every problem—a point of view held by most of the people with whom she was in contact. As a modiste, she catered to the whimsical demands of Black women whose husbands had "made it." In such a world, money was the only key to the door marked "Exit." Minnie saw in me a young lawyer who—if I kept my nose clean, my feet dry and my eye peeled for the dollar—might make considerable money, perhaps even secure a Tammany Hall nod for a small judgeship. What more could one want? That was the one way out!

Time after time Minnie asked me how and why I looked at life as I did. As my reading continued and my understanding grew, I became more and more impressed with the importance of the liberation struggle as a way out. My full commitment to that course became more and more compelling. But I did not lightly dismiss my wife's view. To put money in one's purse was not out of order. But how does one acquire money in large amounts? At what cost? From whom does it come? To what purpose was it to be used? I had no intention of betraying my people in exchange for a handful of silver from a Tammany Hall "wardheeler." I could see little attraction in a life devoted to its pursuit or acquisition.

Nevertheless, my discussions with Minnie did not build up into nasty quarrels—I was ill-equipped for a drag-out fight in any area of human relations save politics. And in spite of our differences, I don't believe we would have parted so soon had not another event occurred. A telegram had come from my sister Alberta in California: "Mother died today funeral Wednesday." My mother had died of a heart attack. Her body was found on her doorstep, the key inserted in the lock.

Since there was no way I could have reached California in time for the funeral, I did not try to make the trip. There was one thing I could do, however. Before this, my sister had intimated that she wanted to come East. I could now help her by inviting her to come to us, and that was what I did.

In my youth Alberta had been wonderful to me; I regarded her as a dear, close friend and counsellor; I wanted to talk over many questions with her. I consulted Minnie and suggested that "Bertie" should live with us for a time. Minnie was strongly opposed to the idea and, as the discussion developed, other issues arose, and many things were said in anger. I packed my belongings and moved out.

CHAPTER 4

Practicing Law In Harlem

WHILE I was still working on the docks I had become acquainted with some young law students who told me about the law firm of Billups and McDougald, on lower Broadway right off Park Place. At that time there were very few Negro attorneys, and even fewer who had offices outside of Harlem. Billups and McDougald were among the most prominent.

Pope Billups was active in real estate matters. He had acquired title to several houses on 135th Street and was trying to juggle them and get into "the big money." Cornelius W. McDougald enjoyed a general practice; he was regarded as a capable criminal lawyer. Shortly after hearing about them, I went to see them and expressed my interest in a clerkship.

It was late afternoon and we sat and talked in the library of their four-room suite. I told them of my experiences, of the reasons why I had left the United States and why I had returned. After they expressed their opinion that there would be a tremendous growth and development in Harlem (they said nothing about my political views), Pope, a small man badly crippled by polio, said they would take me on, help me prepare for the New York bar examinations and give me $35 a month. I was elated. I was launched again on a law career!

Our offices were a rendezvous for young, ambitious Negro lawyers and law students. Both partners enjoyed good reputations and I expected to get some needed experience. Yet, despite my elation, I could not help noting one fact: All of these young men were on the make, ambitious for themselves. Money was to be made out of the development of Harlem; money was to be made out of the yearning of a people to escape from racist misery. I heard no talk of a fight for the rights of Black people.

It was obvious that $35 a month would not be enough to live on. I would have to draw on the small reserve I had. I sold my railroad ticket to Seattle—I don't know why I had held on to it for so long. I was not going West, at least not in the immediate future.

Billups had a car and, despite the ravages of polio, drove it himself—his physical infirmity had taken nothing from his courage. We almost immediately struck up a warm friendship. He began showing me the sights of the city. My talk about the necessity to fight for the people only drew the response that money came first. Yet he was a fighter.

I remember an incident which impressed me greatly. It occurred when, together with two of his clients, Billups had driven us out to Westchester County. We stopped at a nightclub for a drink. The bartender, a white man, refused to serve us. Billups pulled out a revolver and laid it on the bar. He said, "We want to be served, and we want to be served here." Some of the white patrons made for the door, but one of them, a well-dressed, middle-aged fellow, stood up and said, "These people fought together with me in the Argonne. I don't see why they can't drink with me here. Serve them."

The bartender did.

I had not been with Billups and McDougald long before becoming acquainted with two younger lawyers who had passed the New York bar and were preparing to enter practice. The elder of the two was Thomas Benjamin Dyett, a young West Indian, a graduate of Boston University. From all I could determine from my talks with him, he was a capable, level-headed and ambitious man. The other, George Hall, was born in the South; he had graduated from the law school at Howard

University. One of his teachers there was Charles Houston, who became dean of the Howard Law School and an outstanding expert on civil rights law.

We became fast friends. Dyett and Hall talked to me about organizing a law firm with them, asking my opinion. Since I had not yet passed the New York bar, I was reluctant to commit myself as to the prospects of a young Negro law firm. I considered the work my bosses were doing, and I was not greatly inspired. My own interests lay in constitutional law.

Then Dyett and Hall invited me to join them in establishing a firm, even though I was not yet a member of the bar. We discussed the question thoroughly. I was doing all of the brief writing for Billups and McDougald and had gained something of a reputation among the younger lawyers. They insisted, and I pondered the matter. What would be the name of the firm, what would be my share of the income and expenses, since I could not do any courtroom work; where would we establish our offices?

Dyett and Hall had ready answers: the firm would be Dyett, Hall & Patterson; I would be given an equal share in whatever moneys came in; we would set up offices in Harlem. (The matter of using the law as a weapon with which to intensify the battle for Negro rights was not resolved.) I argued that this was too generous an arrangement, but they beat me down, and the law firm of Dyett, Hall & Patterson was born in New York City, in 1923. No partnership agreement was drawn up—our word was enough.

I had talked the matter over with Billups and McDougald and both of them approved the undertaking but thought we would have a difficult time at first. I also discussed the matter with Paul Robeson, Minnie Summer and Eslanda Goode, whom I saw quite regularly, and they urged me to go ahead.

We set up our offices on the second floor at 2303 Seventh Avenue, just north of 135th Street, in a building owned by the Duncan Brothers, proprietors of a large funeral parlor on the lower floor. On the same floor with us was the dental office of

Dr. "Hap" Delaney and his sister Bessie, both graduate dentists and very fine individuals. They were ardent nationalists.

Our office soon became the gathering place of young lawyers and other young professional men. A whole corps of young Negro attorneys was springing up. They included Harry Bragg, who early became one of the local Democratic machine politicians; William Andrews, later to be a state assemblyman; Percy Ifill, a brilliant young West Indian; and Vernal Williams, also a West Indian who later became an ardent Garveyite. They were young men on the make and most young men on the make had to turn their eyes toward the political machine that ran the city.

With all the discussion that went on almost every evening at our office, when the bar exams came, although I passed the written test, I was not prepared for, and flunked the oral. It was then that the bar examiners appointed Henry L. Stimson (later Secretary of State under Herbert Hoover and Secretary of War under F. D. Roosevelt) to be my mentor. In many ways it turned out to be a good thing for me.

When I met Stimson for the first time in his palatial Wall Street suite, his approach was kindly. "What's the matter, Patterson?" he asked. "Didn't you get a fair deal?" I certainly wasn't going to make that kind of complaint. "As to that, I don't know," I answered. "But I wasn't prepared for such an arduous, far-ranging oral test."

"Tell me something about it," he said. I gave him a resume of the questions that had been asked, and he said, "We'll go over these and a few other questions. I think we'll be prepared for the gentlemen next time out."

My contact with Henry Stimson was an eye-opener. Everything he talked about dealt with matters far beyond the ghetto. His starting point was the broad sweep of white American bourgeois life. My experience was severely limited in comparison, and the limitations were imposed by racism. As I listened to him I saw the bar examination in a new light. It was not a question as to who was the better thinker, the white or the Black aspirant. The test reflected one's entire previous environment and contact, and the Black man started with a handicap

created by whites. Stimson discussed matters that come up in
the bar examination because the test was given by white men
who lived in a larger world than that of the Blacks. I began to
understand the monumental handicap under which Negro
science students labored as they emerged from college. I
thought of my earlier experience with Senator Shortridge
of California. The superiority which the white man attributed to his innate capacities was not that at all; he had
advantages due to wider opportunities in a less constricted
environment.

Under Stimson's coaching I absorbed some of the necessary
background, and the following year I passed the oral exam. By
then our firm was already in full stride and I now began to take
an equal part in court work.

A word here about the Garvey movement would be in order.
Led by a West Indian, this "home to Africa" program had
stirred up wide interest. Marcus Garvey, a short, strongly built
Black man with an extremely persuasive voice, had originally
supported a plan calling for the unity of Blacks and whites in
the United States. Meeting with formidable opposition from
white racists, he turned to the idea of building a powerful
Black state in Africa. He argued that the United States belonged to white men and that its 17 million Negroes should
voluntarily surrender their heritage and get out. They were
supposed to forget the blood spilt by their forefathers in five
wars and their contributions to building the United States into
a world power; to forget the 300 years of unrequited toil as
slaves.

It was a fantastic dream—one that the American ruling class
joyfully endorsed. In fact, Garvey won the endorsement of the
Ku Klux Klan and of other forces of American reaction. It has to
be admitted that he was also attempting to create in millions of
Negroes a sense of pride in being Black and that, to the degree
that he succeeded, a great spurt was given to the Negroes'
renaissance.

"It is idle—worse than idle," said Frederick Douglass, "ever to think of our expatriation or removal. . . . We are rapidly filling up the numbers of four million, and all the gold in California combined would be insufficient to defray the expense attending our colonization."

It was Garvey and, somewhat later, Adam Clayton Powell, who was emerging as a foremost political figure in the Harlem ghetto, whom we discussed in the offices of Dyett, Hall and Patterson during the long evenings and weekends. Lawyers, politicians-to-be and others seeking escape from the fate of the masses gathered to argue politics, morals, economics, the problems of the Black people of Harlem, anything and everything that bore on our lives. At the time I wasn't aware that these talks were to have a decisive influence on all our lives. One cannot argue politics and respond to the challenge of other minds without sooner or later realizing that he must take sides. Whom should we back in the next race for mayor or governor? Weighing the merits of the various candidates made us throw on the scales such diverse issues as schools, transportation, health facilities, jobs and, always, the ghetto.

Was Garvey right or was Dr. W. E. B. Du Bois, who opposed the propagation of a separatist movement? Neither of these leaders took an openly anti-imperialist stance.

Naturally, our discussions were not all abstract—they led us to re-examine our own positions. My colleagues never thought of asking, "Which side are you on?" "What's in it for me?" was the unspoken watchword. Although I was part of the group, I could not go along with its self-centered thinking. I became more and more concerned with Harlem's poor. Digging into their problems made me realize that they were related to a larger whole—the salvation of the United States.

Looking back at those talks in our office, I recognize that by and large we did not realize the limitations ghetto-living had imposed on the nature of our thinking and the consequent shape of our political actions. The ghetto was a prison. What we needed at that time was talks about a prison break. Whatever the talks did for the others (some of them ended up

in well-paying offices serving the Establishment), they turned
me more and more toward the realization of myself as a social
being with social responsibilities.

During this really formative period of my life when I was
working, courting, marrying and discussing the day's chal-
lenging issues, I saw a great deal of Paul Robeson. We became
lifelong friends. Paul and I argued over the nature of the Black
man's struggle. How was he to attain to a status that was
durable and substantial? Was the Constitution more than a
scrap of paper to the Negro? Was it more than a scrap of paper
for anyone who did not control the courts and the government?
Certainly our oppressors' disregard of it made the Constitution
sometimes seem little more than a scrap of paper.

Paul had graduated from Rutgers University and then went
to Columbia University's Law School, from which he was to
graduate high on the class roster in 1923. He had been an
outstanding athlete at Rutgers, making the varsity baseball,
football and track teams, while winning high scholastic honors. In 1916, Walter Camp, then regarded as the leading
authority on football, declared him one of the greatest ends the
country had ever produced and named him for the All-
American team.

It appeared, beyond the shadow of a doubt, that Paul was
marked for great success. Wealthy white students at Rutgers
sought to bask in his reflected glory. Through his prowess as an
athlete, he was well known to the school alumni and to the
wealthy men who controlled the world of sports. But his
physical skills were only a fraction of the gifts with which
nature had endowed this young black giant. He was a gifted
singer with a baritone voice of great beauty. Very early, he
displayed extraordinary histrionic ability, and later he became
a speaker of great emotional intensity and power.

It was natural that there would be those who were to
intimate that a place be found for him with one or another of
New York's leading white law firms. He was not, of course,

invited to join any of Rutgers' leading fraternities. In the press there was also the subtle intimation that his future depended upon his ability to accommodate himself to the world beyond the ghetto. That world could always use a docile Negro who did not concern himself with his true place in the changing world.

Robeson's white friends did not want him to become mixed up with social crusaders; they wanted a man who would proclaim and glorify those who would pave the way for him. But Paul took a very realistic view; he often said to me, "Yes, Pat, the door's open for me, but it's closed to my brother." He knew that it was a far cry from a "Hi, Paul, how goes it?" on campus or in a classroom, and a "Good morning, Mr. Robeson, I want to discuss some matters with you," in a downtown New York law office. And he knew how he would be expected to react if the subject to be discussed were the human rights of Black people.

The Negro press also recognized Robeson's great potential as a leader. It admired him and did not want him to clash seriously with the existing order. They would not, of course, object to his fighting for the Negro bourgeoisie to win greater opportunities to exploit its own ghetto market. If he were fired with zeal to effect a fundamental change in race relations, Robeson could prove a foe of no mean proportion.

Life was soon to prove these and other things to Paul. The path that led from Harlem's litter-strewn streets to an oak-paneled Wall Street law office was not as easily traversed as Paul's well-meaning white friends in Rutgers and law school had made out. He recognized that not all of his classmates were fair-weather friends. But they knew only their own world; their ignorance of a less privileged life dampened any desire for change.

My mind went back to my experience with Senator Samuel Shortridge in San Francisco. Paul and I discussed this. Shortridge did not want me around because I would have been bad business for him—money came first, last and always. American big business was really not going to need the services of a

Negro on a higher level than elevator operator or janitor until some world changes were made. Paul's grasp of the situation was extraordinary. The cream of the racists offered him a place in their world. If he took it, he would have to play their game. He saw the role assigned him and rejected it.

Paul decided to turn away from the law as a profession. He was not, however, ready to move into the political area. The theater attracted him, and he was given a tremendous welcome in that milieu—many now believed that Paul was safely out of the liberation struggle. He chose to go in the direction in which his militancy would, he thought, have the greatest impact on the freedom fight.

In fact, we had both begun to see the courts as one of the instruments the establishment uses to sustain racism—it has been so since before the Dred Scott case.

Heywood Broun, who was later to organize the Newspaper Guild, was at that time very friendly with Paul. He declared himself a socialist and tried to convince Paul that the Socialist Party position was the one he should follow. I myself was not then identified with any political party, but I had begun a study of the Soviet Union. My studies naturally led me into the Marxist-Leninist philosophy, and I found it harder and harder to argue against its principal tenets. It seemed to me to have the support of historical and objective truth—a truth that corresponded with the needs of the great majority of the world's people and especially Black people.

I think it was through the good offices of Heywood Broun that Paul got started in the Greenwich Village Theater. Later he played Simon the Cyrenian in a play by Ridgely Torrence, staged at the Harlem YMCA. In the play, Simon the Cyrenian was a Black man who, out of sympathy and compassion for the martyred Christ, carried the Savior's cross to Calvary. The Black man is portrayed as gentle and kindly. Undoubtedly, Mr. Torrence was trying to make cross-bearing a noble endeavor for Blacks. Although the Black man was in the course of a cultural renaissance, at that stage there were no organizations sufficiently developed to be critical of the content of a production so long as a Negro was cast in a leading role.

Eugene O'Neill got Paul to play the "Emperor Jones," a black emperor on a Caribbean island who wanted to rule and mercilessly exploit what O'Neill presented as ignorant Blacks. *Emperor Jones,* with all its failure to understand the Black man, was typical of the dramatic material which white playwrights wrote for Black artists. Paul expressed his distaste for parts like these.

Paul was moving steadily ahead in the realms of music and theater. If he did not have the material to work with that some of us would have liked, we thought it would surely come as the arts began to reflect the political demands of Blacks.

It was during this period that I met a number of theater people, mostly Afro-Americans. From them and through their varied experiences I was to learn how racism permeated every phase of American life. The results of corruption and debasement were not only to be met in the courts and in daily political and industrial life, but also in the world of the arts. Black artists were assigned the roles of maintaining the images of a Black man and woman in degrading roles. If it were not as a buffoon, a razor-wielding rapist, or a head-scratching, eye-rolling, superstitious moron, the Black actor did not get on stage. They could accommodate themselves—or else. Racism pervaded everything, but few Black artists knew how or were ready to fight.

For the Black artist to fight back successfully, there would have to be a broad political struggle projected by dedicated and far-seeing Black leaders. Paul and I spent many hours discussing this state of affairs—particularly in the field of the arts. The discussions we engaged in were sharp, but the dialogue helped make clearer for both of us what had to be done.

"The politician who represents us must go beyond the rules set up by the white folks; he has the duty to create new methods, beat new paths; he's got to have our freedom in mind," Paul observed in the course of one of our talks.

"You're not talking about the old-line politician, Paul, are you? Aren't you thinking of a new kind of Black representative who will work outside the old machines, who is free to explore all roads to freedom without having to consult his white bosses or to get their consent?"

"Precisely," said Paul in his booming voice, and with the familiar smile forming, he added: "Now that we know what kind of politician we need, we will have to get a new kind of organization to support him."

In the 1920's, the formation of such an organization seemed far away.

It was during this period in the early 20's that I went to an NAACP meeting on Fifth Avenue near 23rd Street. On this occasion I recall that Mrs. Bernice Austin, a socially ambitious and quite attractive woman, sold me my ticket. She was married to Harry Austin, one of Harlem's most prominent lawyers. The Austins, like thousands of NAACP members, could by virtue of mere membership be called fighters against racism who never had to go into battle.

A number of Black artists were participating, and the place was crowded. Among those sitting at my table was a Negro woman whose name seemed to be known to the others but not to me. Nora Holt was a vivacious and witty woman with a delightful figure, copper-colored skin and hair. Conversation at our table swirled around her as she talked about music, the entertainment world, with an insider's knowledge. She was a night club entertainer who was already as successful as Black artists were permitted to be.

As soon as I had an opportunity I asked her whether I could see her home. This was agreeable to her. She was living with the Austins. It was the beginning of a long friendship.

Around this time I also met a young pianist—Lawrence Brown—who was to become one of my dearest friends. When I met Larry, he was the accompanist of Roland Hayes, the celebrated Black tenor, and was a pianist of the first order. I had never met anyone who knew more about Negro folk music and loved it as deeply as Larry. A brilliant accompanist, he later accompanied Paul Robeson. He loved sports and there we met on common ground. He was not only a spectator at the main New York sport events, but did everything in his power to keep himself fit physically and mentally. He was deeply interested in politics, an interest that grew out of his experience and observation of the exploitation to which Black musicians were subjected. But he was not a political activist, and he could not throw himself into the arena of day-to-day struggle.

He and Nora Holt and I became fast friends. We attended fights, concerts, the theater and often dined together. There was always a barrage of questions addressed to me about how Black people were going to end the nightmare of racism. More and more my answers revolved around the nature of the social changes and the kind of political organization I felt were necessary.

Changes, I had come to believe, could not be confined to reforms achieved by legislation or through court action. One who accepted reforms as the only expedient would find himself in a blind alley. A fight for reforms was needed under the existing conditions, but reforms would not bring about full equality. The social system of the United States was geared to absorb all manner of reforms.

I was being guided to a specific line of political action and thought by the universal complaints of Black men against racism. They came from every source, every person I encountered. It was Nora who brought me into contact with many of the leading Negro artists—among them Florence Mills, who rose to stardom in *Bye, Bye Blackbird;* Abbie Mitchell; Rose McClendon, a truly great dramatic artist.

For all of these women, the road to stardom was paved with insults, humiliation and degrading sex demands. Rose McClendon, whose talents were respected by her Broadway fellow-artists, never got the roles she deserved. The managers saw to that, always placing the blame on the white theater-going public.

The Cotton Club, where Lena Horne worked, was owned by gangsters; not the duly elected gangsters of the political world but the professional thugs of the underworld who worked with their political counterparts. It was located in the 140's on Lenox Avenue, the heart of the ghetto, yet no Black guests were allowed inside. It served the elite of gangsterism, legitimate and illegitimate. It was an insult to the people of Harlem, yet none of the white liberals who were promoting the "cultural renaissance" at that time made the slightest protest.

Most of the clubs helped to reflect the image of the stereotyped Negro—amoral, happy-go-lucky and sexually uninhibited. In fact, the show was run to titillate the jaded appetites of the supersophisticated guests.

This was the period of prohibition. The owners, as well as many of the patrons of some of the clubs, made their money from the sale of illicit liquor and drugs. Indeed, drugs were sold in volume in the streets of Harlem. One could observe the open promotion of vice. Politicians, naturally, fattened on the business.

Most of the performers were, of course, far from happy-go-lucky and footloose; many of them were later to reflect the influence of Paul's political views in their own activities; many freely offered their services at fund-raising campaigns of the left. Aubrey Lyle, of the famous Negro team of Miller and Lyle, was the sharpest and angriest protester I had met. He was not publicly outspoken, but he did not hesitate to let his hatred of the conditions in the entertainment world be known; he hated those who were robbing him, and his partner Florence Mills was later sent to an early death by racism.

Several days before I left for Europe in 1927, on my first trip to the Soviet Union, Lyle gave a dinner for me and some of our friends. Among the most outspoken on that occasion was Jack Carter, a very light-skinned, promising young Negro actor, who later went to Hollywood, changed his name and became a noted white actor.

In retrospect, I would say that everywhere I turned—toward professionals, lawyers, doctors, artists, business men, working men and women, the men on the docks among whom I had worked—hatred of racism prevailed. Most of these people were

from the South, and all were as one in declaring that the main
difference between the South and the North was that "the
South put up public signs proclaiming segregation," but
jimcrow ruled supreme, South and North. There was no clear
understanding as to the true identity of the oppressors, why
they acted as they did, and whence came their power. The
segment of black society which W. E. B. Du Bois had labeled
the "talented tenth" was to prove unable to lead the Negro to
liberation. A politically enlightened talented tenth did not
exist—no one had found the road.

The grandparents of the men and women among whom I
mingled had been moved through war out of slavery into a
capitalist society about whose class character their offspring
were taught nothing. The former slaves had tried to exploit the
limited social and economic gains during the Reconstruction
period. But they were mercilessly attacked by terrorist gangs
which the new government did not restrain. The transition
from chattel slavery to wage slavery was planned only insofar
as the needs of rising capitalism were concerned. The poor
whites and Blacks knew nothing of this. The Blacks, being
ex-slaves, workers on the land, wanted and needed land and
the means by which to cultivate it. They could not see far
beyond their need for "40 acres and a mule."

The demands of the new economic overlords were concerned with absolute power and the command over cheap,
docile labor. The measure of political power won by the former
slaves in the course of Reconstruction was cancelled out; their
political activities were brought to a halt through naked
terror—night riders, members of hooded orders wielding dag-
ger and gun, rope and faggot.

The descendants of the slaves knew little or nothing about
the real reasons for their betrayal; they emerged from schools
that taught them that their fathers and grandfathers had failed
to meet the demands of leadership when they were given the
chance. Their schools deliberately concealed the heroic efforts
of Black men and women and some poor whites during the
Civil War and Reconstruction to build a new world. The

outstanding contributions of Black people toward making Reconstruction the golden era of American democracy were ignored.

As the son of a mother born a slave, I became aware that the history textbooks I had studied contained no names nor faces of Black achievers or heroes. The young men with whom I now associated were all products of these schools programmed to prepare Black men to play the roles assigned to them by their white oppressors. Thus our discussions were limited by the nature of the miseducation we had received.

While I was becoming acquainted with Harlem, money began coming into the offices of Dyett, Hall and Patterson—we were getting more than our share of the legal business of the community. For example, we were retained by a group of Negro businessmen of Chicago and New York who were eager to establish an insurance company in New York State. The firm—the Victory Life Insurance Company—was already licensed in Illinois but up to then no Negro insurance firm had been licensed in New York and our client saw limitless possibilities. It was a move by Black men into a field dominated by big business. I knew that if Victory Life came in, it would be through the agreement of the giant insurance monopolies and by the good graces of powerful Tammany politicians.

Through the initiative of Tom Dyett, we were also involved in creating cooperatively owned units out of a number of Harlem apartment houses; we were among the first in Harlem to develop this kind of activity.

In connection with the insurance case, I went to Chicago under an excellent contract to look things over. The insurance company was sound in every way; there was no reason why it should not have been licensed immediately by the Insurance Commissioner of New York State. But that wasn't the way the law operated. This case was to emphasize for me the principle of bourgeois society that a legal matter involving hundreds of thousands of dollars and a Black man is determined not by law but by color and politics. My clients could do business in New York only if the big white companies monopolizing the field could work with and through them. The financial stability of the Black promoters or their rights under the law did not have any bearing on the situation. It was rather the question of what advantages and benefits would accrue to white companies; what was in it for white politicians if the Victory Life's petition was approved.

There was no exception to this condition; no tribute a Black American could pay to escape the color of his skin when the matter at issue in court involved a white man or property.

One of the best actuarial firms in New York City had been retained to prepare all the paper work needed to show the eligibility of Victory Life Insurance Company for a New York State license. I went to Albany to talk with the Insurance Commissioner. In New York I discussed the question with Ferdinand Q. Morton, a leading Negro spokesman and fixer in Tammany. As we shook hands, I left two five-hundred-dollar bills in his palm—a small amount in his eyes, no doubt, but a token.

A young black lawyer who was moving up in machine politics, Harry Bragg, was with me. He had arranged the meeting. The stage was set for the admission of Victory Life; the license was indeed gained—but by then I was out of the picture. I did not stay for the celebration. By the time it took place, I was out of law as a business for good, and traveling in my chosen direction.

My reasons were not unfathomable—if I were going to become a politician, I would not accept as my objectives a Sugar Hill abode and fistsful of five-hundred-dollar bills. Politics, for me, had to mean more than that. If it was a game, as some of my friends had said, then it had to be a game played for meaningful prizes—freedom, dignity, democracy, socialism—and an end to the whole of the corrupt and depraved system that had cowed, cuffed, disfranchised, exploited and oppressed me and my people for generations.

CHAPTER 5

Sacco And Vanzetti—
A Turning Point

ONE OF the regular visitors to our law office was Richard B. Moore, a wise and learned man. He called my attention to the way in which the political contributions and gains of Black men during the Civil War and Reconstruction were wiped from the slate of history. He pointed out how racism demolished the new constitutional provisions. Moore forced me to seek answers to some basic questions: How could the political gains be restored, consolidated? Who in society would undertake the monumental task involved?

On each visit, Moore presented one legal case after another in which the law was used to deny the Black man his constitutional rights. He proved how futile it was for a Black American to rely solely on U.S. laws—administered and manipulated by racists—as liberating instruments. What he said made sense: Those who sit in the judicial seats of the mighty, deciding today's crucial problems on the basis of ancient precedents, can seldom decide in favor of progress: the search for precedents leads them to those decisions by which the ruling class has established its power.

Moore then began jogging my conscience about what he called the legal lynching being prepared for Nicola Sacco and Bartolomeo Vanzetti, two Italian workers whose execution by

Delegation leaving New York for the Save Sacco-Vanzetti mass gathering in Boston, August 1927. *Standing in doorway,* Alfred Wagenknecht, leader of the Emergency Committee; *standing left,* Rose Baron, International Labor Defense. I am leaning out the window.

the State of Massachusetts was nearing. As an oppressed Black fellow-American, Moore argued, I should be interested. I decided I had no other alternative: I had either to join the battle for the lives of two innocent Italians or to ignore my kinship with these men.

I had come to the crossroads. Every step along the capitalist road seemed to lead to the swamp of moral and political corruption. The first stop on "freedom road" was Boston, Massachusetts, where thousands of concerned and earnest men and women were fighting to save two white working men whose ideology threatened the status quo. In another part of the country, the setting might have been a tree with stout limbs and a rope all ready for a Black man who would "dance on air." As a Black man and as a member of the human family, I was compelled to join the Sacco-Vanzetti freedom fighters.

Along with the millions of immigrants pouring into the United States during the early years of this century were two young Italians—Vanzetti was 20, Sacco, eighteen. Both young men were poor, both hoped to find in America something of that dream of prosperity and freedom that made this country in those days the magnet for the downtrodden of the world. Both men were dedicated to working-class solidarity and all that was humanist in the traditions of their former homeland. They loved people, they had sympathy and understanding of workers' problems in the United States. And they never hesitated to come to the aid of a neighbor in trouble or of workers fighting against the brutal exploitation then practiced in the factories along the Eastern seaboard.

Vanzetti loved to read. He knew Dante's work, the pride of Italian literature. He loved Puccini's music. His mind was always reaching out to grasp the deeper meanings of life, to understand why in a country as rich as ours workers were driven to exhaustion while others did nothing but clip coupons; why racial hatred and discrimination existed against their Black brothers.

If Vanzetti had little formal education, he read widely—

Marx, Charles Darwin, Leo Tolstoi, Victor Hugo, Maxim Gorky, Emile Zola and scores of others. "I learned," he was to write later, while he was in his death cell in Charlestown prison, "that class-consciousness was not a phrase invented by propagandists, but was a real, vital force, and that those who felt its significance were no longer beasts of burden but human beings."

Sacco and Vanzetti became friends during World War I. Rather than go to war to kill their fellow-workers, they had joined a group of anarchists who went to live in Mexico for the duration of the war. Their friendship continued when they returned to Massachusetts.

In the police files there was quite a dossier under the designation "agitators" concerning these two men. Vanzetti had led a strike at a cordage factory for which he was blacklisted. Sacco had raised money to fight frame-ups, he had walked picket lines, had been arrested for demonstrating. Both were very active in the defense of the foreign-born, who were at that time the targets of a sweeping witch hunt, under the guidance of U.S. Attorney General A. Mitchell Palmer and J. Edgar Hoover. The two friends had organized protest meetings, raised defense money, distributed handbills. They were often followed by spies hired by the federal government.

A protest meeting that Sacco and Vanzetti were organizing for May 9, 1920 never came off. On May 5 they were arrested, charged with dangerous radical activities. But even the authorities must have felt this an insufficient charge, for they added another—they associated them with a payroll robbery at South Braintree, Mass., on April 15, 1920, in which two guards had been killed.

At their trial, Judge Webster Thayer, who presided, revealed at every turn his marked hatred for the two Italians. Every effort was made by the press and the authorities to whip up mass mob hysteria. The courtroom was surrounded with extra guards, and everyone entering it was searched. Suborned witnesses calmly lied on the stand, with the knowledge, undoubtedly, that even if they were charged with having given perjured testimony they would go free. On July 14, 1921, a jury pronounced Sacco and Vanzetti guilty and they were sentenced to be executed. But the fight to save them was to go on for six years, and the marching feet of the protestors shook cities all around the world.

The trial was to reveal to millions the class nature of justice in the United States. It was a mockery of the word "justice"— no less than had been the trials of hundreds of Blacks who fought for their rights. The Massachusetts State Supreme Court disgraced itself by turning down the appeal. When, in order to quiet the mounting indignation, Governor Alan T. Fuller appointed three of the state's most "distinguished" men (A. Lawrence Lowell, president of Harvard; Samuel Stratton, president of Massachusetts Institute of Technology and Robert A. Grant, a retired probate judge), they went along with the frame-up.

I was not surprised. For, after all, who were Sacco and Vanzetti? Poor immigrants, members of a national minority that had not yet established any political power; no aura of prestige or heroism surrounded them as they moved to the front of the stage of history; they had been virtually unknown; they were anarchists but there was no anarchist movement.

It was three years since a working-class government, in alliance with the peasantry, had come into power in Russia; socialism, which had been haunting Europe since 1848, now had flesh and blood; it had a voice in the councils of nations. In the effort to enlist the support of the working class in the war, the capitalist rulers, under pressure, made promises of a better life. After the war, workingmen all over the world were calling for the redemption of these promises. They were prepared to fight for a better life.

The situation was worst of all for Negroes; it was also bad for other minorities; the differences were only those of degree. In the labor markets the Italian was a rung above the Black man. Because he was dark-skinned and a South European, he was catalogued below the Anglo-Saxon, the Scandinavian and other Western Europeans. I have sketched in this background to emphasize my identification of the victimized Sacco and Vanzetti with the poor and exploited everywhere and with my own betrayed people. I was standing on the threshold of understanding that the struggle of the Blacks was inseparable from the class struggle.

In *The Case of Sacco and Vanzetti*, Felix Frankfurter had written: "By systematic exploitation of the defendants' alien blood, their imperfect knowledge of English, their unpopular social views and opposition to war, the District Attorney invoked against them a riot of political passion and patriotic sentiment; and the trial judge connived at—one had almost written 'cooperated in'—the process."

Here was the challenge I had evaded when the Mooney case came into my life. Would I sidestep it again? Or would I face up to the challenge? What Frankfurter called "alien blood" might well have been "black skin." Although the attack on Mooney was an attack on the trade unions and on all oppressed people, he himself did not associate his persecution with the injustices perpetrated on Black people. The case against the two Italians was an attack on the foreign-born, the members of a minority, designed to create fear and prejudice among native-born Americans, to discredit the influence that revolutionary ideas might have on the working class—perhaps especially on the Black masses.

I discussed these questions with my partners. Both men were deeply moved by what I said, but they were of the opinion that any effort on our part in behalf of the accused men would wreck the fortunes of our firm. Dyett and Hall were looking forward to a future in which they might receive high posts from the Democratic party political machine. They did not want to become involved in unorthodox crusades.

The final argument was: "Pat, those guys are Communists! The freedom you talk about is beyond me. I want to be free; if the other guy does, let him earn it like I expect to."

If Communists were to be denied constitutional rights

because they were Communists, and Negroes were to be denied those rights because they were Blacks, where would political persecution end? Would only those who were white and Anglo-Saxon and who accepted the gospel of the rulers of the United States be entitled to the protection of the Constitution? If so, the Constitution became the property of only those with economic and political power.

I called meetings in the office. To these came young lawyers, doctors, even members of the clergy, but most of them were against my position. Among those with whom I now discussed the case were a number of leading Black Communists— Richard Moore, Cyril Briggs, Otto Huiswood, Lovett Fort Whitman and Grace Campbell. Grace was a magnificent Black woman, a school teacher, who had been dismissed because of her political views. These friends talked to me, strengthened my morale with plenty of facts. The powerful writing of Art Shields in the *Daily Worker* also affected me deeply. I was convinced I had to use my profession as a weapon for freedom. If this case were won, that victory in itself would be a blow in behalf of all those seeking equality of rights.

History records the final fight for Sacco and Vanzetti and how it rallied the support of good people around the world. In Paris, London, Madrid, Havana, Mexico City, Buenos Aires, Bombay and Moscow, there were massive rallies. Of course, those who led them were accused of being Communists. Romain Rolland, George Bernard Shaw, Albert Einstein, John Galsworthy, Martin Andersen Nexo, Sinclair Lewis, H. G. Wells and hundreds of other world citizens sent impassioned pleas for their lives, as did Eugene Debs and Anatole France. Were all of these distinguished men following the lead of Communists? I did not believe it.

Vanzetti himself had called for unity in the struggle of white and Negro and for white support of the Negroes' political demands. His position was far more advanced than that of most American labor leaders and that of the American Federation of Labor.

In May 1926, Vanzetti wrote to the International Labour

Council as follows: "I repeat. I will repeat to the last, only the people, our Comrades, our friends, the world revolutionary proletariat, can save us from the powers of the capitalist reactionary hyenas, or vindicate our names and our blood before history. . . .

"There are some who think that our case is a trial for a common crime; that our friends should contest our innocence but not turn the case into a political issue, because it would only damage us. Well, I could answer to them all that our case is even more than a political case; it is a case of class war in which our enemies are personally interested to lose us—not only for class purposes but for personal passions, resentments and fears. . . ."

I decided to go to Boston.

It would have been unwise for me to go alone. I was not known outside Harlem and I would have been lost in the zealous but largely disorganized forces in, or hurrying toward, Boston. There was one direction in which I could turn.

The International Labor Defense, a working-class organization, had been a party to the creation of a Sacco-Vanzetti Emergency Defense Committee; Vito Marcantonio was its president. This fearless lawyer and humanitarian was later to serve with distinction in Congress. Communists, too, were an accepted and conspicuously active part of the committee, which was organizing people to go to Boston. I went down to the ILD office and signed up for the trip.

Rose Baron, the head of the defense committee, greeted me warmly and was one of the people who accompanied me on the trip. She and a jovial Communist leader, Alfred Wagenknecht, made sure that stops for lunch and other needs were made where I would not be refused and insulted because of my color. I made a mental note of that and vowed never to forget it. It was an evidence of sensitivity that touched me. I was being made part of a great struggle without the slightest trace of prejudice.

We arrived in Boston in the evening and drove to Hanover

Street, where an office of the defense committee was located. There was just time to wash and get a bite to eat before assignments to cover meetings were handed out. I was assigned to speak at a meeting covered by Paxton Hibben, one of America's outstanding liberals. Other speakers included Ella Reeve Bloor—Mother Bloor—a revolutionary spirit of amazing energy and wisdom, known from coast to coast as one of the great fighters for human rights. There was also Mike Gold, one of the most noted writers on the Left, an editor of the *Masses* and author of *Jews Without Money*.

I was to learn more about Mike. He was seeking a new way of life, a new America, and he believed that he saw in socialism the goal through which all he dreamed of would be attained. Both his prose and his poetry were dedicated to the revolutionary path of struggle. Mike was a friend of Claude McKay, Langston Hughes, Jean Toomer, and other Negro writers whose voices carried overtones of militancy.

On the platform Mike Gold was a deeply earnest speaker. He drew a parallel between the great mass of Jewish immigrants and the Italians, who were also newcomers to the promised land. He read the famous poem of Emma Lazarus telling of the "huddled masses yearning to breathe free" and of the Goddess of Liberty "lifting her lamp beside the golden door." Mike told the story of the Jew and the Italian as garment workers, and his description of their common plight showed how most of the rosy promises had been broken. He called attention to my presence on the platform and spoke of its significance. Then I was called upon to speak.

The plea for unity which I voiced contained a somewhat different message. I tried to show why I had come to Boston to throw myself into the case of Sacco and Vanzetti. I wanted to help unify Americans in opposing the persecution of these two members of a minority group; I wanted to associate the struggle for their lives with that which Negroes had waged to save their sons and daughters, condemned to ostracism and worse for the crime of being born Black.

Mother Bloor, following me, linked the arrest, trial and conviction of Sacco and Vanzetti with the Palmer raids and the rise of J. Edgar Hoover. Thousands of men had been arrested; hundreds of the foreign-born, who had been welcomed so long as they accepted the ideology of capitalism, were now being deported. But, she pointed out, the slander of the U.S. Department of Justice against the Communists had failed to stampede the American people. The effort to whip up anti-Red hysteria even against Sacco and Vanzetti had fallen flat.

The meeting was a milestone for me. After accepting Mike Gold's invitation to share his room, the next day I was assigned to the picket line on Boston Common. On the Common stood a statue of Crispus Attucks, a Black man who was said to have been the first man to die in the Revolutionary War. I looked into the bronze face and thought what a great and far-sighted American this Black man had been! It was doubtful that this former slave could read—but he could think. He was against slavery and for the independence of this land. He must have seen in the Revolution a step toward the ending of slavery.

Among others in that picket line were Edna St. Vincent Millay, Clarina Michelson, John Dos Passos, John Howard Lawson and my new friends, Mike Gold and Mother Bloor. Had I been brought forward because of my color? No matter, I was proud to be there. To many of the liberals I know I was something of a curiosity—Negroes were not regarded as an organic part of the progressive people of the land. Was that our fault or theirs? Perhaps it was only a result of centuries of miseducation, of lies that maligned Black men and denied the great role they had played and could play in the battle for freedom.

It was not long before the attack came. Soon, beside the picket signs reading "Save Sacco and Vanzetti," other signs were held up, "Down with the Communists," "Lynch the Reds." These were Boston's hoodlums mobilized by the police, and believing the most slanderous of the lies. Then came the cops themselves—mounted and afoot—the city's upholders of law and order.

A notable passage in Upton Sinclair's *Boston,* a semi-fictionalized account of the Sacco-Vanzetti affair, gives this description of that day's events on the Common:

"There was John Dos Passos, faithful son of Harvard, and John Howard Lawson, another one of the 'New Playwrights' from Greenwich Village. There was Clarina Michelson, ready to do the hard work again, and William Patterson, a Negro lawyer from New York, running the greatest risk of any of them, with his black face not to be disguised. Just up Beacon Street was the Shaw Monument, with figures in perennial bronze, of unmistakable Negro boys in uniforms, led by a young Boston blueblood on horseback; no doubt Patterson had looked at this, and drawn courage from it. . . .

"The trooper speeds on; he has spied the black face, and wants that most of all. The Negro runs, and the rider rears the front of his steed, intending to strike him down with the iron-shod hoofs. But fortunately there is a tree, and the Negro leaps behind it; and a man can run around a tree faster than the best-trained police-mount—the dapper and genial William Patterson proves it by making five complete circuits before he runs into the arms of an ordinary cop, who grabs him by the collar and tears off his sign and tramples it in the dirt, and then starts to march him away. 'Well,' he remarks sociably, 'This is the first time I ever see a nigger bastard that was a communist.' The lawyer is surprised, because he has been given to understand that that particular word is barred from the Common. Mike Crowley was so shocked, two weeks ago, when Mary Donovan tacked up a sign to a tree: *'Did you see what I did to those anarchistic bastards?*—Judge Thayer.' But apparently the police did not have to obey their own laws."

But it was not the policeman's name-calling that surprised me—I expected that, law or no law. It was the source of the policeman's annoyance that set me thinking, the fact that he had never before seen a black Communist. I pondered this situation. The National Association for the Advancement of Colored People had never sought to align the political struggles of the Negro people with those of another group. They had sought to draw white men into court campaigns which they had organized and led in behalf of Negroes. But they had mounted no political campaign, participated in no mass demonstrations and had confined themselves to legal action. The Garvey movement, of course, was strictly a separatist movement. In it, the Negro rejected his heritage in America, won in labor and blood.

Now the cop had seen something new. He had seen a Black man concerned with the legal persecution of white Americans who were foreign-born—this Negro had to be something special. Nothing less than "a Communist bastard."

The patrol wagon came, and the police of Boston now found themselves confronted with another dilemma. They had a Black man to take to the Joy Street station house along with a white woman, Clarina Michelson. But they could not allow him to ride on the inside of a patrol wagon with a white woman. So I was walked to the jail; and, of course, I was not permitted to share a cell with a white American. The other men with whom I had marched on the picket line made a fight to have me changed over to the pen they were in, but this was no go in Boston, the cradle of the American Revolution.

We were all bailed out and immediately went back to the picket line. I suppose if we had not been so close to the tragic outcome, we would have laughed at our jailers. They were acting in mechanical obedience to the racist teaching that was the only brand of democracy that made sense to them.

The creative artists were the backbone of the picket line. The learned professors and the leaders of organized labor were missing. America's labor leaders were to permit the framed Italians to go to the electric chair without mobilizing for the life-and-death struggle. The absence of the NAACP could be understood, as could that of the Urban League and the Garveyites. But how explain labor? Thousands in the rank and file fought for Sacco and Vanzetti; almost no officials.

Powers Hapgood, a brilliant young Harvard graduate, was everywhere, speaking and agitating. Three times he had been arrested, each time returning to the picket line upon his release. The fourth time he was shunted by a police captain to a psychopathic ward.

It usually took at least ten days to get in and out of Boston's psychopathic ward. The police did not hesitate to send people there who were obnoxious to them. Hapgood was held for only one day. After my third arrest the same captain threatened that if I were arrested again he would take care of me in the same manner—no doubt with jimcrow accessories. My presence in Boston was becoming a positive annoyance.

Arthur Garfield Hays, one of the country's best civil liberties lawyers, handled the affair in court. He was the legal adviser to most of those arrested, and it was his opinion that I had better not get arrested again. My new friends agreed, and so I stayed off the picket lines.

Shortly after midnight, August 22, 1927, the Commonwealth of Massachusetts executed Nicola Sacco and Bartolomeo Vanzetti. Who could doubt that it was at the behest of those industrialists who wanted to do away with anything that seemed "communistic" to them, and that they were aided and abetted by the Department of Justice and the Supreme Court? And everything was done in accordance with law and order.

I stood in the crowd outside the Charlestown prison, as close to the gates as the hundreds of armed guards would permit. The lights in the prison windows dimmed three times, ending our last hopes.

For me, the world had changed. American reaction had won a victory over the bodies of two men, but its effort to stampede the people had ended in utter failure. In every capital and large city of the world there were mass protest meetings. Men everywhere around the globe came together—unbelieving. They stood in the market squares of little Italian towns; they packed the streets not only in Paris, New York, Berlin and London, but in provincial towns along the Rhine, in the Alps, along the Mediterranean, in Rocky Mountain mining camps, and on the pampas of Argentina. Hundreds of thousands went on strike, in New York, Pennsylvania, Colorado, Illinois, New Jersey. Police clashed with a throng of 50,000 gathered in New

York's Union Square; there were similar gatherings in Chicago and Philadelphia. Communists led these demonstrations. Most of my Negro friends couldn't see the political significance of all this! Japanese labor leaders sent a deputation to the American Embassy in Tokyo. In the Soviet Union there were hundreds of meetings, and in Latin America there were tens of protest rallies. If there were none in the ghettos of America, I think I knew the reason why: The thinking of our people had been ghettoized; they had been alienated from their white fellow-workers. They had been made to feel themselves apart from the general stream—inferior.

I returned to New York and the office of Dyett, Hall and Patterson, but the fact that Sacco and Vanzetti had been executed stayed in my mind. They would have no more to say and yet what they had said would live with me forever. My faith in the law as a weapon of democracy in the United States was gone. I could not practice law again, at least not as I had before. The prestige that came to the Black lawyer came too often at the expense of his people's rights and of his own integrity.

I reread Vanzetti's testimony to the white American jury that had condemned him to death. It was a document that few columnists had paid attention to, with the honorable exception of Heywood Broun. In it Vanzetti scathingly analyzed and dissected our society; he exposed the class character of those who were to murder him and his comrade. I cannot refrain from quoting some passages:

" . . . I teach over here men who is with me. The free idea gives any man a chance to profess his own idea, not the supreme idea . . . but to give a chance to print and education, literature, free speech. . . .

"I could see the best men, intelligent, education, they had been arrested and sent to prison and died in prison for years and years without getting them out, and Debs, one of the great men in his country, he is in prison, still away in prison, because he is a socialist. He wanted the laboring class to have better conditions and better living, more education . . . (so he gets) prison. Why? Because the capitalist class . . . they don't want our child to go to high school or college or Harvard College . . . they don't want the working class educationed; they want the working class to be low all the time, be under foot, and not be up with the head. . . .

"So that is why I love people who labor and work and see better conditions every day develop, makes no more war. We no want fight by the gun and don't want to destroy young men. The mother been suffering for building the young men. . . . No war for the civilization of men. They are war for business, million dollars come on the side. . . .

"That is why my idea I love Socialists. That is why I like people who want education and living, building, who is good, just as much as they could. That is all."

That was Vanzetti's testimony—a small part of it. And just before the sentence had been passed, when he was asked whether he had anything further to say, he replied:

"This is what I say: I would not wish a dog or a snake the most low and unfortunate creature of the earth—I would not wish to say of them what I have had to suffer for things that I am not guilty of. I am suffering because I am a radical and indeed I am a radical: I have suffered because I am an Italian, and indeed I am an Italian: I have suffered more for my family and for my beloved than for myself; but I am so convinced to be right that if you could execute me two times and I could be reborn two other times, I would live again to do what I have done already.

"I have finished. Thank you."

The speaker belonged, as he himself has so magnificently said, "to nations."

The significance of the case was tremendous. Sacco and Vanzetti belonged to white and Black, Italian, German, English, Jew, Russian, American—they belonged to progressive mankind. That was why the ruling-class scavengers did them to death. This kind of belonging led to unity. Success in the people's cause lay in unity in the struggle of the world's oppressed.

The more I thought of the beautiful words Vanzetti had spoken, the more clearly I saw that some of the eloquent and articulate intellectuals who had been my fellow-protesters had not grasped the essential meaning of my presence in Boston. They saw me only as a Black man who, out of common decency, had come to help rescue these brave men who were fighting for a better America. I hope I was that, but the dominant feature of the step I had taken was political not moral.

Certainly I was more than the "dapper" figure which Upton Sinclair had drawn to represent me in his novel. Mike Gold and Ella Reeve Bloor had, of course, seen me for what I thought I was—a new link in a chain that would help hold the progressive forces of our country together and bring white and Black *en masse* to see the mutuality of their interests. I had come back to New York as from a university—but a people's university. Far from being a graduate student, it was the beginning and not the end of the course. I would follow another road of struggle. My law career had come to an end.

The last words spoken by Vanzetti rang in my ears: "If it had not been for these things, I might have lived out my life talking at street corners to scorning men. I might have died, unmarked, unknown, a failure. Now we are not a failure. This is our career and our triumph. Never in our full life could we hope to do such work for tolerance, for justice, for man's understanding of men as now we do by accident. Our words—our lives—our pains—nothing! The taking of our lives—the lives of a good shoemaker and a poor fish peddler—all! That last moment belongs to us—that agony is our triumph!"

My Political Education Continues

I RETURNED from Boston profoundly shaken. The coldly calculated official murder of Sacco and Vanzetti made no sense except as it served the purposes of the ruling class to intimidate and silence (in this case forever) fighters for true democracy. Unsuccessful as the outcome of the battle had been, I learned lessons of struggle that would ordinarily have taken years to acquire. And this crime was directly related to the legal lynchings of Black people. The same forces that denied Negroes jobs in mills and factories wreaked their vengeance on Sacco and Vanzetti. I began to realize that if Black men were to concern themselves exclusively with the problems and needs of the ghetto, they would never gain the insight I had found in Boston—that the struggle was between the rich and powerful on one side and the poor and exploited on the other.

It was then that the mists of confusion compounded of questions concerning racism, class oppression, exclusive preoccupation with Negro persecution were to be cleared away. I began to read and study political science, to learn that not all whites were responsible for bigotry and discrimination, to realize that generalizations about all those who were not Black could only serve our common enemy. It became clearer and clearer that somebody up there didn't want white and Negro to join in a common cause.

Why had I not recognized this before? Had my enforced confinement in the ghetto closed my mind to the truth of class relationships? Was practical experience gained through sharp democratic civil strife a necessary component of the educational process? Why did white liberals and labor leaders who had broad experience in legal defense matters fail to see what was beginning to be so obvious to me? I had come face to face with some of America's leading white liberals: Edna St. Vincent Millay, Paxton Hibben, John Dos Passos and a host of others. They had come to Boston and labored sincerely to save the lives of two Italians. They had looked me over—some with curiosity, some with admiration. But I did not represent to them the emergence of a potentially new social force—unity between Black and white in the fight for justice—people's justice.

When I returned to the firm of Dyett, Hall and Patterson, I talked with Thomas Hall, our law clerk, about my dissatisfaction with practicing law along the old lines. He expressed deep regret, said he believed I had a splendid future in law. But what I wanted and needed was a complete change in my way of living. I turned my law books and my desk over to him.

One day, while I was still nominally with the firm, Cyril Briggs, a West Indian whom I had met through Richard Moore, came to the office. In the course of our conversation, he reached down into his briefcase and brought out a book. "I want to suggest that you read this," he said. "It won't take anything from your law practice—it could add something to it."

It was *The Communist Manifesto,* which many years before I had tried to understand. I began slowly to thumb through the pages as Briggs sat there watching me. I glanced more closely at a passage: "The history of all societies since the break-up of the primitive has been the history of the class struggle." Turning the pages, I realized that I was ready now to grasp its meaning. I bought the book, took it home and read it. A door opened for me.

Soon after, I read the speeches of Maxim Litvinov, representative of the USSR, delivered before the League of Nations. He called for an end to colonialism and racism, for complete disarmament and an end to aggressive wars. His speeches made a lasting impression on me. Here was a new voice in the family of mankind calling for the liberation of the oppressed. How could I use his wisdom in the solution of my own problem? I determined to find out. I was reading feverishly now. The *Manifesto* had pointed the direction.

With all my reading and thinking, I continued to be troubled by questions like: How could a Negro understand and seek class identity, when even white workers were seemingly among the bitterest enemies of their Black working-class brothers? How could a Black person be concerned with the country's fate when 90 per cent of it was fenced off with signs reading, "For Whites Only"? It took me years to realize the endless convolutions of "divide and rule"—the social, psychological, political impact of jimcrow and how it can blind and confuse one at every level of his thinking.

Richard Moore, Cyril Briggs and one or another of their friends were seeing me regularly now. One of them brought me *State and Revolution,* by one of the truly great men of the world, Lenin. All through school and especially in law school, I had been taught that the state, the three branches of the government and the many auxiliary bodies surrounding and bulwarking these branches made no distinction between individuals but viewed all impartially. Now the theory of the state's neutrality was shattered; I could even learn the meaning of the term "state" when used in this sense. Lenin proved to me that the state was an organ of class rule.

As I was no part of the ruling class and a Black man, its state could not be mine, but that did not make the country less my country and if I had nothing to say about its management, I was being robbed of my heritage. *State and Revolution* went on to deal with the difference between bourgeois and working-class democracy. Since I was beginning to identify my interests with those of the working class and to recognize that the interests of the great mass of Black people could not be otherwise identified, a study of the meaning of these two kinds of democracy was called for.

With great clarity the book treated the question of alliances among those who had mutual interests—class alliances, those of the oppressed against the oppressor. It showed why the oppressor would seek desperately to keep the oppressed divided and just how he pitted one against the other. Life began to take on clearer meaning as I read. It pointed in a direction which began to be mine. My whole being was possessed by the desire for equality as I now began to see it. My short sojourn in England, the meetings with Robert Lansbury and McCant Stewart had influenced me to believe that the center of the struggle for me would be in the United States.

Before long I had met white Americans who saw my ghetto clearly in the light in which I was beginning to see it—in terms of class conflict as well as color oppression. They were eager to join with me as a human being in the work of remolding the ghetto and the society that had created ghettos and slums. I had to stop, look and listen. Karl Marx, the great philosopher, had written that the philosopher's and social scientist's efforts to explain the world were all very well, but that the task of the people was to change it. That made sense.

I began to attend classes at the Workers School, conducted by the Communist Party. Its head instructor, Jacob "Pop" Mindell, was one of the most intelligent and kindly men I had ever met—and yet he was a strict disciplinarian. And this school was new to me—students were actually taught the science of society as it revealed itself in life, in social struggles and in the contradictions between democratic preachments and practices.

No one came out of the Workers School without having learned that in getting jobs they would be confronted by owners of mines, mills and great industries seeking profits and, directly or indirectly, linked with banking consortiums by all manner of social and economic ties. The students were shown why they faced rapacious landlords, insurance collectors, agents from credit houses—men seeking to sell them anything and everything except freedom. They were shown how the credit system operates; how if one were caught in it, it never lets one go. Compare this with what passed for education in the public schools and colleges where the relation of forces was distorted and misrepresented from beginning to end, and reality was turned into its opposite. The myths of white superiority in general and that of the Anglo-Saxon in particular were implicit in every course. The "best" (and most successfully miseducated) students among the non-whites got degrees and were hoisted up as cultural leaders so that they might become spokesmen for imperialism among their own people.

After several months in the Workers School, I was informed that I was being considered for a trip to the Soviet Union. I was amazed—and pleased. Two of the leaders of the Communist Party (which I had joined not long before), William Weinstone and Jack Stachel, came to speak to me about the trip. (I tried to imagine the leaders of the bourgeois parties coming to the home of a rank-and-filer, especially if he were black, to inquire as to whether he was willing to go abroad to study.)

Briefly, I was to study the source and nature of racism as an ideology and its political and economic aspects, including the causes of slums and joblessness. I was to observe the country where the working class had come to power, under the leadership of their Communist Party—the greatest victory won by exploited peoples in centuries of freedom struggle.

I talked over my plans with my sister and others in whom I had confidence. All were in favor of my making the trip. Interestingly enough, none of them saw it as a matter in which only I and my sponsors were concerned—they viewed the trip as being related to the further development of the Black liberation struggle. I agreed to go.

I thought later that I should have made arrangements with the Negro press to send them articles describing my trip. Yet, what ghetto paper could have carried my stories and retained its advertisers? What section of the Negro press was ready to give the Black people a clear picture of the social forces, ideas and ideals involved in the Revolution of October 1917 in tsarist Russia? The condition of the people before and during the Revolution and the unprecedented achievements since those momentous days?

I could not help comparing my coming departure with the trip I had undertaken in 1919 under my own initiative. At that time I was in flight from my country's pervasive racism; I had been driven from home by a feeling of being unable to cope with the situation, of lacking the understanding that would help me direct my own effort to combat the evils. Now I was going to learn from those who had defeated their oppressors. That I was invited at all was living proof of the universality of that struggle and of the concern of those who had won their freedom with those who had it still to win.

In the eight years since my first trip abroad, I had gained some knowledge of what made the wheels of our world go round. I had become part of a collective of mighty proportions, comprised of workers, Russians, Anglo-Saxons, French, Germans, Italians, Jews, Negroes, Mexican Americans and others. In every country in the world, Communists were emerging from among the peoples to give leadership to liberation struggles. The whole of mankind had entered the era of the world socialist revolution. I had found comrades with whom I now believed any freedom-loving individual could identify, regardless of color or nativity.

I could not help wondering what would have happened eight years earlier if George Lansbury had been more persuasive in his suggestion that I go to Russia. But if, as McCant Stewart had bluntly told me, Liberia did not need me, I thought ruefully that this was also true of Russia in 1919—I would have had little or nothing to offer it. Association with the Communist Party and participation in the defense of Sacco and Vanzetti had prepared me in some degree for the trip, and what I learned would be tested in the crucible of struggle when I returned.

Before I left, Jay Lovestone, at that time one of the influential leaders of the Communist Party, condescended to visit me in Harlem. In the course of our brief conversation, he notified me not to expect to return as one of the leaders of the Party. His admonition was an insult to my intelligence and to that of the Communist Party. Lovestone did not favor my going abroad, but Jack Stachel, William Weinstone and Richard B. Moore overcame his objection. And, to my surprise, Lovestone's attitude had strong overtones of racism. I was not dismayed— enemies of racial unity were to be found in the ranks of any American organization and institution. But in the Communist Party such elements were sure to be detected and judged by their actions. Lovestone was, shortly after, to prove himself a careerist as well as a racist. In 1929, only a short time after his gratuitous warning to me, he was to be expelled from the Party.

The day came for my departure. I sailed on the *Île de France,* tourist class. I was booked for Southampton, England, where I was scheduled to board a Soviet ship for Leningrad. The trip across the Atlantic took nine days, and I enjoyed every one of them.

On the second day out, a group of passengers strolling on the deck greeted me with a "hello" spoken in an obviously foreign tone. They were members of a Moscow trade delegation which had been visiting the United States. I told them that Moscow was my destination, and their warmth expanded. The leader of the group gave me his home address on Tverskaya Street and urged me to visit him. They, too, were going from London, through the Baltic Sea and the Finnish Gulf, to Leningrad, and then by rail to Moscow. We traveled most of the way together.

They made no pretense of knowing the United States, although they had been in the States two months. They were anxious to know about my life. What had I been and done? Where did I live? How did I expect to find life in the Soviet Union? To this last question they addressed themselves at length. It was soon clear to me that they did not want me to have any illusions. The Soviet Union was not a Utopia; I was not going to paradise. There was famine in some parts of the country along the Volga. But the power was in the hands of the people; the class enemy, within and without, had been beaten.

About my life in my own country, there was nothing to conceal. I was a Black man—that they could see. They had seen some Negroes as they traveled about the country, but had had no opportunity for serious conversation. I talked freely and frankly. I was never one to feel that evils from which Black folk suffered in their home land should be concealed to save the "good name" of a country where such evils were officially tolerated. Of course, it wasn't the country that was responsible—it was the ruling class.

The Soviet citizens knew full well that American troops had fought against the Russian revolutionaries after the October Revolution. They were not fooled about the good will of American businessmen—it had a dollar tag on it. And they did not want me to labor under illusions which reality might dispel. They did not know that I did not expect to see Moscow a reconstructed city. Years of revolution, civil war and blockade must have taken a fearful toll in a city that had never given serious thought to the welfare of the masses.

For me, one thing stood out: the people led by Communists had taken power. After the American Civil War Blacks and poor whites had met the greatest obstacles in their efforts during Reconstruction. Undoubtedly the Soviet people would make mistakes, their work might be sabotaged, but they owned and controlled the government. They had drafted rebuilding programs and would correct their own mistakes. In my own country, on the other hand, the mistakes made by the former slaves and the poor whites during Reconstruction were thrice compounded by the betrayal of the democratic forces and the establishment of the dictatorship of capital over the lives of the oppressed.

To me, the Soviet Union was a new world in the making. This called for the making of a new man, a new people. That would not be easy because the remnants of old ideas and customs recede slowly. How long would it take us to make a

new man in Mississippi, a new Black man in the ghettos of the
United States? How long to humanize millions of whites?

These were among the thoughts that raced through my mind
as we sailed from the Finnish Gulf into Leningrad. We had left
Southampton on a Soviet ship. The attitude of its officers and
crew toward me had been a heart-warming experience. Some
Americans to whom I later told the story of that passage said
cynically: "Of course, they treated you with great hospitality.
Their responsibility was to win you. They had a job to do."

I didn't believe this. Only the most skillful, sophisticated
deceivers could feign such a welcome and sustain friendliness
over a period of several days without any condescension or
phoniness being revealed. There was in the treatment accorded
me a wholesomeness born of the new freedom they were
experiencing and wanted for others. I was to meet this kindli-
ness and consideration from persons in all walks of life.

CHAPTER 7

First Visit To
The Soviet Union

WE LANDED in Leningrad and although there was no time for sightseeing, I was thrilled to be in the city where Alexander Pushkin, the world-renowned poet, had lived. As a Black man I had reason to be proud of Pushkin. He was of African lineage, and he had taken his place alongside the progressive forces of history. To the Russians, Pushkin was a Russian, a great Russian poet—to me he was also a Russian-African. That is what the quest for identity in the United States had done for me. My country's lies about the history and culture of Black men, unrelieved by any acknowledgment of their contributions to the development of mankind, were circulated in order to justify slavery and, later, discrimination and exploitation. This shameful distortion of history forced the Afro-American to emblazon on his banner all great men with Black ancestry. Pushkin loved his African background no less than he loved Russia; he loved all men seeking liberation, and under Russian skies that love for humanity had flowered.

Leningrad was the expansive window to the West opened by Peter the Great, and it was indeed like a Western city in many physical respects. We freshened up at the Hotel Europa on Nevsky Prospect, one of the great highways of the world. The hotel had once been one of Europe's most luxurious hostelries,

but the terrible battles that had taken place in and around
Leningrad had caused so much devastation that priority had to
be given to other tasks of reconstruction. The rehabilitation of
the hotel had been left to a later date.

On the overnight trip to Moscow in the early morning there
was little to see save the snow-covered village fields. We came
into the Yaroslavsky Station, which stands in an enormous
public square housing three railroad stations. There an auto-
mobile awaited me, and I was driven to a building on Tversky
Boulevard, a short distance from Pushkin Square. The large
building known as the Tversky Boulevard Building was now a
student dormitory. Before the Revolution it had been a fash-
ionable school for the daughters of the aristocracy. It now
served as the University of the Toiling People of the Far East,
as well as for students from India, Africa and the Near East.

Here I was to meet hundreds of young men and women who
were later to become part of the adminstrative and cultural
institutions of countries freed from colonial oppression. The
students were by no means exclusively Communists; by and
large they were children of workers denied educational opportunities in their homeland.

Why did the leaders of the Soviet Union go to such expense
and trouble to establish a school for foreign students at a time
when they scarcely could provide for their own? The imperialists had refined the techniques of miseducation to a fine art.
Afro-American, African, Indian, and East Asian colonial youth
had the slimmest chance of winning through to a college
degree. The master class in Europe's capitals used schooling in
their colonies with the shrewdest calculation. A very limited
number of their victims were trained in simple clerical work,
bookkeeping and so forth—just enough to hold some minor
jobs in the cities. A few, sons of chiefs and other powerful men
whose friendship was useful to their rulers, were allowed to
attend the great universities in London, Paris, Berlin. But for a
great majority of the colonial people, their chances of education beyond the earliest grades were as remote as those of the

At the World Conference Against Racism and Anti-Semitism in Paris, 1930. Louise Thompson, later to become my wife, is in the first row, third from right; I am in the second row, center.

children of a Mississippi sharecropper. To many thousands of
Black, Brown and Yellow students, the effort of the USSR to
give them a chance to become acquainted with the real world
and with objective truth was a priceless gift. And to the USSR
it represented the acceptance of responsibility to mankind, to
international working-class solidarity—the essence of their
philosophy.

My first day at the University of the Toiling People of the
Far East was a day of getting to know one another. Not just
exchanging names—some did, some didn't. I met a young
Black woman whose name was Maude White; she told me she
has been a student at Howard University in Washington, D.C.
Another person I met was a Black man about my own age who
used the name Otto Hall. He and his brother, Harry Haywood,
were later to become leaders in the Negro liberation movement
in the United States. Then there was a chap known as Denmark
Vesey, a slender young Black man eager to learn what had
taken place in Russia and why.

Among the Chinese there was a son of General Chiang
Kai-shek and among the Indians a niece of Pandit Nehru. Both
were studying the science of social development.

I formed a habit of getting up early and walking about this
800-year-old city. Time and again I walked around the Krem-
lin. From that structure for hundreds of years men had
controlled the destiny of millions of people in Russia and the
Asian lands. Now it housed the people's elected representatives. Everywhere in the city there was evidence of the ravages
of war and civil war. Ochotny Ryad (Hunters' Row), a main
thoroughfare, was an array of shacks just outside Red
Square—one of the most colorful public squares in the world.
But the shacks were not to remain there long—the huge Hotel
Moscow was to rise on the site before long. Across the street,
offices of the various ministries of the government were to be
housed in a splendid new edifice. Moscow was building
anew—and building and building.

Nearby was the world-famed Bolshoi Theater, home of the

Russian Ballet and opera. Central Moscow was circled by the famous Sadovaya (garden) Boulevard. I walked around the circle many times and I grew to love the city. Everywhere steps were being taken to eradicate the ravages of time and war; and in the transformation of the conditions of living, one could see the transformation of a whole people rebuilding their lives and laying new foundations for their children's lives.

I made many acquaintances at the University. A large percentage of the students were one day to become freedom fighters in some faraway land. Some were to come through savage struggles and become leaders of their people in many avenues of work and life. I was also to see some of them again at the United Nations.

We called the University KUTVA—the Russian initials of the long name it bore. Among my instructors was one man, Endre Sik, whom I shall never forget. A refugee after the first Hungarian revolution had been crushed, he had somehow reached the USSR. He was tall and slender, with one unforgettable physical feature—a magnificent shock of white hair. He was a doctor of philosophy, a dedicated scientist. He lived to help others understand the ways in which to fight exploitation and to work for the liberation of man. But had you asked Endre Sik where he most wanted to serve, I believe that he would have answered, "In the liberation of Black men."

Sik lived with his wife and a young son and daughter in a Quonset hut near the railroad station from which trains left for Leningrad. The large hut was built from stores captured from Americans when they had joined in the attempt to crush the October Revolution. It housed four families, which, in the light of the great housing shortage, was not as bad as it sounds.

Sik was a very busy man. He taught at more than one school and also met with other Hungarian refugees to discuss their national problems. We students were busy too, but as often as possible I visited Sik's home He spoke English as well as French, German, Russian and, of course, his native tongue, and so he had little difficulty in discussing economics, politics and ideology with most of his students. I never met a man for whom I had a greater respect.

I never learned what had first turned Sik's attention to so intense a study of the persecution of Black men. He was, it is true, a profound humanist; there were many Bolsheviks who were, yet not all of them were so deeply concerned with Africa or Afro-Americans. Perhaps it was because he saw the African peoples, especially those who lived south of the Sahara, as amongst the most maligned and vilified of all the peoples of the earth. Foreseeing at the same time the vital role Black Africa would play in its liberation struggles and the future development of mankind, he became extraordinarily concerned with the history and struggles of Black men.

He was greatly desirous of blasting the lies and propaganda of the pseudo-historians, biologists and sociologists of the West who went to great lengths to show Black Africans as being inherently inferior. In the late 20's he had begun a history of Africa. Now completed, it treats of the evolution of the African peoples and the role of the imperialists in their subjugation and in the partition of the African continent (*The History of Black Africa*, Academiai Kiado, Budapest, 1966).

The Republic of South Africa already had a Communist party and so did several other African countries. There was also a Pan-African movement, fathered by Dr. W. E. B. Du Bois. The African people were not asleep; they were destined to move into the orbit of world revolutionary struggle.

The talks with Sik were extremely profitable, not only for me but for all the Black students who participated in them. We understood that the ideology and philosophy of the Revolution that had deposed tsarism had far-reaching influence: they were sapping at the foundations of colonialism. The Socialist Revolution had added new dimensions to all the liberation struggles of mankind.

Studying at KUTVA was a fascinating experience, the more so because no one was seeking an education for purposes of self-aggrandizement. Everyone there was seeking to break with an ideology that had kept him tied to colonial oppression. Combined with formal study there was practical experience. Students traveled throughout the Soviet Union to see the national development at many levels. They studied and observed the problems of the colonial peoples who had been held in the tsar's "prison of nations" and how they were solving them in the "family of nations" for which the Revolution had laid the foundation.

I traveled to many of the Eastern Socialist Republics and what I saw amazed me. What was taking place in Uzbekistan, Azerbaijan, Georgia and other nations of the USSR would knock the props out of the arguments of every racist. The national budget of the USSR was divided so as to give to those people who had been kept in a backward state by the tsars a larger share than would strictly have been theirs. Equality of rights and opportunities could be available to them only if they received a larger share at the outset. Those who had been held back had to be helped to catch up.

Wherever one traveled, the picture was one of tremendous movement in culture, industrial development and participation in politics. Schools were literally springing up everywhere. I will be forgiven if my thoughts returned time and again to Mississippi, Georgia, Alabama, South Carolina, Texas and all points South to review the efforts to keep the Negro from securing an education—especially in his own history and heritage. Here I was in a democracy with a new kind of content, little more than a decade old and yet seeking with all its resources to wipe out illiteracy and to educate all of its peoples.

The trips to the various sections of the country were eye-openers. Witnessing the application of new relations was the only way to determine how the new social attitude really worked. I took notes in the course of the many discussions I sat in on where criticisms and decisions were weighed and in many instances applied. I would, of course, be expected to make a report on my return, both to the school and later to the

Party. The reporting-back assignment was remarkably helpful in sharpening the students' powers of observation. The reports were studied by Soviet authorities in reviews of the correctness of their theory and course of action. It was a two-way street: the teachers became pupils and the students, teachers. From these trips there came a deep sense of the world role of the USSR.

What one saw was a multinational effort. Production was based upon the character of the natural resources of each republic, with the all-union government lending every possible aid to the development of water power, irrigation, health and education. The determination and vigor with which the fight against racial and religious prejudice was waged were truly remarkable. A factor of great importance was the fight led by the central government and its leadership against what was known as Great Russian chauvinism, a tool of the ideologists of the tsarist empire much like the myths of white superiority that are used to brainwash and dehumanize the white masses in America.

A new life was flourishing in the countryside, in the villages and towns; the people had acquired land; new cities were coming into being. The veils had been lifted from the faces of the women in the former Moslem colonies. Myths about woman's place in society that had flourished for hundreds of years were being banished from the minds of both men and women. The creative genius of these once stultified peoples had been released and they proved to be as gifted as any other people on earth.

In the meanwhile, the political leaders of England, France and the United States were taking no effective steps to check those powerful men who in Italy, Germany and Japan were openly talking about the need for the re-division of the world by force. The politicians and powerful monopolies that backed them wanted not only colonies in Asia and Africa, but political dominance in Europe as well. In spite of the fact that these forces menaced the interests of the U.S. monopolies in the world market, American imperialism was gambling recklessly by supporting them, seeking always to turn them against the USSR.

It was evident to those who read *Mein Kampf* or saw and heard Hitler in his rantings that he was a maniacal racist as well as a warmaker. Hitler's fascism threatened the very existence not only of all Jews, all revolutionaries, all progressive whites, but also that of every Black man in the world.

The Soviets alone raised the cry "Stop fascism!" The Sixth Congress of the Communist International met in Moscow in 1928 to discuss the rise of fascist ideas and actions and how to organize for successful struggles against them. Nicolai Bukharin of the Soviet Union made a major report on the situation in the colonies. But Harry Haywood, James Ford and I, who attended, were not satisfied with the way in which Bukharin handled the relationship of the Black man in the United States to the colonial movement and what should be the tasks of all Communists in that situation. It was our opinion that it was necessary to stress the position of the Afro-American and the role that Negroes could play in the struggle—especially in the light of the magnitude of American imperialism's menace to the world.

We discussed the matter with Otto Kuusinen, Dmitri Manuilsky and a number of other comrades who were handling the program. A meeting was arranged with Bukharin before he made his summation. Our position was that the United States in its historical development was somewhat unique, due to the contradiction of slavery and the post-Civil War freedom conflicts. The Black man had paid for his freedoom with his blood, playing a decisive part in winning the war.

Naturally, we did not expect Bukharin to go into the details of the Negro's struggles—only that he deepen and expand upon the subject. After considerable discussion, the correctness of our position was admitted and an agreement was reached to include the matter as we saw it in the summary.

I was impressed by the manner in which Jim Ford handled

himself at that discussion. Ford was an American Negro, born in Alabama in 1893. He lived and worked for the liberation of Negroes from jimcrow restrictions and the achievement of their constitutional and human rights. He worked also for the deliverance of mankind from the tyranny of economic over-lords who had appropriated the natural resources of the world, whose wars were fought to redivide the world's wealth, and who threatened the very existence of the Black peoples. Jim Ford was a dedicated man.

Trips abroad to attend international conferences were also part of the broad education I and my fellow-students were receiving at KUTVA. Another gathering that I attended was the Second Congress of the Anti-Imperialist League, which met in Germany in July 1929. I was nominated to go by my class.

But before I left for Western Europe, I embarked on my second marriage. At one of the school's social affairs I had met Vera Gorohovskaya. A most attractive and cultured woman, she spoke several languages, among them English. After our first meeting, we began to see each other regularly. Her home was in Leningrad but she was spending her summer vacation with an aunt in Moscow. After a brief courtship, we decided to get married. (We were to have two daughters, both of whom now reside in Leningrad. The elder, Lola, is now an engineer and the mother of six children; the younger, Anna, is a newspaper correspondent for Tass.)

Vera and I were amicably divorced several years later. She thought it would be harmful to my work if she came back to the United States to live with me—considering the rampant racism here. We remained good friends, however, and my love for the children never waned.

At that time, in 1928, two events were being organized: one was the second Congress of the League Against Imperialism that I have referred to; the second was the First International Negro Workers Congress. The proposal to hold the latter meeting had been raised by Ford, who had organized an office for the International Negro Workers Trade Union Committee in Hamburg, Germany, from which he had begun to make contacts with Negro workers in all parts of the world.

Working together with Ford was George Padmore, a British West Indian freedom fighter who had joined the American Communist Party while studying at Howard University. *The Negro Worker,* a trade union publication organized by Ford and edited by Padmore, had its office in Hamburg. At that time no fixed date or place had been determined for the International Negro Workers Congress. But it was obvious that both the League Against Imperialism and the trade union congress would deal first and foremost with the growth of fascism. Above all, the Communists would place the question of fascism and the dangers of war before the people with all their ability.

James Ford and I left the Soviet Union together for Frankfort-on-Main, Germany, near the end of July. We went as observers to the Second Congress of the League Against Imperialism, hoping and expecting to speak with as many delegates as possible and, above all, to talk with the Black delegates from Africa and the Americas, North and South. Obviously, as participants in a Congress described as anti-imperialist, we wanted to meet with the other delegates and specifically discuss the economic needs of each country.

The *New York Times* (July 22, 1929) reported that nearly 400 delegates from the oppressed peoples of all lands attended the Congress. Among them there was the Negro leader William Pickens of New York and several other Americans. Pickens was destined to become one of the leaders of the NAACP. A brilliant speaker, he was a graduate of Yale University, among the top ten of his class. He had won the Ten Eyck Prize. In the United States he was regarded as a militant and ardent fighter for the rights of Negroes.

Ford and I made every effort to contact Pickens, but he studiously avoided us. This seemed strange to me, since he had been speaking about the horrors of racism in the United States. But, as I discovered later, he had also spoken against the Communists. Pickens addressed the Congress in German and left almost immediately without exchanging a word with his colored brothers.

While not a delegate, Ford was able to get the floor and deliver a splendid anti-war, anti-imperialist statement. He and I had the opportunity of talking with a number of Africans. We spoke of the forthcoming First International Congress of Negro Workers. We were now more than ever certain that a gathering of Black men from all parts of the world was necessary if a united anti-imperialist position was to be taken. Mindful of Pickens' anti-communist attitude we felt that a consistent anti-imperialist position could not be taken by one who was anti-Soviet or anti-communist.

What was demanded was an objective appraisal of history. The peoples of the Tsarist Empire had won a monumental socialist revolution and civil war. During the civil war period they had fought heroically against the interventionist troops of the erstwhile allies of Russia—England, the United States, France and others. They had called for peace among the peoples of the world; they had demonstrated their courage and self-sacrifice and their respect for oppressed mankind. They had established the first fortress of a new world. Like it or not, there it stood, the first socialist state in the world, a rallying point for the progressive forces of mankind.

As my return to the United States approached, I began to evaluate many aspects of the socialist country in which I had had the good fortune to study, to travel, to learn, to participate in the anti-fascist struggle. The peoples of the USSR were faced with a mountain of problems in the building of a socialist society. The tsar had bequeathed them a heritage of poverty, ignorance, medieval farming techniques, racial and national prejudice. In addition, World War I, the international enemies of the Revolution, and the defeated counterrevolution had wrought wide devastation. Millions of families were homeless, tens of thousands of orphaned children wandered across the land, stealing to live.

It is difficult to convey the impact of a place like Moscow in

1927, particularly on a Negro. Just the strangeness of the city—the architecture, the foods, the clothes, the customs. The quiet darkness of the streets at night. There was nothing to compare with the massive explosion of neon signs in New York, the sidewalk pitchmen, the blaring music, the flags and bands of our hard-sell society, the general Main Street hysteria—nor the river of autos, taxicabs and trucks that fill our own downtown streets with the roar of a giant waterfall.

The second impact, if one is an American Negro, comes in the discovery that there is no racial tension in the air. One looks at, talks to, works with white men and women and youth as an equal. It is as if one had suffered with a painful affliction for many years and had suddenly awakened to discover the pain had gone. The Russians seemed to give a man's skin coloration only a descriptive value, looking immediately past this attribute to the significant human differences of character, mind and heart.

I saw the people of the USSR facing up to the tasks of removing the ruins of the old and building the new. Under the leadership of the Communist Party, an awe-inspiring creative explosion was under way, touching every aspect of life. From their western borders to the Pacific, the people were mobilized to solve their tremendous problems.

There were four jobs waiting for every available worker. Yes, there were homeless children but homes and work and educational camps were being built for them and they were becoming citizens of their motherland. Here was a people who had found a way to throw the fantastic power of their collective strength into solving the basic problems of living. In the process, the participants were remaking themselves; learning to think and work collectively—for the benefit of all. The remnants of racism and religious bigotry of tsarism was being fought tooth and nail.

I had seen a new man in the making and I liked what I had seen.

CHAPTER 8

Return to
The Great Depression

THE GREAT bubble of U.S. prosperity had exploded in October 1929, while I was still abroad. Twenty-five billion dollars in stock market values vanished almost overnight and things were rapidly going from bad to worse. By the time the landslide hit bottom, 5,761 banks had failed, wages had been cut and cut again until they averaged 45 per cent for all industry. Forty million men, women and children—one third of the nation— were to find themselves ill-fed, ill-housed and ill-clothed—in the words of President Roosevelt. And all this in the midst of a cataclysm that no man could logically explain (except in Marxist terms).

President Herbert Hoover contented himself with setting up commissions to investigate. In place of halting wage cuts, he suggested staggered work weeks to spread employment. Henry Ford, the wizard of mass production, declared, "There is plenty of work to do if people would do it." And a few weeks after this profound observation, he closed down the Ford plant, putting 75,000 more men out of work.

Indeed it seemed that no one among the leaders knew what to do. The distinguished bourgeois economists could only mouth meaningless rationalizations. The leading industrialists and financiers presented the government with angry demands.

The President responded by setting up the Reconstruction Finance Corporation, which loaned two billion dollars to banks and industries to spur the recovery that he said was "just around the corner."

In itself the depression was not unique—there had been one ten years before and depressions at fairly regular intervals before that. Once started, their effects spread throughout the world—England, France, Germany, Italy slid down into the slump along with the United States. But the 1929 situation was different: For the first time in history, there was one country that did not sink into depression. In the USSR there was no unemployment—actually there was an acute shortage of manpower. In some key industries, workers were doing overtime to meet the soaring demands. While miners in the United States were jobless and starving, the USSR was forced to launch a drive to mechanize their coal mines. While factories here lay idle, production in the USSR was not only going full draft but increasing at fantastic rates! Over-all production in 1931 was 19.4 per cent over 1930.

Those years of the depression could have had an even more tremendous impact on workers throughout the world; suffering poverty and depair, they would only have had to turn their eyes to the East to see that workers could solve their problems without benefit of the banks and industrial rulers who owned everything, decided everything and steered the nation onto the rocks of disaster. But the American people were kept from a full knowledge of the socialist state by anti-Soviet propaganda that was sustained at a hysterical pitch.

I found on my return to New York that, as usual, the Negroes were bearing the brunt of the depression. Not that millions of their white fellow-citizens were not also on the absolute rock bottom of poverty—it was just that a larger percentage of the Negro population was numbered among the victims.

My comrades in New York, as well as across the country, were up to their necks in work, helping to organize hunger marches and tenants' protective groups, as well as fighting to build union strength against the endless waves of wage cuts. There was work to be done wherever one turned. Certainly the huge Harlem ghetto could use all the talent and training I and others could bring to it.

Black people had turned in great numbers some years before to the movement led by Marcus Garvey, to which I referred earlier. Because he stressed the Black man's African heritage, much of what he preached answered the deep psychological hunger within the Black community for a meaningful past. The movement that he led had a paramilitary character and a titled hierarchy which at least simulated the outer trappings of power. One could understand its appeal to the Black masses who had known only white power and white overlords for generations. But the trappings could not hide the basic despair and hopelessness. With no perspective of alliance with the white exploited masses, and fearing defeat in competition with the middle classes for a just share of the market, Garvey and his followers hit upon the Utopian slogan, "Back to Africa!"

By 1930 the Garvey movement had declined. But in its dispersal there were left many small groups that persisted, preaching the gospel of nationalist, Black separateness. They would leave to the white capitalists the enjoyment of the Black people's inheritance won by toil, sweat and blood—and lost through the chicanery and trickery of bourgeois law and justice.

It was March 1931. I had behind me three years abroad devoted to the study of imperialism and to anti-imperialist activities. I had met leaders and liberation fighters of almost every country in the world, representing all colors and nationalities, united in the common fight to liberate their countries from political bondage. I had been able to study documents showing the value of U.S. loans abroad and the growing export of dollars. Here was the basic proof that the long arm of U.S. imperialism was grasping for the control of more and more of the world's resources and governments. American monopoly was associated with the rise of fascism in Western Europe. Of course, there were pious phrases of condemnation, but the appeals in the League of Nations and elsewhere for a united front against fascism put forward by the Soviet Union met with apathy. Indeed, the Soviet calls for action were termed alarmist by the U.S. press.

I was glad to see my sister again. She had not had an easy time in New York but was now adjusting herself. She had secured a room with Dr. and Mrs. Charles Ford and I visited her there. Of course, there were long talks about my travels and experiences, especially in the Soviet Union. They knew that the reports they read in the papers were slanted so as to prejudice the people. I remembered how Dr. Du Bois had on one occasion been asked why he discounted so much that the metropolitan press reported about the Soviet Union. He had replied unsmilingly: "Well, for 400 years the press has systematically lied about my people: I am satisfied that it would lie about anything that would be good for black folk."

Harlem was growing at a furious pace. Negroes were seeking escape from the ghetto death traps downtown. In comparison with the downtown slums, Harlem seemed a heaven to the newcomers. Black folk from the South were heading North by trainloads—the second wave of an exodus from Dixie that had begun during World War I. Black men and women from the British West Indies poured into Harlem despite the restrictions. Harlem was becoming the capital of Black America; it was already the largest Black community in the world. This city within a city was astir with many political currents. Its inhabitants comprised a conglomerate mass of the old, long-time Northern Negroes, the newly arrived Southern Blacks, and the West Indians. The continuing influx of Black and Brown families into this "promise land" and the practices of the real estate sharks created a competition for living space. Unbelievably high prices were asked for homes. Racism was rampant, and police brutality was on the order of the day.

The community was also gaining recognition as the cultural center of Black America. Black culture—painting, literature, music and sculpture by Blacks, about Blacks, was beginning to come into its own. There were protesting voices being raised in Harlem, but there were few that went beyond the emotional pitch and tone to analyze scientifically the causes of Black exploitation and poverty in this land of inestimable wealth and influence.

Among the writers, Claude McKay and Langston Hughes were emerging as spokesmen for Black freedom. The voice and writings of Dr. Du Bois were countering in the sharpest terms the "Back to Africa" program of the Garveyites. The young Communist Party, which was gathering its forces and forging the program that was proving so effective in the Great Depression, also opposed the "Back to Africa" concept.

Harlem did not have a basic working class. There was little heavy industry in and around New York City, but there were Black railroad workers—mostly in the public services section of the railroads—textile and garment workers in bottom-rung jobs; there were jobs in other fields, and then there were the domestic workers. It did not take the mass of Blacks long to learn that Harlem was quite a bit on the hellish side of heaven; they were dissatisfied, bitter and discontented with their lot, hungered for release from the prison of asphalt and stone in which they were trapped. The white bourgeoisie recognized the revolutionary potential here and used every known device to prevent it from attaining unity in struggle. The West Indian Black, who was part of the majority in his native island, exploited this advantage in the States and became an entrepreneur. Envy of the West Indian arose among some Black Americans, fanned into enmity by the white rulers' crediting West Indians with more enterprise than other Blacks. Then there was also the fact that Blacks who had lived a long time in the North feared that the influx of Blacks from the backward South would threaten their own social and political status.

My first assignment after my return was to the post of

Communist Party organizer in Harlem. Of course, I tried to bring the message of hope I had found in the USSR. I told how the people over there were proving every day that workers were far more capable of ruling the land than the upper classes. I told them how discrimination on the basis of color, class, sex, religion or nationality could be eliminated; that socialism was the answer to the depression as well as to other problems plaguing our land.

My work in Harlem was demanding, rewarding and, I think, helpful to those whom I was able to influence. When I was called away for a "brief" teaching job in Pittsburgh, I had no idea it would keep me from Party organizational work for a score of years!

The project in Pittsburgh was a school—a school of a brand-new kind, in which miners and steel workers were to learn the techniques of organizing, to study the history of the labor movement and to analyze our society and find out the "whys" behind the monstrous destruction being visited upon our people by the depression.

I was excited by the prospect of teaching such students. And I was convinced that one of the most effective roadblocks to progress for the workers of the United States was the carefully maintained hatred that separated whites and Negroes. Pittsburgh was one of the main headquarters for the activities of some of the most rapacious operators in the history of labor exploitation.

Pittsburgh, Pennsylvania! What a city! An artery to the "industrial heart" of the nation. The area where Morgan, Frick, Carnegie, the Du Ponts, the Mellons, Pitcairns, Rockefellers and others of the most powerful and ruthless robber barons had fought it out for the enormously lucrative industries centered there—steel, coal mines, iron ore, railroad equipment, aluminum processing, food products, electrical products. During World War I, Pittsburgh had produced 58 per cent of the munitions manufactured in the country.

The combination of key heavy industries and boards of

directors made up of big league pirates could only mean superexploitation to the workers of Pittsburgh. Working conditions in some of the plants were a cross between a madhouse and hell. Steel workers put in ten and twelve hours a day for an average annual wage of around $900. Safety devices were unknown. One mill was called the slaughter house. "They kill a man in there every day," the saying went.

Any attempt on the part of the workers to organize for better conditions was met with instant repression. Company unions, labor spies, terror campaigns—the whole catalogue of techniques developed to hold down workers. The big corporations maintained an organization called "labor adjusters," which was only a euphemism for a goon squad. The leader of these "adjusters" boasted he could mobilize 10,000 men on a few hours' notice, armed and ready to smash any attempt to strike.

When I came to Pittsburgh, the population was around 650,000, of which 150,000 were foreign-born men and women from Europe, Canada and a dozen other nations. Negroes comprised about seven per cent of the total, about 40,000. Superexploitation had created unimaginable slum areas— workers were packed into hovels; rats, bedbugs and cockroaches flourished in the dark and ancient buildings with their moist walls, cracked doors and floors, primitive toilet facilities; the "heating systems" would have frightened an Eskimo. Children slept eight and ten in a room; adults fared little better, and God help the old or ill!

Hundreds of men and women were sleeping in public parks and scrabbling in garbage dumps for food—devoid of hope, jobs, or the prospect of finding help anywhere. Some literally starved to death. For Negroes, conditions were even worse—difficult as this is to imagine. They held down the most dangerous, lowest paid, dirtiest and most exhausting jobs in the various plants—that is, those who could find any work at all. They were always the first to be laid off.

When I arrived in this paradise, I had secured a room in the jimcrow YMCA at the edge of the ghetto, in an area known as the "Hill." Here Black people were paying exorbitant rents for houses not fit for human habitation. Unable to break out of the ghetto, Black families were renting one or more of their rooms to lodgers in order to meet the demands of the landlords.

I did not live at the YMCA for long. Actually, it was not in the heart of the ghetto district, and the young men who lived there were, for the most part, students at the University of Pittsburgh. Few of them understood the ordeals and problems of the working class; when I tried to draw some of them into an awareness of the effects of the depression on the Negro people, I got little or no response.

The school I was assigned to was being held in a hall owned by one of the Jewish fraternal organizations. Twelve students had been signed up and all of them were living on the premises. There wasn't room for one more, so I had to look for a place close by. I ended up renting a room from a Mrs. Lulu Clark.

Earlier I referred to the massive attacks on the Soviet Union that filled the news media, but here I found a notable exception to the brainwashing. In Pittsburgh, as well as in Detroit, Chicago, Cleveland and other great industrial centers, millions of foreign-born workers believed that socialism was helping to solve the problems of the people of the USSR. In those days each national group was likely to have its own hall, association, newspaper and spokesmen, as well as its own cultural activities—dances, choral groups, study groups. And thousands of them were ardent reds. Many of the foreign language papers read like the *Daily Worker.* Open members of the Communist Party were union officials; top labor leaders deliberately hired Communists to do organizational work.

It was these foreign-born groups that gave power and thrust to the organizing campaigns in auto, coal, steel and other industries during the depression years—and later. They poured out in thousands to back unemployment demonstrations, hunger marches and other campaigns. It was from the same groups—the conscious militant workers—that support came in the drive for unity of the oppressed Negro and white depression victims.

The rulers of America feared this developing unity; they looked with horror on the mass demonstrations in which Negroes and whites participated. Every device of the government and the corporations was brought into play to keep the whites and Blacks divided; Negroes were beaten, threatened, jailed, and so were whites. When possible, the whites were deported.

This budding unity was, of course, aided by the depression—a situation in which thousands of poor, native-born whites began to realize from the privations of their own lives that they held much in common with their poor Black brothers. They shared freight trains, park benches, breadlines, haystacks, hobo jungles, hospital charity clinics, the dirt-poor life in shantytowns called "Hoovervilles"—those edge-of-town camps with houses made of tin salvaged from oil drums, walls made of cardboard, dirt floors, jungle sanitation.

For myself and other activists in those days, life seemed to involve no end of arrests. The men who held power in the cities refused to offer more than token aid. The only recourse left was to bring mass pressure on City Hall, on the sheriff, to halt eviction; and on the courts to free prisoners. One of these experiences became a milestone in my life.

I was working with a friend who headed up an unemployed council. Those about to be evicted for failure to pay the rent turned generally to the unemployed council for aid. Neighbors were organized to thwart an eviction by rallying around and putting the furniture back into the house. But often the sheriff's men came in droves and this called for a much wider mobilization.

The unemployed council mimeographed and distributed leaflets throughout the neighborhood, calling the people out. Speakers were assigned to explain to the crowd who were the real villains—the landlords and other big businessmen who sought to fasten the burden of the depression on the already

over-burdened poor. We would explain how their only hope
for improvement lay in bringing the power of their numbers to
bear in mass protest demonstrations and other activities.

One demonstration involved a family that had been very
active in various struggles. When this came to the attention of
the bosses, the landlord ordered them evicted and the family
turned to the unemployed council for support. In view of the
limited forces available, students from the workers' school had
to be mobilized along with tenants and others. I was mustered
in and placed on the steering committee of the demonstration.

Hardly had the sheriff's men finished dumping the furniture
on the sidewalk than people under the direction of the steering
committee began putting the furniture back. A young Black
man by the name of Ben Carreathers headed the action
committee. I've seen few men like Ben in my life. He was more
than six feet tall, a splendid specimen of manhood. His face
was sharp, he had deep-set eyes and a voice that was low and
gentle until he grew angry. He feared neither man nor the imps
that man had created.

As Ben exhorted the crowd to get things moving, the furniture was going back faster than it had come out. Then policemen on foot and on horseback came down like an avalanche on
the demonstration. Clubs began to fly in every direction.
People fought back. Ben was like a raging lion. I saw him
toppling cops as one would tenpins. The leaders, including
Ben, were brutally clubbed and then arrested. And although I
had been specifically instructed not to get into the demonstration, it was clear that if the action were to be successful I had to
take leadership. I must confess I had been nervous, but the
courage shown by Ben calmed and steeled me.

I elbowed my way through the crowd in an effort to get onto
the porch of the house from which the eviction was being
made, and as I mounted the front steps I started to speak. I was
able to say only a few words before I, too, was seized by the
police and thrown into a patrol wagon. Some 20 or 30 men
were carried down to the Blawnox Street jail. Only five were

held. We were booked under an old sedition law that had been
pulled out of legal mothballs.

An indictment was handed down within a few days and the
trial began. Negro lawyers had crowded into the courtroom to
hear the trial. And the people who had been part of the
demonstration were also there in full force. We had decided
that as an attorney I would represent myself and the rest of the
defendants.

The first day I was called to the bench, the judge surprised
me by telling me in the same tone he would have used to
explain some rule of evidence: "I think you should know that I
was once a coal miner." There was no elaboration and my
response to this bit of judicial intelligence was something like:
"I hope your rulings will reflect it, Your Honor." This had
absolutely nothing to do with the case, and it did not alter the
judge's role as a dispenser of bourgeois justice.

The second day he summoned me to expand somewhat on
his theme, confessing: "I once joined the Socialist Party when
I was a young man."

At the end of my presentation of the case to the jury, I was
called to the bench for the third and last time and was told:
"Do you know I have been more than a Socialist—I've thought
of myself as being a Christian Communist." I mumbled
something like, "I would never have thought so, Your Honor,"
but back of my mind was the thought that if the case had lasted
one more day he would have greeted me as "Comrade" and
confessed to having participated in the Bolshevik Revolution.
It was interesting to speculate on what lay behind his admis-
sions to me. Perhaps he needed to reassure himself—just in
case in his chosen course he were to be overtaken by the
workers' total victory.

The trial lasted five days—three days for argument and two
days for the jury's deliberations. The Pittsburgh newspapers
were full of scare headlines about the "Communists Attempt to
Incite a Riot." In the tense atmosphere created by the press, the
testimony of the state's witnesses—all of them police

officers—sought to give "evidence" that we had not only
incited to riot but were guilty of insurrection.

As the prosecution presented its case to the all-white jury, I
noticed that the foreman—a woman—seemed to question with
her eyes and facial expressions some of the prosecutor's
contentions. So when I presented the case for the defense, I
consciously directed my attention to her. I painted a picture of
families living in daily fear of having to sleep in the streets and
how this common fear had forged a bond between neighbors
for the defense of their homes. "A man's home is his castle."
Citing this well-worn concept of Anglo-Saxon common law, I
asked how anyone could expect self-respecting Americans, no
matter what the color of their skins, to give up their homes
without resistance, willingly accepting the role of aimless
wanderers and panhandlers?

As for the charge of inciting to riot and resisting arrest, I had
elicited from defense witnesses that no one was armed, nor had
there been any discussion of violent actions. There had been
only one objective—to place the furniture back into the house.
How could there be a charge of inciting to riot or of promoting
insurrection when there had been no disturbance at all until
the police officers intervened?

At the end of two days of deliberation, the jury returned and
the lady foreman announced a verdict of "Not guilty." This
was the last case I was to participate in as a lawyer for many
years.

The mine and metal workers school lasted six intensive
weeks. Directing the school had been a stimulating experience.
I was later to derive much satisfaction from seeing many of the
graduates of that short session go on to become militant union
organizers of steel and coal—two of the toughest industries in
the United States. Looking back at my short stay in Pittsburgh,
I realize that I was both teacher and student. Much that I had
learned has helped me through many rough spots. The most
important lesson I learned was that the organized power of the

workers, when directed by class-conscious leaders, is irresistible, even by the most formidable corporate combinations. As a Black man I had also learned that the Black people were part of this power that must inevitably prevail in the United States if the nation was to survive.

It had been exhilarating to witness the mass response to the call of the Communist Party to fight back against capitalist efforts to solve the crisis at the expense of the people. Millions of Americans, for the first time in their lives, were learning the true role and meaning of government. The harsh struggle to stay alive from day to day was teaching Americans what no amount of formal education could—that the government was *not* above classes, that it always served those who owned and managed the corporations; that the workers got only what they fought for as a class. For the Communists, mass organization was the order of business—the organization of unemployed councils, the mobilization for hunger marches and for thwarting the seizures of farms by the bankers, the defense of the workers' leaders who were persecuted for leading these activities, the involvement of the Black people in mass struggles, the education of the working class in the fight for survival.

I had seen millions of workers, Black and white, speaking a dozen languages, sunk in desperate poverty, rise in militant struggle. I saw new leaders springing up overnight out of those same ranks of labor—brave, brilliant men and women who put their lives on the line over and over again. I had witnessed the first skirmishes initiated by the workers against some of the most powerful industrialists in the land. These skirmishes were part of the preparation of the great battle to come in which the organized workers—Black and white—forced the corporate giants of steel and coal to share with them a larger portion of the profits coined out of labor's toil, sweat and misery.

CHAPTER 9

The Scottsboro Case

A TELEPHONE call from Rose Baron of the International Labor Defense resulted in my return to New York. The ILD executive was in session, she told me. A multitude of pressing problems were before it; the organization was busy on many fronts, especially in defending and supporting the leaders and the rank-and-file union members who were being arrested in the fight for bread and employment. City, state and federal governments were taking part in these harassments, resorting to widespread terrorizing tactics in and out of court.

Rose Baron was one of those people who had persuaded me to go to Boston in August 1927, to join in the last-ditch fight for the lives of Sacco and Vanzetti. I recalled with warmth her sensitive efforts on that trip from New York to Boston to protect me from racist insults and indignities during rest stops. Born in tsarist Russia, she had learned the ways of religious bigots first-hand under the whiplash of the tsar's Cossacks.

She now informed me that the organization had come into the Scottsboro Case and I was tremendously elated at this news. It seemed to me it would mark the beginning of a new era in the fight for Negro rights. Rose stopped the words of congratulations with which I had greeted her announcement. She had a specific question to ask me.

It seemed that J. Louis Engdahl, National Secretary of the ILD, was preparing to leave on a tour of Europe, accompanied by Mrs. Ada Wright, mother of Andy and Roy Wright, two of the Scottsboro boys. Their aim was to expose the frame-up and to arouse international protest against the threat of mass murder planned by American reaction. The Executive Committee, therefore, wanted to know whether I could take over the organization leadership until Engdahl's return. I was honored and pleased beyond words. I had some misgivings as to my ability to handle the job, but I accepted.

Nevertheless I wanted to talk the matter over with Ben Carreathers, one of the courageous Negro leaders and a dominant figure in the Pittsburgh area. We saw eye to eye, but I never regretted leaving any place more than I regretted leaving Pittsburgh. I believed that the city was destined to be one of the fiercest battlefields for American democracy; the organization of the steel industry was to be undertaken before long, and Ben Carreathers was to play a conspicuous role, particularly in the organization of the mills in Aliquippa.

As I prepared to leave Pittsburgh, I went over the details of the Scottsboro case in my mind. It had begun March 25, 1931, when nine Negro lads were dragged by a sheriff and his deputies from a 47-car freight train that was passing through Paint Rock, Alabama, on its way to Memphis. The train was crowded with youths, both white and Black, aimlessly wandering about. They were riding the freights in search of food and employment and they wandered about aimlessly in the train. There was a fight, and some white lads telegraphed ahead that they had been jumped and thrown off the train by "niggers." At Paint Rock, a sheriff and his armed posse boarded the train and began their search for the "niggers."

Two white girls dressed in overalls were taken out of a car; white and Black youths alike were arrested and charged with vagrancy. But the presence of the white girls added a new dimension to the arrest. The girls were first taken to the office of Dr. R. R. Bridges for physical examination. No bruises were found on their bodies, no were they unduly nervous. A small amount of semen was found in the vagina of each of them but it was at least a day old.

The doctor gave his report to the sheriff and obviously it

ruled out rape in the preceding 24 hours. But for the Alabama authorities that made no difference—they came up with a full-blown charge of rape. The nine Black lads stood accused.

The second day after the arrests the sheriff tried to get the girls to say they had been raped by the youths, and both refused. They were sent back to jail, but a Southern sheriff can exert a lot of pressure, and on the following day Victoria Price, the older of the two women (who had a police record), caved in. Ruby Bates, the 17-year-old, an almost illiterate mill hand, still refused to corroborate the charge. But on the fourth day she, too, succumbed to the pressure. The Roman holiday could now be staged.

On March 31, 1931, 20 indictments were handed down by a grand jury, emphasizing the charge of rape and assult. The nine boys were immediately arraigned before the court in Scottsboro. All pleaded not guilty.

The first exposure of the infamous frame-up appeared April 2, 1931, in the pages of the *Daily Worker,* which called on the people to initiate mass protests and demonstrations to save nine innocent Black youths from legal lynching. On April 4, the *Southern Worker,* published in Chattanooga, Tenn., carried a first-hand report from Scottsboro by Helen Marcy describing the lynch spirit that had been aroused around the case. The trail began on April 7—with the outcome a foregone conclusion.

Thousands of people poured into Scottsboro—if there were "niggers" to be lynched, they wanted to see the show. A local brass band played "There'll Be a Hot Time in the Old Town Tonight" outside the courthouse while the all-white jury was being picked. The state militia was called out—ostensibly to protect the prisoners. Its attitude toward the lads, one of whom was bayonetted by a guardsman, was little different from that of the lynch mob. In short order, Charles Weems, 20, and Clarence Norris, 19, the two older lads, were declared guilty by the jury. On the same day, Haywood Patterson, 17, was the next victim. And on April 8, Ozie Powell, 14; Eugene Williams, 13; Olin Montgomery, 17; Andy Wright, 18; and Willie Robertson, 17, were declared guilty. The hearing of Roy Wright, 14 years old, ran into "legal" difficulties. The prosecution had asked the jury to give him life imprisonment, but eleven jurors voted for death, and it was declared a mistrial.

Stephen R. Roddy (a member of the Ku Klux Klan, it was said) had been retained by the Black Ministers Alliance in conjunction with the NAACP as a defense attorney. At the trial he said he was present only as an observer. But he had advised the boys to plead guilty so that he could try to get them off with life imprisonment. The court duly appointed another lawyer, Milo Moody, to act with Roddy as a defense counsel. His attitude was similar to that of the NAACP appointee and augured ill for the defendants.

Not one witness was called by counsel for the defense; the jury was not asked to acquit the defendants; indeed, there was no summation by the defense counsel in behalf of the boys. Nor was there any real cross-examination of the two women involved, and neither of the lawyers consulted with the defendants until the day of the trial.

The day after the trial ended, the ILD entered the case. George W. Chalmers of Chattanooga, armed with a battery of fellow-lawyers that included Joseph Brodsky and Irving Schwab of New York, interviewed the lads in their prison cells. After being retained formally, Chalmers entered a motion for a new trial, stating that the boys were clearly innocent, that they had not had counsel of their own choosing and that they were the victims of a monstrous frame-up.

The very next day, April 11, the Chattanooga *Times* revealed inadvertently the true role of Roddy and Moody in the following statement: "That the Negro boys had a fair trial even the defense counsel fully admits. Stephen Roddy, chief defense counsel, declared: 'Judge Hawkins was most fair and impartial.'"

The sentence pronounced by this fair and impartial judge was death in the electric chair.

After I had become involved in the case, I began to examine all the available evidence, as well as the alignment of the social forces arrayed against the youths. In reading the very first lines of the indictments, I read: "The People of the State of Alabama against—" and then the name of each defendant followed. The people of the State of Alabama, indeed! Almost half of the people of Alabama were Negroes, while those who were calling themselves by that name included the white sheriffs drunk with racism; the police who believed that their guns were synonymous with law and order; a press steeped in racism; landlords, bankers, businessmen and a racist white community. Both of the pathetic accusers were prostitutes. "They told me," Ruby Bates said later, "I must work with the police. What could I do?"

On the other side were tens of thousands of Alabama white workers, who had no leadership, and many honest white liberals who did not know how to organize themselves for this kind of struggle. And as the story of the case spread far and wide, there were hundreds of millions of Europeans, Asians, Africans and Latin Americans—among them hundreds of thousands of Communists who were firm in the knowledge that defeat for racism in Scottsboro would mark a progressive advance for the entire world.

How did the NAACP fit into this picture? It was the largest and oldest organization of Blacks and whites active on the civil rights front. The Communists had broken the case open and called for a united defense. State and federal authorities, with their strong allies in and out of office throughout the South, feared that call for unity—it threatened to undermine their carefully built plot. And they hated the Communists; indeed Alabama law called for the ousting of Communists from any part of the case. The NAACP did not hesitate to lift every voice to certify their equal hatred for the Communists and also called for their exclusion from the defense. They demanded the exclusive right to handle the case.

But one think was certain: The ILD had no intention of

turning its back on the Scottsboro boys. It had neither the time
nor the money to enter a fight with the NAACP. But it could
not evade the ideological battle, for only thus could the
government's role be exposed. If the NAACP leadership had
been ready to go all out to save the youths, the ILD would have
welcomed them as they would welcome the aid of any and
every one who could help in the fight. We felt that the case was
not primarily a legal matter; it was a political struggle of
national and international import; the courts were being used
as a shield to conceal the racist policy of government. Alabama
knew nothing of justice for Black men, and anyone who was
seriously aiming at the freedom of the Scottsboro boys was
inevitably labeled "Red."

For all these reasons, the ILD continued working for the
mass defense; to settle *some* of the slanders, we made our
support official. On April 24, the ILD received the following
letter signed by Mamie Williams, Ada Wright and Claude
Patterson—all parents of Scottsboro boys:

"Although our sons are minors, we were never consulted as
to the retaining of Steve Roddy either by the Ministers Alliance
or by Mr. Roddy.

"We know that the ILD has engaged for us as good a lawyer
as there is in Chattanooga, and we do not want Mr. Roddy to
have anything more to do with our boys.

"The Ministers Alliance by sending a Committee and Attorney Roddy to Birmingham in an effort to have the boys
disown the ILD is really helping to send the boys to the
electric chair.

"We call upon everyone to give full support to the International Labor Defense."

On the same day the boys sent the following statement to
New York:

"We, Haywood Patterson, Andy Wright, Roy Wright and
Eugene Williams, after a conference with our parents, desire to
reaffirm our written contract with the International Labor
Defense to engage George W. Chamlee as chief counsel in our

defense, and we, Ozie Powell, Olin Montgomery, Clarence Norris, Willie Robertson and Charlie Weems, join with the above named defendants in ratifying our written statement to the ILD concerning the employment of counsel for us.

"A statement yesterday obtained from us by Steve Roddy, W. M. James, L. P. Whitten and H. Terrell, under circumstances we did not understand, indicated that we were not satisfied with the ILD. This statement was obtained without the consent or advice of our parents, and we had no way of knowing what to do. We completely repudiate that statement and brand those who obtained it as betrayers of our cause."

These facts were made known to the world through the medium of the daily press. But the NAACP wanted the case confined to the courts and not made the property of the people who would carry the struggle to the streets. The NAACP therefore practiced every device to get the ILD removed from the case. That is why it became necessary to release statements like the above on May 14 and 18; October 1; December 27 and 28 in 1931; and once more on January 2 in 1932.

It was all the more impressive to read a letter to the *Daily Worker,* written April 19, from William Pickens, Field Secretary of the NAACP:

"I am writing from Kansas City, where I have just seen a copy of the *Daily Worker* for April 16th and noted the fight which the workers are making through the ILD to prevent the judicial massacre of Negro youth in Alabama. . . .

"In the present case the *Daily Worker* and the workers have moved, so far, more speedily and effectively than all other agencies put together. . . .

"This is one occasion for every Negro who has intelligence enough to read, to send aid to you and the ILD." (Alas, Mr. Pickens was later forced to recant by the NAACP leadership.)

The meaning of the fight to free the nine defendants was best expressed by Richard B. Moore, who had criss-crossed the country as a national board member of the ILD to bring the story of the boys to the American masses. In 1940, speaking in Washington, D.C. before a meeting of the National Conference of the ILD, Moore said:

"The Scottsboro Case is one of the historic landmarks in the struggle of the American people and of the progressive forces throughout the world for justice, civil rights and democracy. In the present period, the Scottsboro Case has represented a pivotal point around which labor and progressive forces have rallied not only to save the lives of nine boys who were framed . . . but also against the whole system of lynching terror and the special oppression and persecution of the Negro people. . . .

"Last year we came to a new development in the Scottsboro Case which shows more clearly than ever before the fascist nature of this case. Governor Graves (of Alabama) gave his pledged word to the Scottsboro Defense Committee and to leading Alabama citizens at a hearing to release the remaining Scottsboro boys. . . ."

Among the leaders of the NAACP, Henry Lee Moon was one who revealed that he recognized the international character and significance of the Communist defense. It was not, however, until 1948, after the fierce heat of battle had subsided that in his book, *Balance of Power,* he said:

"It was during this period, in the spring of 1931, that nine colored lads, in age from thirteen to nineteen years, were arrested in Alabama and charged with the rape of two nondescript white girls. The defense of these boys was first undertaken by the NAACP. But the Communists, through the International Labor Defense, captured the defense of the imprisoned youths and conducted a vigorous, leather-lunged campaign that echoed and reechoed throughout the world. The Scottsboro boys were lifted from obscurity to a place among the immortals—with Mooney and Billings, Sacco and Vanzetti—fellow-victims of bias in American courts."

As for the "vigorous, leather-lunged campaign," the ILD saw the battle for these nine lives as a fight for America's honor and integrity—besmirched by every branch of its government in its relations with Negro citizens. Betrayed by those in power, the Scottsboro boys were "to be lifted to a place among the immortals." Lifting them meant lifting 15 millions of Black people.

To quote Moon further: "The Communists maintained that legal defense had to be supplemented by international propaganda; American consulates, legations and embassies were picketed and stoned in many parts of the world. Mass meetings of protest were held in the capitals of Europe and Latin America at which resolutions demanding the freedom of the Scottsboro boys were passed. Letters, telegrams and cablegrams poured in upon the President of the United States, the Governor of Alabama, the presiding judge and other state officials, demanding the immediate release of the boys."

And then Moon added: "This propaganda was effective in exposing the hypocrisy of American justice, but it did not gain the freedom of the boys." Nevertheless, when the NAACP left the case, the boys had been condemned to death. It was the fight waged by the ILD that saved their lives by refusing to be bound by the restraints of the narrow, legalistic arena. And it was the ILD that lifted the nine Negro lads from an ignoble grave "to a place among heroic figures."

Moon himself says later: "the black masses seemed intrigued by this bold, forthright and dramatic defiance. Offering no quarter, the Communists put the South on the defensive in the eyes of the whole world. They stirred the imagination of Negroes and inspired the hope of ultimate justice. In churches, in conventions, in union halls, in street corner meetings, Negroes were clamorous in expressing approval of the campaign."

It was this reaction of the Negro masses that was the acid test of the correctness of ILD policy. It laid the foundation for the monumental united front that secured the release of all the boys. It was this mass united front that the NAACP leadership was forced eventually to join.

As Moon himself sums it up: "To the Communists . . . the whole campaign was much more than a defense of nine unfortunate lads. It was an attack on the system which had exploited them, fostered the poverty and ignorance in which they were reared and finally victimized them by legal proceedings which were a mockery of justice."

Candor compels me to add that in spite of these noble words Henry Lee Moon was a Red-baiter par excellence when the exigencies of his job demanded it, even though at an earlier stage he had observed that the masses "while not flocking to the Red banner, have refused to be stampeded into an anti-Communist bloc. Politicians seeking Negro support need more than the Red bogey to garner this vote. . . . Communism is not regarded as the enemy. . . ."

Another figure of note, commenting on the significance of the Scottsboro Case is of singular interest. Nancy Cunard in her book, *The Negro, an Anthology,* writes:

"To bring out the absolute fiendishness of the treatment of Negro workers by the governing white class in America, more specifically but by no means restricted to the Southern states, I am going to start with what may seem a fantastic statement—I am going to say that the Scottsboro case is not such an astounding and unbelievable thing as it must seem, as it certainly does, to the public at large. Why? That nine proven innocent Negro boys, falsely accused of raping two white prostitutes, tried and retried, still held in death cells after 2 1/2 years. . . . It is unparalleled. It is not primarily a case that can be called political, as is that of Tom Mooney, still held for 18 years in San Quentin . . . on an equally vicious frame-up because he was an active strike-leader; nor at first sight do the same elements predominate as . . . in the murder by law of Sacco-Vanzetti. But the same capitalist oppression and brutality are at the root—because every Negro worker is the potential victim of lynching, murder and legal lynching by the white ruling class, simply because he is a worker and black. No, this frame-up is not unparalleled, though the scale of it and its

colossal development into what is now really a world issue, are
so. No previous Negro case has aroused such universal outcry
against the abomination of American 'law.' "

As the ILD increased its efforts to bring the true character of
the case before the peoples of the world, it won ever more
support. The flood of letters and petitions pouring in on the
officials involved continued to mount; the people rose to
defend their hard-won rights against the attack of their enemies.

After the trial, the convictions and sentencing, the ILD
leadership was more than ever convinced that only world
protests would save the condemned youth. Protests were called
for from all parts of the world—and they came from such
eminent men as Albert Einstein, Thomas Mann, Maxim Gorky,
Theodore Dreiser, Waldo Frank and many others. The voice of
the Scottsboro lynchers, *The Jackson County Sentinel*, declared that the mass movement to save the nine boys was "the
most dangerous movement launched in the South in many
years."

On May 1, 1934, the NAACP, over the signature of Walter
White, issued a press release announcing that "The NAACP
. . . had no connection whatsoever with the efforts of Communist groups or with the International Labor Defense in the
case and that it would have no such connection."

In the June 13, 1934, issue of the *National Guardian,* a New
York liberal weekly, this note appeared: "The National Equal
Rights League invited the ILD and the NAACP to meet in
conference in New York City this weekend with the League.
Walter White, Secretary for the NAACP, declined on the
ground that the Association had tried for a united defense and
because, he claimed, 'the ILD was out for propaganda purposes and would never harmonize.' "

The ILD *was* out for propaganda—it was out for propaganda
against racism and extra-legal lynching; propaganda against
the racist policy of government; propaganda vital to the
struggle for the lives of the intended victims; propaganda

against the conspiracy to slaughter the boys as an act of terror calculated to quell the unrest of the Negro masses and to throw up a barrier to Negro-white unity.

Senator Walter F. George of Georgia, in a moment of candor, said (in 1936): "Why apologize and evade? We have been very careful to obey the letter of the Federal Constitution but we have been very diligent and astute in violating the spirit of such amendments and statutes as would lead the Negro to believe himself the equal of the white man. And we shall continue to conduct ourselves that way."

But no American writer I know of has exposed in a more forthright manner the basically criminal attitude of government toward Negro citizenry than Gustavus Myers in his *History of the Supreme Court.* In a chapter treating of the role of the Fourteenth Amendment, he said:

"Now this Amendment has been one of the Amendments adopted to secure the full freedom of the Negroes and to safeguard them from the oppressions of their former owners. Yet for more than twenty years the Supreme Court of the United States, in deference to the demands of the ruling class, had consistently emasculated it. . . . It had declined to give the Negro protection of the National Government when it decided that 'sovereignty for the protection of rights of life and personal liberty within the states rests alone with the states.' This meant that the former slave states were empowered to abridge the liberty of the Negro as they pleased. . . . Using the Fourteenth Amendment to load the helpless Negro race with the obloquy of prejudicial law and custom, and to snatch away from the white worker what trivial rights he still had, the Supreme Court availed itself of that same Amendment to put corporations in a more impregnable position in law than they had ever been before."

Thus the Scottsboro Case had to be fought in such a manner as to save the lives of those innocent young men and at the same time expose the forces involved so clearly as to make a recurrence of Scottsboro difficult indeed.

It took seventeen years! It took all kinds of court maneuvers, all kinds of struggle outside the courts; it took tremendous sacrifices of time and energy by thousands of good people around the world—many of them Communists, many of them not Communists—to win that great battle. But at the end, not one boy was lynched. All were freed. And the South has not been quite the same ever since.

Patterson in the 1930's.

CHAPTER 10

The Chicago Years

IN 1938 I went to Chigago as associate editor of the *Daily Record,* established to present the Midwest public with an organ reflecting a working-class point of view. It would concentrate on reporting and analyzing labor-industrial disputes, jimcrow and racial segregation, unemployment problems, peace, education and other issues of special interest to the people.

Before I left for the Soviet Union I had again met Louise Thompson, whom I had first seen in 1919 at the Oakland Auditorium. I was acting as chairman of the local NAACP and introducing James Weldon Johnson when I especially noticed the young high school girl in the audience. (This was just before my own graduation.) I was to see her on various occasions and in 1927 she came to New York enroute to a teaching assignment at Hampton Institute. Chicago was her native city but she had grown up on the West Coast.

I took pleasure in showing her all over New York. I loved to dance and I took Louise on her first visit to the Savoy Ballroom. While she lived in New York she had a kind of salon for young artists, who gathered around her. I even remember trying to persuade her to come to the Soviet Union with me. When I returned, she helped to organize groups whom I would address on my experiences.

From then on we met in various campaigns, or I would meet

her at such international gatherings as the Paris World Assembly against Racism and Anti-Semitism. After I came to Chicago to work on the paper, Louise came on vacation and we were married over the Labor Day weekend. Paul Robeson and his accompanist Larry Brown were present, as were the Rev. Archibald Carey, who married us, Horace Cayton and John P. Davis. (Our daughter, Mary Louise, now a physician, was born in 1943.)

For a while we had to put up in the Vincennes Hotel but we soon found an apartment in Maryland Avenue near 51st, on the Eastern edge of the Southside ghetto.

Chicago was indeed, as Carl Sandburg had described it: "A sprawling, two-fisted slugger" always spoiling for a fight; it also devoted itself to being "hog butcher of the world." One thing Sandburg doesn't mention—it was a hotbed of racism and anti-union labor activity.

The Poles and Czechs who had fled political and religious persecution and economic exploitation in the old country flocked to Chicago. They were to furnish much of the labor power for the packing and steel industries. In the factories and neighborhoods they met both Black and white Americans who had fled intolerable political and economic conditions in the Southern states. This three-way confrontation of foreign-born white, native white and native Black in the Chicago labor market presented the big industrialists and their propagandists with a perfect setup. Groups could be pitted against one another. Churches and schools were enlisted in making racial hatred, religious bigotry and national chauvinism significant factors in Chicago's human relations.

While racism was being consolidated among the whites, including the newcomers from Europe, the local governments on the one hand maintained a democratic pose toward the Blacks and, on the other, practiced ruthless police terror. Chicago was a democracy of profit; I learned from my Chicago experience valuable lessons on the class nature and development of bourgeois democracy.

Perhaps no other large city outside the South had ever been so thoroughly and systematically looted by political gangsters as had Chicago. Political gangs vied with each other for control; all were subservient to the anti-labor meat packers, the steel magnates and the farm implements producers. Big packers sold rotten meat, and big steel hoisted prices; both had their own racket to protect—the ruthless exploitation of Black and white labor. And state and city governments protected them. Gambling, prostitution, crime in every conceivable form flourished; police corruption was directed from City Hall. (Upton Sinclair and Theodore Dreiser have dealt realistically with this phase of history.)

After six months of struggle, the *Daily Record* ran into insurmountable financial difficulties and passed off the journalistic stage. We had learned a lesson from the experience: a labor paper must secure for itself a readership base in the community as well as in the factories if it is to succeed.

By 1940, when we were winding up the affairs of the newspaper, the Black community had pushed back the walls of the ghetto beyond Garfield Boulevard, beyond Washington Park. Westward and northward sizable Black neighborhoods had been established. The *Record* had left at least one heritage, a campaign to get Black baseball players into the Big League ball clubs. The campaign had also been persistently pursued by the New York *Daily Worker.*

I myself had pushed the campaign vigorously, and not only in the pages of the *Record.* Leaflets were distributed in white and Black neighborhoods. Communists everywhere were active.

This talk of baseball was not the usual statistical chit-chat of earned runs, runs batted in, home runs and fielding averages. There was a side of baseball more important to the Blacks on the Southside than the pitching of Bob Feller of the Cleveland Indians and the bats of the famous "murderous row" of the New York Yankees. Black sport fans were talking about the conspicuous absence of Black ball players. Jimcrow had kept Black Americans out of its higher and most lucrative echelons.

Black Americans were aware that there were players among them who were the peers if not the superiors of any white player. Black fans following the Negro League teams knew players like Satchel Paige, Josh Gibson, lanky "Bullet" Rogan and others whom they recognized as being better players than many white professionals drawing five-figure salaries in the Big Leagues.

A group of us, including Paul Robeson, Gil Green and Claude Lightfoot, discussed carrying the issue further. The decision was reached that we had to intensify the campaign. To this end, we would confront directly one of the Big League club owners or Baseball Commissioner Kenesaw Mountain Landis, or both. I was asked to handle this phase.

I wondered whether I should seek a conference with William Wrigley, owner of the Chicago Cubs, or Charles Comiskey, owner of the American League team, the Chicago White Sox.

The White Sox home grounds, Comiskey Park, was on the Southside. Wrigley Field, the Cubs' home ground, was located on the Northside, outside the Black community, but this did not exempt the team from pressure, picket lines, leaflets and letters. The campaign, when it went into full swing, was fed by articles and editorials in the *Daily Worker* and a number of Negro weekly newspapers.

After consultation, I wrote for an appointment with William Wrigley and at the same time sent a letter to Baseball Commissioner Landis, outlining the issue I wished to discuss. Favorable replies came back from both offices.

I spoke by telephone with Paul Robeson in New York and with Earl Dickerson, an acquaintance of many years before, who was now chief counsel for the Liberty Life Insurance Company of Chicago. With their agreement and in their names, I arranged the conference with Judge Landis. I decided, however, to speak with Wrigley myself.

I arrived promptly at the appointed time and entered Mr.

Wrigley's suite after getting a breath-taking view of the city and Lake Michigan before being ushered into his private office. I had expected to see an office that could have been used as a Hollywood set—and I did. Mr. Wrigley's greeting was cordial; he invited me to sit down and indicated that I "had the floor."

It was high time, I told him, that the jimcrow pattern of baseball was changed. Black baseball fans were no longer willing to support a national game from whose ranks one-tenth of the nation was excluded. . . . If Black players were brought into the Big Leagues, an untapped reservoir of Black baseball patrons would be opened up.

I reminded him of the calibre of the Black players in the Chicago American Giants, a Black team, and of players in other Negro league teams; their exploits had not gone unnoticed in the metropolitan press. He nodded agreement. And he listened without an outward show of irritation. He knew the value of the perspective I had outlined—perhaps he saw a pennant or two in the offing. Yet he was afraid to commit himself. Here was a new angle—white racism could be a barrier to greater profits. And yet, business was afraid of the juggernaut it might create.

When he spoke he expressed agreement with what I had said and deplored the existing situation. He buzzed for his secretary and asked her to get "Pants" Rowland on the telephone. Rowland was manager of the Los Angeles Angels, a Cub farm team in California. He informed Rowland of the discussion that we had just had and asked him to come to Chicago. As he hung up the phone, he turned to me and said he would give the matter his sincere attention. He invited me to return upon Rowland's arrival; I assured him I would be there and left the office feeling I had accomplished a good first step. I than returned to the Communist Party office and reported what had happened. There was some feeling that reporters should have been present, but Wrigley did not want them.

The next order of business was to set up a date for Robeson and Dickerson with Judge Landis. That meeting took place before Rowland could come to Chicago. It turned out that Dickerson did not appear so we decided that Paul should talk with the commissioner alone. Judge Landis gave him more than an hour. Paul later told us that he had raised two questions: the absence of Black players from organized baseball and the Commissioner's responsibility to remedy this situation. The Commissioner acknowledged the first point but said that while he might not have been sharp enough, he had raised the question at the club owners' meeting. Robeson replied that it was not enough to have discussions—"it was time to act." The Commissioner promised to "see what could be done."

My second meeting with Wrigley was most interesting. Wrigley introduced me to "Pants" Rowland, and the talk opened with Wrigley asking Rowland if he knew of any Black baseball players who were ready for the big time. Rowland replied bluntly that there were probably several, but the person he regarded as having the greatest potential was a young man who had been a most outstanding athlete at the University of California at Los Angeles. His name was Jackie Robinson.

There was talk of Jackie Robinson being acquired by the Angels, but that was not what we wanted. He had all the qualifications of a Big League ball player. Wrigley did not openly discuss any decision he had made to secure Jackie's signature to a contract. What would Rowland do when he returned to Los Angeles, I wondered? We didn't know. But within a few years from that conference in Wrigley's office, Jackie Robinson was playing in Ebbets Field with the Brooklyn Dodgers, after a short probationary period with Montreal, Brooklyn's farm club. And just as quickly as one could say his name, Robinson was established as one of the country's outstanding baseball players.

I am not saying that Jackie Robinson got to the Big Leagues only through the good offices of the Communist Party. But I

Above, with James W. Ford, Communist Candidate for Vice President, 1940; *below,* on a picket line in Chicago, December 1940, with Vito Marcantonio, New York's American Labor Party Congressman, and a striker of the National Association of Die Casting Workers, CIO.

With Louise, after our marriage in Chicago; Louise Thompson Patterson, 1940.

say, without fear of refutation, that the *Daily Worker,* under the direction of its sports editor, Lester Rodney, and the Chicago *Daily Record* were second to no other voices in the United States in the fight to get Negroes on the rosters of Big League baseball clubs.

What was most important was the repeated proof that democracy in every sphere of human relations had to be fought for. Where Negroes were concerned, they had to lead that fight and help educate white Americans to their responsibilities.

When the Chicago *Record* folded early in 1940, the staff was released and naturally I, as associate editor, was jobless. Our "operation bootstrap" had proved inoperable. We had no credit; the newsprint people and the printers wanted their money guaranteed before they would supply paper or get our sheet ready for the street.

Every government agency set up to save the country from the Reds harassed us and stayed on our tail. We were fighting so that Black Americans might enjoy equality of rights and opportunities. We were pro-labor, the foreign-born, the unemployed, older citizens, jobless youth. We were opposed to wars of aggression and colonialism. Ergo, we should be forced out of business.

I reported to the Chicago Party office ready to go to work, and there was plenty to do. Gil Green and Claude Lightfoot were in charge of the office. The Southside ghetto was bursting at the seams and white reactionaries in housing and real estate were trying to close every avenue of escape. The Communist Party was fighting to break down the walls of the ghetto. Since I had already won a reputation as a public relations man, I was assigned to this area of work.

The capitalist press is venal everywhere in the United States, but Chicago could easily have won first prize in this department and among all others the Chicago *Tribune* ranked high as an example of yellow journalism. In simple language and with vivid pictures it fed the masses of the people spiritual corruption. It was shot through with subtle racism and not-so-subtle anti-labor and anti-foreign-born propaganda. It was therefore all the more regrettable that the *Record* was not able to survive. It could have been a powerful force in the ideological battle in which the white bourgeois press strove—at times successfully—to pit white against Black and the entire community against labor. It was this reactionary poison that we now prepared to fight.

Louise and I moved closer to Washington Park, where the Black Nationalists, Garveyites, Muslims, Communists and others had weekly forums and free-for-all debates. There was no attempt to keep anyone from speaking, although the FBI agents who moved among the audiences always tried to create hostility when a Communist was on the platform. To their chagrin, of all the speakers the Communists were the most popular; they dealt with the realities of American life and with international as well as national issues. It was at this period that I met Gus Hall, who was to become Secretary of the Communist Party.

Best known among the Communist speakers was a man named Poindexter. He had learned his oratory right there in the park. A dark, brown-skinned man of medium height and pleasing personality, he possessed great natural ability as a speaker. He had found the arguments of the Communists unassailable and had joined the Party. Earlier he had been influenced by the Garveyites, but he came to regard them as sectarian and utopian. Among the arguments advanced by the Communists that had convinced him was the necessity for the unity of Black and white here in the United States in the struggles ahead. The Africans, the Communists contended, would take care of colonialism in Africa if we were able to take care of U.S. imperialism, the friend and supporter of South Africa and all reactionaries on the African continent.

There were Black trade union leaders among those who often took the platform, including Hank Johnson and Sam Parks, both of the Packinghouse Workers Union, and Tom Bell

of the Railroad Cooks and Waiters Union. Ardent trade unionists, their knowledge of the trade union movement was linked
with an understanding of its relation to politics.

On Sunday afternoons, especially in the summer, South-
siders crowded into the park and formed a circle around the
speakers. There were often well over a thousand listeners in
the audience. It was here that Richard Wright, the famous
Black writer, first encountered professional revolutionaries. It
was from such gatherings that he came to the Communist Party
and was inspired to begin his career as a writer. Later, for other
than political differences, he broke with the Party. Although he
was convinced that the political philosophy of Communism
was correct, he did not see a book as a political weapon. He
thought that the creative genius of a writer should be freed
from all restrictions and restraints, especially those of a political nature, and that the writer should write as he pleased.
Unfortunately, Harry Haywood, then top organizer on the
Southside, did not exhibit the slightest appreciation that he
was dealing with a sensitive, immature creative genius with
whom it was necessary to exercise great patience. He criticized
some of Wright's earlier characters sharply and tried to force
him into a mold that was not to his liking. Name-calling
resulted and Haywood used his political position to get a vote
of censure against Wright, who thereupon resigned from the
Party.

It was from listening to these discussions that I conceived
the idea of opening up a broad, nonpartisan school for workers,
writers and their sympathizers. The thousands of Blacks who
had migrated to Chicago from the deep South to escape
oppression knew little or nothing of the class essence of the
struggle against racism, and the white Europeans who had fled
religious and economic persecution knew little or nothing of
the racial factors that permeated every phase of the class
conflict in the United States. The gulf between these two
groups, which could only serve the forces of reaction, had to be
bridged. The school, I hoped, would help build a bridge that

would link together these two groups of newcomers to the American urban industrial complex.

I had in mind a school in which we would teach how society had developed its class structure, how it functioned and was held together, what social forces dominated it and how those who were exploited and oppressed could escape. Above all, I believed that the many and varied contributions of Black Americans to the economic, political, artistic and social life of our country had to be uncovered. In a word, the acquisition of knowledge that would make it easier for those who fought together for better conditions on the job to see the dire need that they also fight together on the political front. We would explain what lay behind the hostility to the Soviet Union and point out that although the rulers of the West had joined with the Soviet Union to crush Hitler, they had never had serious differences with Hitlerism; that, in fact, they were protagonists of both racism and of anti-Semitism in their own countries.

The launching of such a project was a herculean task. I talked it over with Party leaders and with a number of my Black friends, especially several of the newspaper men on the *Chicago Defender*. It found favor with them, but they said they were not able to halp materially.

I then took the train to New York to talk the idea over with Earl Browder, at that time General Secretary of the Communist Party, and with Henry Winston. Both of them approved of the steps I had taken and urged me to go full speed ahead. I also consulted with Paul Robeson, who promised to do all he could to help promote the program. I left New York determined to push the school to the best of my ability.

Upon my return, I sat down to write a prospectus, a plan of operation and a budget, based upon what I could now foresee as the initial expenses. At that time I had the good fortune to meet a woman whose name was Clara Taylor. She was, among other things, an interior decorator. A small group of public-minded business people had been brought together to discuss the school plan. An appeal for money ended with moderate success. Mrs. Taylor expressed a desire to work on the project.

She said nothing about a salary and I warily expressed my appreciation.

Mrs. Taylor wanted to know whether premises had been rented. They had not been acquired as yet, and she suggested that she be given that assignment. We sat down to talk and she expressed the opinion that the space we rented should be decorated in good taste. Then out of the blue, she said: "Why don't you go and talk with Marshall Field? He might help you. He's not a racist and, despite his wealth, his thinking is on the progressive side."

I had never been one to hesitate at asking any person to help financially with any project with which I was associated. A revolutionary must see himself as a people's agent. The money he solicits is not for himself—it is for the people's cause. But not all revolutionaries can ask financial aid, so those who can, must, I had often told myself. I did not scoff at the idea of going to see Marshall Field, a merchant prince who headed one of the largest department stores in the country. He was many times a millionaire but was still liberal enough to contribute to progressive causes. In fact, he had financed *The Compass,* a left-of-center daily newspaper in New York.

I went over to the Field building and without any difficulty was ushered into Mr. Field's office. He invited me to sit down and speak out. I did. Drawing out the prospectus for the school, I presented it to him. He read it carefully and then looked at me and smiled.

"Rather an ambitious undertaking," he said. I agreed.

"What experience have you had in building schools?"

I told him of my experience with the miners and steel workers school in Pittsburgh in the 20's. "What drives me is the depth and expanding character of our system of miseducation. Think of a people exploited mercilessly, denied their rights in the courts and at the polls, denied opportunities for cultural advancement and taught that this situation is ordained or that the responsibility rests at their own doorsteps.

"Millions of whites, many of them graduated from famous universities, are without knowledge of why and how the Black

man's position is what it is. These whites have the contempt of
the ignorant for fellow human beings whom they neither know
nor even see in human terms, and they themselves are gradually being dehumanized.

"I want to see a school that dispels lies and myths and
soberly deals with realities."

I stopped, afraid that I had gone too far. But Mr. Field only
repeated "an ambitious undertaking." Then he asked: "Do you
know anything about the Roosevelt School of Social Science?
There are a group of men planning it and they already have a
site on Michigan Boulevard." I told him that I had heard about
it.

"Well, you and Mr. Gosh ought to get together. Let me see if
I can arrange a meeting. I will get in touch with you."

Two days later the call came. Mr. Field wanted to know if I
could meet with him and Mr. Gosh at his office on the
following afternoon. I phoned and informed his secretary that
I would be present. It was a short meeting; Marshall Field
asked me to present my prospectus. Mr. Gosh listened. When I
had finished, Field expressed approval, and turning to Gosh
asked him what he thought of the plan. Gosh had no particular
criticism to make, but when Mr. Field quietly said: "Why can't
you two join forces?" Gosh replied just as quietly: "That's
impossible." He had a long explanation; he wanted to develop
a university, it appeared.

I expressed my agreement with much of what he had said.
Roosevelt College was going to be a bourgeois college of a new
type, which rejected much of the mythology to which the old
schools still clung: the myth of white superiority. The growing
signs of revolt among Blacks and the resentments of students
to courses barren of any relation to life made Roosevelt College
a necessity. But it was not out to oppose the existing order.

Later I heard that Dr. St. Clair Drake, an outstanding Black
scholar, was to be on the Roosevelt staff. Together with Horace
R. Cayton, another able Black scholar, Drake had produced
Black Metropolis—A Study of Negro Life in a Northern City. It
was a book of vital significance, detailing the reality of the

economic, political, spiritual and cultural life of Blacks in
Chicago, and it was prophetic in its predictions of the ills to
emerge from the cauldron of white racism.

But the program I envisaged for the Abraham Lincoln
School went beyond what Gosh had in mind; we were going to
have a college without entrance requirements, open to all.

Marshall Field put several thousand dollars into the project.
Clara Taylor found an ideal spot at 30 West Washington and
decorated it beautifully.

The school got off to a splendid start. I had secured the
unqualified support of Si Wexler, a La Salle Street broker. He
opened an extension class in his own home, to which a number
of his business colleagues came. I lectured there on the
political significance of the rise of Hitler. The course dealt
with the support Western imperialism had given to the National Socialists and why. I elaborated on Hitler racism, then
on white supremacy and anti-Semitism in the United States,
emphasizing the fact that these were twin evils. "Dig down
where you find one and you will find the other," I asserted.

Our school had a board of directors of a mixed character.
They came from the ranks of labor, the middle class, the Black
nationalists, and somehow they found in one or another of our
classes a common interest. What made this fact so heartening
was the proof it offered that these divergent groups could be
brought together to learn how to work and fight for common
interests.

Pearl Hart, one of Chicago's best known civil liberties
lawyers, was chairman of the board. Working with her was
Maudelle Bousfield, a prominent Negro school teacher, whose
husband was president of the Liberty Life Insurance Company, a Black controlled and operated outfit; Earl B. Dickerson, chief counsel of the same insurance firm; Dr. Julian
Lewis, a noted Black scientist; Dr. Metz F. P. Lochard,
educator, journalist and diplomat; Harvey O'Connor, well-
known writer on the class structure of American society; and a
number of trade union leaders.

The school's director was British-born A. D. Winspear, an

Oxford University scholar and an authority on Greek history. I was the assistant director, and the staff was made up of men and women expert in their respective fields, all advanced thinkers. The school was vitally needed in the Middle West and indeed in the entire nation. I have never enjoyed any experience more than the building of the Abraham Lincoln School.

When the school was inaugurated, telegrams came from many workers. James E. Murray, Democratic Senator from the state of Montana, made the principal speech. I quote from his address:

"The front on which the Abraham Lincoln School and other similar institutions of learning are today fighting for the protection of democracy is a front that must not be neglected if liberty and freedom are to survive. They are fighting the battle for a better world and for a lasting peace. . . . The Abraham Lincoln School has been established to train your fellow-citizens in sound democratic principles and in the maintenance of national unity so necessary for the winning of the war and the preservation of democracy. Today the people are often confused by the great welter of propaganda they encounter in the press and on the air and find it difficult to form sound judgment on national problems. I think you are giving the best answer to that question right here in Chicago through the Abraham Lincoln School, dedicated to the preservation of the people and for the people."

The school gave impetus to the cultural and educational life of Chicago. One of its staunchest supporters was Paul Robeson, who was under what might well be called national arrest. He could leave his house, city and state but not his country—his passport had been taken from him. The savage attacks upon him by the State Department and other government agencies had virtually put an end to his concert tours and no producer would cast him for a Broadway show. Now almost all his time was devoted to progressive causes, and American imperialism feared and hated him. The racists were trying

desperately to do the impossible, to destroy his effectiveness as
an enemy of racism and a friend of peace.

Among the many events given to raise funds for the school
was a concert by Lena Horne. My wife had met Lena Horne
during a tour that brought the celebrated star to Chicago.
During the first conversation they had, which dealt mainly
with the ravages of racism, Lena Horne had expressed the
loathing of the humiliating conditions under which Black
women in the theater and concert stage had to work. Louise
had been enraptured by Lena's views and came home enthusiastic about her ideas and her personality.

After listening to Louise's praise of the glamorous star, I
determined to try to get her to appear at an affair given to aid
the school. There was no better emissary than my wife, so I
sent Louise to see Miss Horne again and she came back
jubilant. Lena had agreed to appear. An entertainment committee was set up to promote the affair and, after we had decided
on a date satisfactory to Miss Horne, we engaged the Chicago
Opera House for the occasion.

When it was known that Lena Horne was going to be the
stellar attraction, women and men who would have hesitated to
come forward under other circumstances in behalf of our
school were now ready to permit the use of their names as
sponsors. I decided to do the job up brown. I got in touch with
Paul and asked him to come to town to introduce Miss Horne.
It was a gala affair; the house was packed to the rafters.

It was too much to expect that the Abraham Lincoln School
would go unthreatened by reaction. It was a challenge and a
threat to bourgeois institutions. Supporters and students began
to get visits from the FBI. Their jobs were threatened and some
were victimized. Such stalwarts as Pearl Hart could not be
shaken but there were others who felt far from secure. They
were frightened and began to drop away. The school closed
after three years.

CHAPTER 11

The Civil Rights Congress

THE CIVIL RIGHTS CONGRESS was formed in 1946, a merger of the International Labor Defense and the National Federation for Constitutional Liberties. It was dedicated to the defense of victims of racist persecution and of those who were hounded for advocating peaceful co-existence. In 1949 I became its National Executive Secretary. I determined to follow the course established by the ILD and make of the CRC a fighter for Black Liberation.

J. Edgar Hoover called it subversive. Every time that gentleman cried out against Communists (while he protected the Klan and the real perpetrators of violence and subversion) Congress voted him ever larger appropriations. Every Attorney General, in his turn, put CRC on the Department of Justice "subversive list," and pressed for legislation to outlaw it.

I recall an incident at about this time when I was called before a house committee investigating lobbying activities. Representative Lanham of Georgia engaged me in a verbal exchange. I had said, "I am fighting for the life of a Negro in Georgia." The Congressman interrupted, "That statement is absolutely false. The State of Georgia has never lynched a Negro." "Georgia has killed only too many," I replied, "as everyone in this country and in the world knows."

When I added that the Negro had no rights in Georgia, Lanham shouted, "That's another lie." "And I believe *your* statement to be a lie," I said. "How many Negroes have you lynched?"

With that, the Congressman could not contain his fury. Calling me "a god damned black s.o.b." he jumped up and ran to the foot of the dais, breaking through the first pair of attendants, intent upon attacking me physically. He was finally held back by two policemen.

Not long after, another congressional committee subpoena'd me because I had refused to turn over the books and records of the CRC, and I was later sentenced to a three-month term for refusing to turn over to the Bureau of Internal Revenue the list of our contributors. (It was not until 1955 that this contempt conviction was reversed by the U.S. Court of Appeals.)

I refer to these incidents to indicate the climate in which we were living then, as well as the vigor and militancy with which CRC conducted its campaigns to enlist the masses in the defense of such victims as Willie McGee, Rosa Lee Ingram, the Trenton Six, the Martinsville Seven, and many others. A brief description of some of our cases follows:

Willie McGee, a 36-year-old Negro veteran, father of four children, was a truck driver in Laurel, Mississippi. Mrs. Troy Hawkins, white, claimed she was raped by a man in a T-shirt with "kinky hair," while a child slept in an adjoining room. McGee was arrested, held incommunicado for 32 days, and tortured until he signed a confession, which he later repudiated.

At his first trial in Laurel, the all-white jury cried "guilty" after two minutes' deliberation, while a lynch mob waited outside. The State Supreme Court reversed the conviction on appeal. But it did not dismiss the framed case. A second conviction at a new trial in Hattiesburg, Miss., was also reversed; a third trial was still in progress when the defense attorneys were threatened by mob violence and had to flee. The U.S. Supreme Court stayed the execution three times but refused to dismiss the case or review it despite new evidence that Mrs. Hawkins had forced McGee to maintain intimate relations with her for several years by threatening him with a rape accusation.

In the course of the trials worldwide protests were organized by the CRC. In July 1950 a mass delegation of prominent Americans went to Jackson to demand a stay of execution and a new trial. On May 4, 1951, hundreds of Black and white Americans gathered for a sunrise prayer meeting in Jackson in one last effort to save Willie McGee's life. But the forces of bigotry and reaction were implacable, and in March, 1951, Willie McGee was put to death in the electric chair.

Twenty years had passed since Alabama's white racists had attempted the legal lynching of nine innocent Black youths in the Scottsboro Case. The intervening years had been filled with war and crises profoundly affecting the lives of millions of Americans and awakening within many of them an awareness of reality. The build-up of Hitler had taken place; fascism had come to power in Italy and Nazism in Germany, and the whole world had been engulfed in war.

The Black liberation movement had advanced during those years, as many Negroes began to appreciate that their fight was not isolated but part of the worldwide struggle of all freedom-loving peoples. Scottsboro had marked a new stage in the fight of Black men and women for equality of rights under the law, for their dignity as citizens. Nevertheless, the case was given no commensurate place in lay or legal history. The men who had attempted that mass murder in Alabama, it goes without saying, were not brought to trial for conspiracy. The men who control the writing and teaching of history are too shrewd to submit such cases to the scrutiny of youth. Scottsboro was pushed into the limbo of forgotten causes so far as history books are concerned.

Scottsboro had revealed the role played by the state—the multiple role—conspirator, judge, jury and executioner. If the state failed to carry through its plans, it was because the progressive world was alerted and had rallied to the defense of

Part of a huge throng in Chicago's Washington Park, 1951, in a rally to save the life of Willie McGee, sponsored by the United Packinghouse Workers Union.

On a picketline for the Martinsville Seven, Washington, D.C., February 1951. With the child is Mrs. Josephine Grayson, whose husband, Francis, was one of the frameup victims.

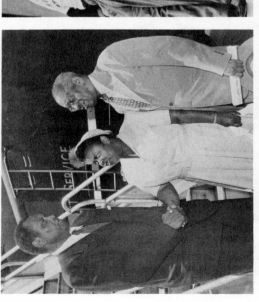

Left, Bessie Mitchell, sister of one of the Trenton Six, greets Paul Robeson; demonstrators for the freedom of Willie McGee chain themselves to the columns of the Lincoln Memorial in Washington, D.C.

the hapless victims. The facts of the case had disclosed the conspiracy of both state and federal systems; the solidarity of the oppressed alone could have saved the Scottsboro boys. The case marked a departure by government from the practices of the post-Civil War Reconstruction period, during which mob-incited lynching bees strung up, shot, tortured Black men. Instead, the forces of "law and order" were given the executioner's job.

All this was vividly recalled to the partipants in another mammoth struggle during the mass trial that was to become known as the Martinsville Seven. Here the federal government was giving a new twist to the doctrine of States' Rights. Each state was licensed to handle its "niggers" as it saw fit as long as it was in the interest of landholders and industrialists. No law protective of the rights of Black Americans to life, liberty and pursuit of happiness applied; the provisions of the Constitution were flagrantly violated and Blacks were denied the equal protection of the laws.

In Martinsville, Virginia, the victims had been arrested and charged with the rape of a white woman. The alleged victim was well known to be a prostitute as well as a mentally retarded person, and there was no evidence that a rape had taken place. Mrs. Floyd claimed that a squad of Negro men had attacked and raped her. Seven men were picked up and confessions were extorted from them—confessions which they all repudiated at the trial before an all-white jury. The defendants were convicted and sentenced to death. Appeals made to the Virginia Supreme Court and the U.S. Supreme Court by the CRC were denied. The mass protests organized by CRC failed to halt the execution on February 2, 1951.

When the CRC plunged into the fierce fight to save the seven men, the anti-black virulence in the small Virginia town had been enough to create a lynch atmosphere, and it was obvious that no white jury would dare to return a verdict of not guilty. The court fulfilled its racist duty and seven Black men were condemned to die. The electric chair was readied.

The victims ranged in age from a 32-year-old father of five to teenagers; the Black community was terrorized during the trial and convictions. More than the lives of seven Black men were at stake; a successful fight to save their lives required a broad, far-reaching alliance of Black and white. White America, however, was not yet ready for a struggle against the masters of racism.

Mrs. Josephine Grayson, the grief-stricken wife of the eldest of the victims, came to speak with me at the CRC office after her husband was sentenced. She was a tall, good-looking Black woman whose dark brown eyes, which must have twinkled merrily in happier times, now betrayed her utter frustration. As she sat across from me with her hands folded in her lap, this question occurred to me: Even if there had been any evidence of guilt on the part of the doomed seven, did the record show that the State of Virginia had ever passed a death sentence in a case where a white man was charged and convicted of raping a Black woman? The record proved conclusively that the death sentence was reserved for Blacks.

Mrs. Grayson told me of the terrible struggle she and her children had undergone to survive without a father and husband at home. Hers was a story of poverty, illiteracy, joblessness, hopelessness and desperation. I was shaken by her story; it produced in me a new level of hatred for my country's rulers.

I agreed that the CRC would seek to save these men from the electric chair, and when I later discussed my preliminary reactions with the organization's resident board, I explained the need to fight this case vigorously if the white supremacists were to be prevented from bringing these macabre mass murder circuses to the courts of the North. The board agreed that we should take the case. Before we could take the defense legally, I had to obtain the signatures of the seven men imprisoned in the deathhouse of the Virginia state prison at Richmond.

Accompanied by Mrs. Grayson, I arrived in Richmond on a sunny, summery day. It was my first visit to the city since I had filled a speaking engagement there during the Scottsboro campaign. That meeting was held in a park the city was building over a garbage dump in the Black ghetto. I saw in my mind's eye the audience of several hundred anxious and worried Black men and women milling around the speakers' platform as I stood talking with Hosea Hudson, who headed my personal bodyguard while I was there. Hosea had organized the guard because white policemen were thick as swarming bees. What a good feeling that meeting had given me as I recognized the fighting spirit of Richmond's Black population!

Now, in 1951, I was there again, and I wondered to what extent, if any, the attitude of the city and state officials and businessmen had changed toward Black people.

Mrs. Grayson and I took a taxi to the prison gate. After stating our mission we were ushered into the warden's office. He had been informed of our coming and was prepared to receive us. His cordiality conveyed the unspoken words: "Someday I'll get you." He was a burly man who looked the part of a "Negro-whipper." We would have been suffering from mental deficiency if we had expected from a Southern sheriff or prison warden a reaction of sympathy or understanding. I answered his "What can I do for you-all?" with "We want to see the men from Martinsville." He rose from his seat, slowly put his coat on and drawled: "You-all come along." We passed down a narrow corridor which ended at a heavily barred door that opened onto the prison yard. It was just after the lunch hour and the outdoor enclosure was filled with convicts.

I stopped before going downstairs from the building in which the warden's office was located and my eyes took in a view of the scene below. At first it appeared as if all the inmates were Black but before long I did distinguish a small group of white prisoners gathered in a far corner. The Negro population of Virginia was then less than 25 per cent and the proportion of prisoners seemed extraordinarily large. We walked through the yard to the death house located in its southwest corner. More

prison guards joined our group as we approached the citadel of
death. Eleven men were imprisoned there, nine of them
Black—including the Martinsville Seven.

Each condemned man had his own cell. We were taken first
to Francis Grayson. He told me how the white woman complainant had come among the group of Black men and boys
while they were "horsing around," and solicited their trade.
Some of the men had accepted her offer, and then a dispute
over money terms arose and the woman went away in a huff.
She soon returned with a few police officers and the Black
group was arrested. It was not clear at the time what they
would be charged with, but it *was* clear that the woman would
testify to anything proposed by the police. The police who
were only the armed agency of those who controlled the local
government, could not decree the murder of the seven men;
nor was the decision left to local authorities; the state officials
also had knowledge of the affair, and the decision was left to
them.

The charge of rape rises naturally in the throat of a Southern
government official in any confrontation between a Black male
and a white female. That was the charge made by the defenders
of the "chastity of white womanhood." The seven victims were
rushed to trial and convicted. Grayson was not certain whether
any of those declared guilty had actually had sexual in-
tercourse with the complainant. He himself had not touched
her. She disappeared from her old haunts soon after the guilty
verdict was returned. The job of terrorizing Black men had
begun; the appeal to the state's high court against the lower
court decision was fruitless, and the U.S. Supreme Court
refused to grant a hearing. The latter would not grant a review,
although from a legal point of view it was certainly within its
jurisdiction.

I spoke to each of the defendants individually and after I had
finished there was no hesitancy. Each of them signed retainers
for the legal service of the CRC.

It is hard to go into a death house and try to buoy the spirits of condemned men without creating illusions. I had discussed the appeal; there was nothing more to do. Of course, you never knew whether you would speak with condemned men again. (In this case I never did.) The appeal was lost; and again the federal judiciary and the president permitted a state to violate the constitutional rights of Black men and to send them to their deaths.

I pondered this case deeply. I compared it to the host of others in which the U.S. Supreme Court had turned its back on Black victims whose rights had been flagrantly ignored. The doctrine of States' Rights had rendered the constitutional rights of Black citizens null and void.

As I walked back to the warden's office the disparity between the numbers of Black and white prisoners struck me again. State prisons in the South were really reservations, concentration camps for Black political prisoners. Millions of Black Americans are aware that when they leave home in the morning they may not return at night if by chance their general demeanor or manner of response to a question rubbed a white person the wrong way. This offense could and often did mean death or imprisonment for a period of years.

What would a count of Black political prisoners on a national scale reveal, I wondered? We were by now back in the warden's office, and as he seated himself, I inquired casually: "Tell me, warden, what is the percentage of Black prisoners in this prison? If I said 75 per cent, would I be wrong?" He rubbed his chin with his right palm, contemplated the question for a moment, and then replied: "I guess roughly a little more than two thirds." After a short pause, he continued: "The niggers keep cutting each other up, you know, they're a real hard lot." That last affront was as much as I could take. I turned to Mrs. Grayson and asked if she had any requests to make on behalf of her husband. She said no, and we left.

The warden was a product of white capitalist rule, a man who had been willingly but unwittingly robbed of his humanism, debased and turned into an animal that walked and talked like a man. He personalized the system he served and under which I was forced to live. His was the mentality that governed the quality of justice to be meted out to Black men. And the voice of the same system that had conditioned him was heard throughout the land—in Congress, in the courts, the press and the pulpits of the nation. I must confess that as I left that office I was just as afraid for my own life under such a system as I had been for the lives of the seven condemned men.

For 20 odd years I had been fighting on the civil rights front and I had learned that the best defense is an offense. This was never an easy task. Official denial of rights was the milieu from which most civil rights cases arose. And not every lawyer wants to become involved in a case in which the state and those who control it are charged with criminal conspiracy. The judge has the power to hold the lawyer in contempt of court and to go so far as to institute disbarment proceedings against a lawyer connected with such a defense.

The development of an offensive movement begins with mass democratic action; the broader and deeper and sharper it is, the greater are the defendant's chances. The forms of struggle, legal procedure and mass action tactics must be coordinated. It is therefore necessary to prepare the state's intended victim for the activities that are an inseparable part of the campaign. It is a matter of relating the defendant to the people as a whole.

Whether we would have the time needed to carry this case to the people worried me. Would there be time before the executions for the weight of people's reaction to have any impact on the state?

We were riding away from the Virginia prison as I reviewed the elements of our struggle. Mrs. Grayson and I reached the railroad station. It was time to part. It was hard to smile; I could not bring myself to utter some trite remark about courage. I told her simply that the next step, appeal, lay ahead of us. She was a brave woman; there were no tears in her eyes when we parted.

Back in the CRC office in New York, I assembled the staff and put two matters before them: first, the appeal of the death sentence; second, I outlined the questionnaire that in my opinion should be sent to the attorney general of each state calling for statistical information regarding the Black inmates and their conditions in the prisons. The appeal was agreed upon, lawyers retained and the questionnaires sent out. Within a matter of weeks some of them began to come back into the office. They came from all parts of the country and the information they contained confirmed the conclusions I had reached.

There was not a single state in the union in which the Black prison population was not in excess of the Black man's percentage of the general population. I even discovered one prison in Georgia that did not have a single white inmate! In Chicago, the Black population of which was less than ten per cent, youth reformatories had a Black population of 50 per cent!

Together with Dr. Oakley Johnson, an able sociologist from the University of Michigan, and Elizabeth Lawson, who specialized in historical research, I produced a brochure entitled "Genocide Under Color of Law." We never got it to the printer. Before it was completed, despite all our efforts to mobilize a worldwide protest movement, the state of Virginia had sent the seven innocent Black men to their deaths. Their crime: being born Black.

The murder of the Martinsville Seven fitted into the national social and political mosaic as neatly as patches fit into an intricate quilt pattern. And the institution geared to murder was moving north. It reached New Jersey, where six young men were being threatened with the same fate.

In the case of the Trenton Six, the men were picked up on February 6, 1948, on suspicion of the murder of William Horner, a second-hand furniture dealer killed in his store in Trenton, January 27, 1948. None of the men arrested matched the teletype descriptions the police had sent out on the day of

the crime. A 48-day trial ensued (June-August 1948), and a
verdict of guilty was brought in. In August of that year the
CRC entered the case, throwing all its resources into the
defense and the publicizing of the facts. But it was not until
February 24, 1955 that four of the Trenton six were acquitted.
One of them had died in prison and the sixth had been
resentenced.   And once more the law had proved the nature of
the "even-handed" justice it dispenses to its Black victims.

At my 60th Birthday Celebration, New York, 1951.

CHAPTER 12

We Charge Genocide

AT THE end of World War II, with Germany and Japan prostrate and demoralized, the world powers discussed the imperative need to establish an international organization of nations. Spokesmen at the highest levels declared that such a body should be committed to world peace, equal rights for small nations and take responsibility for "non-self-governing territories"—a euphemism for colonies. The new world body, to be called the United Nations, was to admit as members large and small, strong and weak nations on the basis of equality and without regard to political structure or ideology.

Times and conditions had changed, and the rulers of the United States, who had repudiated the League of Nations, with its expressed intention to outlaw war and colonial exploitation, could not now reject the idea of a United Nations. A new world state, the Soviet Union, had arisen in its socialist might as a serious counterweight to the imperialists and it would have exposed to the world the meaning of a rejection of the United Nations concept as an act of sabotage of world peace.

In the wake of the war, the trauma of mass deaths, personal tragedies, homeless and stateless multitudes dependent on international charity, and the unprecedented destruction of property constituted a background of indescribable misery. An international body devoted to preserving the peace was imperatively needed.

As it was drawn up, the UN charter did not provide for the power of the organization to enforce observance of its provisions or of its conventions, covenants and resolutions. It conferred no police power. Where moral suasion failed, there was left only the power of the people who recognize the justice of a resolution to support it with protests and demonstrations against the recalcitrant state. Although the principal German warlords were tried at Nuremberg, the trials, because of the manner in which they were conducted, concealed more than they revealed about the cause and nature of such wars as the one the world had recently suffered.

I could not fail to recognize that just as the United States, under cover of law, carried out genocidal racist policies in police murders of Black men, framed death sentences, death that came from withholding proper medical care to Black people, just so had Hitler built and operated his mass death machine under cover of Nazi law. It goes without saying that this analogy was not clearly seen by the masses in Western countries and by the masses of Americans. There were profound differences in the character and motives of the states which were promoting the world organization. Not all who agreed to build the United Nations wanted to do away with future wars; some wished merely to consolidate the spoils of their victory.

Nevertheless, the war had brought about profound changes in the way of life and political thought of millions, especially in Eastern Europe, where the peoples had established new and revolutionary governments after Hitler's defeat and the rout of his quislings. These peoples, whose countries had been devastated by the war and who had lived under the rule of the Nazi storm troopers, wanted a secure peace. But they did not associate their own governments with the ultramodern cannibalism that had been the Nazi hallmark. This was also true of the millions of Black men and women who hated white supremacy at home, but did not see in it the seeds of fascism with which every capitalist state is infected. Most Black leaders did not critically examine the world scene; the United

Nations Charter, to these leaders, was a high-sounding document—like the Declaration of Independence and the Preamble
to the U.S. Constitution. They did not draw the conclusion that
those whites in power who had besmirched the Constitution
by practicing racism in its name, were not likely to do more
than pay lip service to the United Nations Charter.

I read the introduction to the historic document with great
interest: "We the peoples of the United Nations are determined
to save succeeding generations from the scourge of war, which
twice in our lifetime has brought untold sorrow to mankind,
and

"to reaffirm faith in fundamental human rights, in the
dignity and worth of the human person, in the equal rights of
men and women, and of nations large and small, and

"to establish conditions under which justice and respect for
the obligations arising from treaties and other sources of
international law can be maintained, and

"to promote social progress and better standards of life in
larger freedom."

While "faith" in fundamental human rights, in the dignity
and worth of the human person had been affirmed and
reaffirmed in the United States, it was largely a faith without
works—indeed golden words were often used to hide the
inhuman deed. What then could be the meaning of the signatures affixed to the Charter of the United Nations by representatives of the U.S. Government? There has never been, is
not now, not can there ever be a reconcilation of the aims and
purposes of a racist state with world peace. I could only
conclude that the Charter, while marking an advance in the
perception of humanity's needs, did not and could not change
the status of Black Americans. I concluded that Black citizens
should utilize the Charter and the provisions of its conventions
to expose their own condition and position. The United
Nations would have increased meaning to Black Americans if
they were to see themselves as one of the peoples whose
freedom struggles had brought the organization into being.

I studied the composition of the delegation chosen by

President Truman to speak for the United States at the 1945 San Francisco conference out of which the United Nations Organization was born. Two of them deserve mention, Edward Riley Stettinius, Secretary of State, and Tom Connally, Senator from Texas. Stettinius was the descendant and reincarnation of a long line of "robber barons;" Tom Connally a spokesman for virulent racism in the U. S. Senate.

For such men, the Charter could only be a shield behind which American imperialism would seek to dominate the century. Behind it they thought they could conceal the international intrigues and machinations of their rapacious class. They sought to formulate a program and create an institution through which this program could be realized; American imperialism could enter its "century of world domination" with the UN as its dutiful puppet.

To me, it seemed clear that the Charter and Conventions of the UN had to be made the property of the American people as far as possible and especially of Black America. It could be made the instrumentality through which the "Negro question" could be lifted to its highest dimension.

How were we in the Civil Rights Congress going to help in the fight to secure the implementation of the provisions of the Charter? It was a task that was not impossible for the CRC, I believed. In opposition to the ruling classes of the United States, England, France, Italy, whose political and diplomatic activities were in no way consistent with the Charter, there were hundreds of honest people who wanted to put an end to wars of aggression and insults to human dignity, and they sorely needed leadership. If the masses of the exploited millions did not fight against its deterioration, the UN would suffer the fate of the League of Nations. Were that to happen World War III could scarcely be averted.

I tried to recall certain aspects of the League of Nations. Afro-Americans, perhaps because they lacked a world outlook at that time, or because of their righteous contempt for President Wilson, were not enthusiastic. They remembered, as I did, how, during World War I, Wilson had gratuitously and arrogantly insulted Monroe Trotter, the editor of the *Boston Guardian,* when that prominent Black leader and scholar had passionately pleaded with him to use his executive powers to put an end to the disgraceful policy of segregation in the armed forces.

Trotter saw nothing inconsistent in fighting against Kaiser Wilhelm and at the same time against lynch-minded landlords, the state officials of the Southern states and their racist representatives in Washington. He insisted that a war of this kind should further the proclaimed liberation aims boasted of in school, church and from public platform. The metropolitan press interpreted his appeal in another light, and so did President Wilson, the "idealist" from Princeton University (at that time a jimcrow institution). In the eyes of these gentlemen, Trotter had stepped out beyond his depth; he was just a "belligerent," "uppity," and "intransigent" Black man. They could not see that what Trotter advocated would, if adopted, serve the national interest.

Wilson, the "liberal," refused to end jimcrow in the governmental departments or in the armed forces—in fact, he extended it. In his view, the Negro was attempting to gain full citizenship too rapidly. In reality, the President was not interested in Black men as American citizens or as human beings—he saw them only as Negroes and expendable.

Like Trotter, I was fed up with such democracy. The rulers of the United States were on the make; they had visions of achieving economic and political world supremacy. Capitalist morality wears the stamp of the dollar sign. In entering World War I, American imperialism saw the possibility of destroying the power of German imperialism, its chief rival, and of grabbing the German colonies in Africa and the Pacific. At the same time, these very racist capitalists intimated that this "war to save democracy" would benefit Black Americans, and some Blacks succumbed to this appeal.

Even the great Du Bois, that man of heroic stature, was

persuaded to write his famous "Close Ranks" editorial for the *Crisis,* organ of the NAACP, in July 1917: "Let us while this war lasts forget our special grievances and close our ranks shoulder to shoulder with our own white fellow citizens and the allied nations that are fighting for democracy."

World War I ended; great changes had indeed come about in the world but these did not include any immediate or profound changes in the status of the Negro. The rulers of the world had not meant their high-flown pretensions. Thus the Negro was justified in his indifference to the announced aims of the League of Nations; the barefaced pronouncements about colonies and subject peoples which had been made by Lloyd George, Georges Clemenceau and Vittorio Orlando—the cynical, arrogant leaders of Britain, France and Italy. But most distressing of all was the attitude of President Wilson, who had categorically refused to use his high office to protect the rights of Negro citizens before, during or after the war. Was such a man going to create an organization for human freedom throughout the world, while he mocked human dignity at home? I could not believe he would. The slogan, "Make the world safe for democracy," was indeed a hoax!

Such were the lessons of which history was reminding me. Was it possible now, under the United Nations Charter for the CRC to open a new vista to the Negro? We felt it was necessary for us to help raise the Black man's struggle to new dimensions, to project it onto the world's political stage.

In truth, the UN Charter represented a great step forward from the Covenant of the League of Nations. For one thing, among the UN's founders was the Soviet Union. The USSGR had inaugurated a new form of society and had unceasingly called for total disarmament and peace.

My friends and I analyzed the substance of the UN conventions. In 1947, the UN Commission on Human Rights met in Paris and submitted proposals to the Economic and Social Council. Under the chairmanship of Mrs. Eleanor Roosevelt, the Human Rights Commission submitted a draft statement to the General Assembly. The proposal, called "The Universal

Declaration of Human Rights," was passed; no nation had voted against it, but the U.S. delegation abstained from voting. This government has, in fact, not ratified that declaration to this day.

We in the CRC decided that the presentation of a petition charging the crime of genocide and thoroughly documenting what we regarded as the genocidal attitude of the U.S. Government toward its Negro citizens was timely. It would be helpful, we thought, to all peoples fighting for freedom, and would be particularly helpful here at home among both Black and white citizens where the potentialities of the UN were not too well understood or appreciated. It would point out to Black men and women the broadening avenues through which their struggle might move forward.

The petition, I thought, should expose the reactionary role that the racists of the United States were preparing to play in world affairs, especially its dangers to world peace. No government bound up with racism could want or seek world peace.

It was in this respect that the CRC petition was to differ from that written by Dr. Du Bois for the NAACP and that presented by the National Negro Congress. These petitions, which preceded ours, sought redress of the numerous grievances from which Negroes suffered, while the CRC petition made a specific charge against the criminal, racist policies of the U.S. Government and the destructive impact this had on national integrity as well as its effect on world peace.

The UN and its organs and agencies could not by themselves effect any fundamental change in human relations within any of the member states. We knew that. These bodies could not pass laws binding upon the United States or any other government. But the UN rostrum was in the center of the world stage. The Black man in the United States could announce to the world audience that until the flagrant injustices of racism had been beaten, no quarter of the globe could be safe for those seeking freedom and the enjoyment of life's bounty.

Within the CRC we read and debated the provisions of the

Charter and the conventions. Every human-rights provision of the Charter, everyone of the conventions on women, children and genocide was being violated in relation to both Negro nationals and poor whites. Concentrating on the Convention on the Prevention and Punishment of the Crime of Genocide, we decided to gather facts to prove the violations of this convention and to formulate a petition revealing its application to the United States that would constitute a new weapon in defense of democracy.

I talked the matter over with many close friends and advisors. Several times I talked with William Z. Foster, national chairman of the Party. He listened attentively and analyzed the project, probing each step as I outlined it to determine as closely as possible for himself what he thought would be the reaction of the government and what were the social forces controlling it. He then urged full speed ahead.

I spoke with J. Finley Wilson, Grand Exalted Ruler of the Elks, an outstanding figure in the Black fraternal field, and with Hobson Reynolds, his chief lieutenant. Both of them, from behind the scenes, supported the project. Rosco Dunjee, editor of the *Black Dispatch,* Oklahoma City, wrote an eloquent endorsement of it. I spoke also with many members of the Negro clergy, including Rev. Charles A. Hill of Detroit, Bishops W. J. Walls of Chicago and R. R. Wright of Philadelphia. They applauded the plan.

In the study that went into the preparations for the petition to the United Nations, I was deeply impressed by the dissenting opinion of Mr. Justice John Harlan in the case of *Plessy vs Ferguson* which the Supreme Court decided just before the turn of the century. Justice Harlan asserted that:

"Exemption from race discrimination in respect of the civil rights which are fundamental in citizenship in a republican government, is, as we have seen, a new right, created by the nation, with express power in Congress, by legislation, to enforce the constitutional provision from which it is derived. . . ."

Harlan continued:

"The one underlying purpose of congressional legislation has been to enable the black race to take the rank of mere citizens. The difficulty has been to compel a recognition of the legal right of the black race to take the rank of citizens and to secure the enjoyment of privileges belonging under the law to them as a component part of the people for whose health and happiness government is ordained. At every step in this direction, the nation has been confronted with class tyranny, which a contemporary English historian says 'is of all tyrannies, the most intolerable,' for it is ubiquitous in its operation and weighs perhaps most heavily on those whose obscurity or distance would withdraw them from the notice of a despot."

In their relations with "citizens of color," city, state and federal governments have violated every provision of law that Mr. Justice Robert Jackson had invoked against the Nazis when he opened the trial of the war criminals in Nuremberg.

We prepared to push ahead. We would be the first organization in history to charge the Government of the United States with the crime of genocide. It was a weighty responsibility; we were mounting an all-out ideological attack and for that firm proof was necessary. We were going to document institutionalized oppression and terror that had spread from the streets to the courts, to the chambers of mayors and governors, to the very executive offices of the Federal Government. Its roots were deep in our economy, but we were going to expose those roots.

Among the statements in our general indictment was the following:

"The wrongs of which we complain are so much the expression of predatory American reaction and its government, that civilization cannot ignore them or risk their continuance without courting its own destruction. We agree with those members of the General Assembly who declared that 'genocide is a matter of world concern because its practice imperils world safety.'" We were not, in FDR's phrase, "out to save capitalism from itself," but rather to save bourgeois democracy from the capitalist machinations which might well lead to fascism.

It seemed to us that it should be a matter of concern to all who were conscious that the evils of racism were among the foremost fruits of capitalism. We polled leading trade unionists, educators and prominent liberals to find out how they would regard such a project. A letter was also sent to a select list of prominent men and women and to a number of the country's leading law schools, over my signature. The letter inquired of the addressee whether he or she believed that the UN Convention on the Prevention and Punishment of the Crime of Genocide would apply to the situation of the Negro in the United States. One letter was sent to Mrs. Eleanor Roosevelt, as head of the U.S. delegation in the UN Human Rights Commission.

Replies came in from all sides. Interestingly enough, they were, in the main, along the color line. A majority of the Negroes polled believed that the Genocide Convention should be invoked; a majority of the white liberals and personalities were of a contrary view. Some stated categorically that only a Communist could think of making such a charge. To me this was a tacit admission that Communists were ahead of all others in developing the fight for the rights of Black people.

Without exception, faculty members at law schools were adamantly opposed to the genocide charges. Most of them were in favor of the Genocide Convention as an abstract statement of law but rejected any attempt to apply it, declaring that such an attack impeached the integrity of our nation. And this was the consensus of the replies we received from white liberals in general.

Among those who replied was Professor Lemkin, "father" of the Genocide Convention, which reads as follows:

ARTICLE II: In the present Convention, genocide means any of the following acts committed with intent to destroy, in whole or in part, a national ethnical, racial or religious group, as such: (a) Killing members of the group; (b) Causing serious bodily or mental harm to members of the group; (c) Deliberately inflicting on the group conditions of life calculated to bring about its physical destruction in whole or in part; (d) Imposing measures intended to prevent births

within the group; (e) Forcibly transferring children of the group to
another group
ARTICLE III: The following acts shall be punishable: (a) Genocide;
(b) Incitement to commit genocide; (c) Direct and public incitement
to commit genocide; (d) Attempt to commit genocide; (e) Complicity
in genocide.

How an honest person viewing the American scene impartially could come to any conclusion other than that forms of
genocide were being practiced in the United States was too
difficult for us to see.

Professor Lemkin experienced no such difficulty. In a considerable correspondence with me, he argued vehemently that
the provisions of the Genocide Convention bore no relation to
the U.S. Government or its position vis-à-vis Black citizens.
Lemkin and other law professors and practicing attorneys were
evidently fearful of criticizing a government whose conduct in
relation to its Black citizens was a disgrace to civilized mankind. This was only one instance of what racism was doing to
the minds and morality of America's men of law and science.
Obviously, no effective support for our petition was to come
from that direction.

Paul Robeson and I sat together many times and discussed
the situation. We finally agreed that a small group of petitioners should be sought to sign the petition to be entitled *We
Charge Genocide: The Crime of Government Against the
Negro People.* The leadership of CRC endorsed this plan.

A staff was chosen to work with me in drafting the petition.
There were excellent writers, research workers and historians,
among them Richard Boyer, historian and author; Elizabeth
Lawson, biographer and pamphleteer; Yvonne Gregory, writer
and poet; and Dr. Oakley Johnson, scholar in British and
American literature; and others. Each made an outstanding
contribution. Aubrey Grossman, a brilliant young lawyer from
California who was then National Organization Secretary of
the CRC, devoted energy and capabilities without which the
petition would never have come off the press. He and I raised
the money.

Among the petitioner's names were many who have an enduring place in American history: Dr. W. E. B. Du Bois; Charlotta Bass, an Afro-American woman who had owned and edited the *California Eagle* (a Los Angeles weekly newspaper that for years had been in the forefront of all progressive struggles); Louis Burnham, a young and valiant Black writer and one of the founders of the Southern Youth Conference (who was later to die a premature death); Wendell Phillips Dabney, of Cincinnati (Negro editor, owner and publisher of *The Union);* Benjamin J. Davis, Jr. (one of the Communist leaders with whom I could not at the time meet, since he was a political prisoner behind bars in the Federal prison at Terre Haute); Roscoe Dunjee of Oklahoma City (owner, editor and publisher of the *Black Dispatch,* one of the most vocal and active human rights fighters of the era); James W. Ford, a leading American Communist (the first Negro leader since the deathless Frederick Douglass to be nominated as candidate for Vice President of the United States); William Harrison, one-time editor of the *Boston Guardian* (whose founder, Monroe Trotter, had challenged Woodrow Wilson); the Rev. Charles A. Hill of Detroit (one of a large group of Negro clergymen who could not be induced to leave the Negro rights struggle to politicians); Dr. W. Alphaeus Hunton (who was later to become a resident of Accra, Ghana, where he worked in the production of the *Encyclopedia Africana);* Paul Robeson (who was to present the Genocide Petition to the UN Secretariat in New York on the same day I was presenting it to the General Assembly in Paris); Mary Church Terrell of the District of Columbia (one of the country's great Afro-American women leaders); the Rev. Eliot White, leading white Episcopal clergyman (an outstanding fighter for democracy); Robert Treuhaft, a lawyer, and his wife Decca, Jessica Mitford (who together shared distinguished reputations as fighters for human rights); my wife, Louise Thompson Patterson, a well known fraternal order worker and outstanding organizer.

In addition, there were Rosalie McGee, heroic wife of Willie

McGee (legally lynched in Jackson, Miss.); Bessie Mitchell, sister of one of the framed "Trenton Six"; George Murphy, Jr., of the *Baltimore Afro-American;* Eslanda Goode Robeson, author and journalist; Elizabeth Keyser, my boyhood teacher at Tamalpais High School in California; Charles Collins, Negro trade unionist; Wesley Robert Wells, who signed while in the death house at San Quentin penitentiary; Albert Kahn, internationally known American writer; Harold Christoffel, leading CIO trade unionist; Harry Haywood, author of *Negro Liberation;* William Hood of Detroit, member of local 600 of the Auto Workers Union and former head of the National Negro Congress.

Among the many others who signed this historic document were Matthew Crawford, militant leader of the liberation struggle in Northern California; Angie Dickerson of New York, an outstanding militant in the civil rights field; Winifred Feise, courageous white woman living in New Orleans; Josephine Grayson, whose husband, Francis Grayson, was one of the Negroes framed in Martinsville, Va. on a rape charge and legally lynched; Claudia Jones, a valiant Communist leader; Maude White Katz, writer; Larkin Marshall, Negro leader in Georgia; Pettis Perry, Communist leader; John Pittman, noted journalist; Ferdinand Smith, one of the founders of the National Maritime Union, CIO—and a host of other fighters for democracy and civil rights.

The petition began with a review of the case against the government and an offer of proof of the charges made. It revealed the scope and historical background of the genocidal practices being committed against Negro citizens of the United States, specifically setting forth the record from 1946 to 1951.

"The responsibility," it began, "of being the first in history to charge the Government of the United States of America with the crime of genocide is not one your petitioners take lightly . . . . If our duty is unpleasant it is historically necessary both for the welfare of the American people and for the peace of the world. We petition as American patriots, sufficiently anxious to save our countrymen and all mankind from the horrors of war to shoulder a task as painful as it is important. We cannot forget Hitler's demonstration that genocide at home can become wider massacre abroad, that domestic genocide develops into the larger genocide that is predatory war" (p. 3).

Here is a part of the Summary and Prayer with which the petition concluded (p. 195):

"There may be debate as to the expediency of condemning the Government of the United States for the genocide it practices and permits against the 15,000,000 of its citizens who are Negroes. There can be none about the existence of the crime. It is an undeniable fact. The United States Government itself, through the Report of President Truman's Committee on Civil Rights, admits the institutionalized Negro oppression, written into law and carried out by police and courts. It describes it, examines it, surveys it, talks about it, and does everything but change it. In fact, it both admits and protects it.

"Thus it was easy for your petitioners to offer abundant proof of the crime. It is everywhere in American life. And yet words and statistics are but poor things to convey the long agony of the Negro people. We proved 'killing members of the group'—but the case after case cited does nothing to assuage the helplessness of the innocent Negro trapped at this instant by police in a cell which will be the scene of his death. We have shown 'mental and bodily harm' in violation of Article II of the Genocide Convention, but this proof can barely indicate the lifelong terror of thousands of Negroes forced to live under the menace of official violence, mob law and the Ku Klux Klan. We have tried to reveal something of the deliberate infliction 'on the group of conditions which bring about its physical destruction in whole or in part'—but this cannot convey the hopeless despair of those forced by law to live in conditions of disease and poverty because of race, of birth, of color."

Our petition was ready for presentation.

Two comments on *We Charge Genocide*, which came soon after its publication in book form,* now seem especially pertinent. The first was from Richard E. Westbrook, a prominent Negro attorney in Chicago:

"I have read with great care the petition relative to genocide edited by the Civil Rights Congress, and I consider it one of the best-prepared publications I have had the honor to read. It is evidence of careful research and sagacity. It demonstrates courage and ability, and is a clear-cut statement of irrefutable facts."

The Rev. Stephen A. Fritchman, minister of the First Unitarian Church of Los Angeles, wrote:

"My deepest thanks to you for *We Charge Genocide.* This is a devastating and desperately needed book for our times. I plan to preach on it soon. I know it will add to the mobilized conscience of America."

Following the much-publicized incident of my appearance before the House Lobbying Committee, I feared that some kind of action would be taken against me for having provoked a member of Congress to expose the manner in which Negro congressional witnesses could be treated by members of Congress. I hardly expected that Congress would act against Henderson Lovelace Lanham, the gentleman from the Fifth District of Georgia who had called me a "god-damned black s.o.b." I was certain that the reactionaries in Congress would act against me, but the action had not yet developed. Nevertheless, we questioned whether, under these conditions, the government would permit me to leave the country on a mission to the UN in Paris. But it was felt that I was the one to do the job and arrangements were made as we had originally planned. Paul Robeson would present the petition to the UN Secretariat

*First published by the Civil Rights Congress in 1951; reprinted in 1970 by International Publishers, New York, with a new Introduction by William L. Patterson and a Preface by Ossie Davis.

in New York on the same day that I presented it to the UN
General Assembly in Paris.

We were worried as to how to get enough copies of the
petition to Paris for me to put one into the hands of each
delegate. It seemed unwise to try to ship them on my ticket and
we therefore arranged to mail 60 copies to be held for me at the
central post office in Paris. For fear that something adverse
might happen to them, an additional 60 copies were sent to
London and 60 more to a friend in Budapest. I carried 20 in my
baggage. I felt that I was at last ready to pass the ammunition. I
was off to Paris on December 15, 1951.

Speaking at the Writers' Club in Prague, after flight from Paris, 1951.

CHAPTER 13

In Paris

I ARRIVED in Paris on the morning of December 16, 1951, and at once took steps to make my presence known to Jacques Duclos, one of the top leaders of the Communist Party of France and a member of the French Senate. It was difficult to reach the senator. Anti-Communist elements had made it necessary for the Party to take every precaution to safeguard the lives of its leaders. One had to have sound credentials before getting into the Party office, but I finally made it. When I met Comrade Duclos I found he remembered me from 1937, when I had visited him in relation to my participation in the struggle against fascism in Spain.

He immediately called a conference, which was attended by Raymond Guyot, Secretary of the International Bureau of the Party, as well as several other leading Communists. The decisions taken were these: That other friends would be notified of my presence; that an English-speaking person would be assigned to work with me; that I would go at once to the offices of *L'Humanite,* the Party paper, for an interview.

The interview took place under the guidance of the editor, Valentine Couturier. The attitude at *L'Humanité* was something to behold. All those on the editorial staff who spoke English were anxious to get *Genocide* distributed among prominent Frenchmen. A glance at the title page had been evidence enough of its significance in the fight against fascism.

I walked out of *L'Humanité's* office feeling happy and deeply impressed by the international solidarity of the French Communists.

When I emerged there was snow on the ground. I secured a room at the Hotel de France, near L'Opéra and the American Express office. There was no time to lose. I set my baggage down in my room and was off to contact friends among the delegation at the UN. The advice they gave me was later to prove invaluable.

The first thing they wanted to know was whether I had a "gray card." A gray card was evidently a permit that enabled one to make instantaneous air-flight arrangements for Switzerland, to ski or skate or whatever you chose to do. I was not at the time interested in those sports, but my friends suggested a more likely use I might have for such a "ticket of leave"—I might have to depart from France suddenly.

"After you have distributed the genocide petition," they said, "your chances of staying in Paris may be seriously curtailed. You know your Uncle Sam well enough to foresee a vicious reaction. The American Embassy may tell you your passport privileges have been canceled; you may have to surrender your passport and go home. Or the French Government, at the behest of your State Department, may order the police to cancel your stay here and you may be ordered to leave. Where would you go if this happens?".

I confessed that I did not know. Friends set about securing a gray card for me, and also urged me to get Czechoslovak and Hungarian visas. I could only agree.

After I left them I hastened to the Palais Chaillot, where the Assembly was in session. I wanted to dispose of the petitions I had brought. I especially wanted to put the petition into the hands of Trygve Lie, Secretary General of the UN; Dr. Padilla Nervo, Chairman of the General Assembly, and Mrs. Eleanor Roosevelt, Chairman of the Commission on Human Rights.

The copies I had were delivered by me personally, together with the following letter to the Secretary General.

Dear Sir:

The petitioners of the United Nations for relief from the crime of genocide have given me the honor to present their petition detailing the crimes of genocide of the Government of the United States against the Negro people.

The petitioners are aware that their government is not a party to the "Convention on the Prevention and Punishment of the Crime of Genocide." They are, as well, aware that the proposed article was rejected which would have allowed the Human Rights Commission to initiate an inquiry on receipt of complaints from individuals, impelled to exercise their inalienable right to petition for redress because of the desperateness of their plight, and their own knowledge of the frightful consequences this crime can have on all people and on world affairs.

While such issues as are set forth in this petition are not specifically on the agenda of the Economic and Social Council, the Commission on Human Rights, or any of the organs of the General Assembly, I submit to you, Mr. Secretary General, that authority to investigate violations of human rights lies, I believe, in the statement of the general purposes and principles of the United Nations as set forth in Articles I and XIII of the Charter. I beg of you, therefore, in view of the urgency and gravity of this matter to use those provisions of the Charter as would enable you to place this matter upon the agenda of the Commission on Human Rights, as a supplementary point.

And, Mr. Secretary General, in view of the fact that questions of a kindred character, and of peace, to which these matters bear the closest relationship, are still under discussion, we would be grateful if you would refer this petition to any organ of the assembly you deem proper, and that you would order the distribution and circulation of the above-mentioned petition as a memorandum received by the United Nations for the use of all delegates.

The letter was signed for the petitioners by me as National Executive Secretary of the Civil Rights Congress.

The following letter was sent to all delegates individually:

Ladies and Gentlemen:

The enclosed letter, together with the enclosed copy of a petition to the United Nations for Relief from Genocide, a Crime of the Government of the United States Against the Negro People, its own nationals, has been submitted to the Secretary General of the United Nations, to the President of the General Assembly, and to the Chairman of the Commission on Human Rights.

On behalf of the petitioners, I would be grateful if you would take all the steps available to see that the matters contained in the petition be brought to open discussion, so as to provide, under existing rules of procedure of the General Assembly, the relief prayed for in the petition.

This was also signed in the same manner as the preceding letter.

I arrived at the Palais Chaillot during a recess. The delegates were gathered in small groups, talking while they walked about, or sitting in the lounge. Walking alone and looking agitated, was Dr. Channing Tobias, a Negro member of the U.S. delegation. He carried a book and I observed on its cover the accusing hand of Paul Robeson. It was, of course, the genocide petition.

Dr. Tobias, a handsome, light-skinned Negro more than six feet tall, with a head of beautiful gray hair, was the Chairman of the Board of the NAACP. He held a degree of Doctor of Divinity, and was perhaps as well thought of in bourgeois circles in the United States at that time as Booker T. Washington had been during an earlier era. Our rulers had, since the Civil War, needed a Black spokesman to caution Negro workers against the dangers of trade unionism and to teach them the necessity for patience. Now it needed a Negro like Dr. Tobias to caution Negroes against the dangers of communism.

Some time earlier, Tobias had been made a member of the Board of the Bowery Savings Bank. He, Ralph Bunche, an American career diplomat, and Edith Sampson, a lawyer from Chicago, were the Negro members of the American delegation headed by Eleanor Roosevelt. That there should be so large a Negro contingent was indeed worthy of note and of study. It was evident that there were special tasks that Negroes were best qualified to perform under existing conditions. One was to create the impression among delegates, especially those from former colonial countries, that the U.S. Government recognized and rewarded "capable" Negroes. It was perhaps also the task of these Negro leaders to convey to UN delegates by their presence that the U.S. Government had as a political objective the achievement of Black-white unity.

Dr. Tobias saw me come in, and he stopped his pacing to beckon to me. We had been only slightly acquainted. After leisurely checking my hat and coat, I crossed the foyer to meet him. His beckoning summons had seemed imperious to me, but I decided that this was not the time to take umbrage at a gesture. Without offering his hand, or even uttering a "how-do-you-do," he demanded, "Why did you do this thing, Patterson?"

"What thing, Dr. Tobias?" I asked politely.

"Make this attack upon your government," he snapped.

"It's your government, Dr. Tobias, and my country," I said quietly. "I am fighting to save my country's democratic principles from destruction by your government."

He kept his temper. "But why," he asked, "didn't you write about genocide in the Soviet Union?"

I had not expected such crude red-baiting. "There are two reasons, Mr. Tobias, the first being that I know nothing about genocide in the Soviet Union, although I have been there a number of times. The second is that I am not a national of that country. I think I would look rather foolish coming here with a petition dealing with human relations in any country but my own."

"Patterson," he demanded, as though talking to one of his stooges, "where do you expect to get with this?"

"That depends in part upon your courage, Dr. Tobias. How far will you help me get?" I added seriously.

Without another word the reverend gentleman turned away. He had not made a convert—neither had I.

Evidently we had been talking rather vehemently. A photographer had come over and taken pictures; several people were looking in our direction, among them Edith Sampson. My wife and I had known Edith very well during our Chicago days. She, too, beckoned to me, and I walked over slowly to where she was standing.

"Hello, Pat," she said, and held out her hand. "I have seen the petition and agree with most of it."

"Will you help me get it before the Economic and Social Council?" I asked.

"Pat, you know how I feel about you and Louise. You're fine people. But this is a delegation matter and I have to vote with the delegation."

"Is it as simple as that, Edith?" I asked. "This petition constitutes more than a pro forma matter. The integrity of our country is involved. So is peace. Racism challenges all Americans. This is an acceptance of that challenge. It is the Negro's entry on the world stage as a fighter for the dignity of mankind, its unification, and for world peace."

She made some noncommittal answer and shook my hand as I turned away. Later Edith and I were to have another talk about the petition. She told me how it had upset the delegation. The debates about it had been sharp. Mrs. Roosevelt was deeply annoyed. I could feel that Edith was torn between the official status she thought she had achieved and her good instincts. But she had to pay a price for serving a government that countenanced terror in its relations with millions of her people.

Having had these encounters with two of the Negro delegates, I left the Palais Chaillot. I wanted to do some walking and thinking. I had not gone to see Ralph Bunche. I recalled the time in 1937 when James W. Ford, a prominent Negro Communist, and I had talked with Bunche in Paris. He had said then that he knew where he stood. He had said: "Go your way. I'll go mine."

Snow was falling softly; I buttoned up my coat and walked a few blocks; Paris was a beautiful city.

Ralph Bunche's attitude toward the petition was negative. Although we did not meet, we passed one another in the halls and lobbies of the Palais Chaillot, and he never took occasion to speak to me. After the meeting of the General Assembly when the petition was discussed, I was told that when he

returned to the states he alleged that I had not made an effort to
contact him. What he meant to imply I do not know but I do
know that he made no effort to contact me.

Across the Atlantic, Paul Robeson and other members of the
CRC who accompanied him had presented copies of the
petition to the offices of the UN Secretariat. The event was
reported in the *New York Times* of December 18, 1951.

The *Times* had also taken the trouble to elicit the views of
Dr. Lemkin at Yale. His anti-Soviet opinions proved of more
significance to the *Times* than the words he had written into
the Genocide Convention. Dr. Lemkin, according to the
Times, said: "The accusations were a maneuver to divert
attention from the crimes of genocide committed against
Estonians, Latvians, Lithuanians, Poles and other Soviet-
subjugated peoples." Lemkin branded Paul Robeson and me
as "un-American" elements serving a foreign power. This was
a procedure that was to be repeated many times. Dr. Lemkin
was attempting to put the shoe he held on the wrong foot.

To go back to my thoughtful walk in the snow, I had become
tired and now hailed a cab and went again to the Paris post
office in quest of the 60 petitions I had mailed to myself. There
were none. I sent a wire to London, asking friends to pick up
the copies that had been mailed there and send them on to me.
Then I headed for a little restaurant on the East Bank where I
often ate. After I had read the menu, I glanced casually around
the room. To my great surprise I recognized Clarina Michelson
sitting at a table in the rear. I had not seen her for years; the
sight of her brought me back to Boston, and August 1927,
when the progressive people of the world were fighting to save
the lives of Sacco and Vanzetti—now almost a quarter of a
century ago.

I went over to Clarina's table; I knew that she had married
again and was now living in Europe. She recognized me at
once and we embraced. She introduced her friend as Barbara
Hirsch. I recalled that Al Hirsch, Barbara's husband, had gone
with me on a delegation to Harvard to solicit the aid of Felix

Frankfurter in the Tom Mooney case, and also on a delegation I had led to Albany, N.Y., seeking the aid of President-elect Franklin Delano Roosevelt in the fight for Tom Mooney's freedom. Barbara had worked as a volunteer for the International Labor Defense years earlier, when I first became its chairman.

Clarina invited me to sit down and we began to reminisce about our arrests at the Sacco and Vanzetti demonstration. The Boston police had refused to allow a "nigger" to ride in the patrol wagon with a white woman. Here in Paris we could sit and eat together in a decent restaurant.

I told Clarina and Barbara of my mission. Clarina interrupted me to say that Mrs. Roosevelt had, on the previous day, made a speech in the Third Committee of the General Assembly, in the course of which she had gone into the question of the status of Negroes in the United States. I knew of the speech but did not know it had hit the press. The records of this Committee, which are available in any sizable library, give an indirect summary of the remarks of each speaker. The gist of Mrs. Roosevelt's words on this subject is as follows:

The allegation that the U.S. Government was disregarding the interests of the Negroes is baseless. True, there had been instances of Negroes being victimized through unreasoning racial prejudice, but such incidents were not condoned, and President Truman himself had on numerous occasions issued executive orders to insure the protection of Negroes in employment under government contract. The official policy of the U.S. Government was that the remaining imperfections in the practice of democracy which resulted from the conduct of small groups must be corrected as soon as possible. . . .

Besides exaggerating the anti-racist role of Harry Truman, it was a poor apology for U.S. racist policy. It not only ignored a hundred years of terror but contradicted the words of the Truman Civil Rights Commission.

The next day the Paris edition of the *New York Times* reported a further portion of Mrs. Roosevelt's remarks:

"Mrs. Roosevelt told United Nations delegates today that Negroes were becoming increasingly active in the political life of the U.S. . . . She was speaking *in reply to Soviet bloc charges of violation of the human rights of Negroes in the United States."* (Emphasis mine.)

The petitioners had friends as well as foes in the UN. The Soviet delegation had copies of *We Charge Genocide.* Its arguments outweighed those of Mrs. Roosevelt and the three Negro collaborators. *Genocide* had not dealt with the racist practices or the "conduct of small groups," but with a *policy.* A hundred years of lynch terror constitutes a policy aided and abetted by a government of force and violence.

Although Mrs. Roosevelt had not overtly taken up the petition we had filed, her remarks were obviously an effort to undermine its effect. I sought a platform from which to reply to her and found a most convenient spot in the columns of *Action,* a Paris newspaper. The editors interviewed me but did not make the interview a direct reply to Mrs. Roosevelt's remarks. Instead, the questions they asked me were based largely on a brochure which had been issued by the U.S. Information Service in Paris and on the material in our petition. Here are portions of the *Action* article:

The condition and the progress of these Negroes, who constitute one-tenth of the American population, awaken everywhere a growing interest.

A brochure published by the American Information Service, dated December 15, 1950, explains in the above sentence the reason for a study devoted to Negro Americans. We recognize the meaning of reality in the U.S. Embassy propaganda: the condition of the Negro is as interesting to public opinion as it should be to the General Assembly of the United Nations, as set forth in the publication *We Charge Genocide. . . .*

The signatories of this petition, a volume of 240 pages which contains proof of the allegations of the plaintiffs, asked one of their number, William L. Patterson, to present it to the U.N. General Assembly. Mr. Patterson has consented to answer our questions. . . .

(We merely repeated the main points which were developed in the USIS brochure and asked Patterson what he thought of them.)

Q. The USIS brochure says: "The U.S. Government thinks it is neither possible nor efficacious to remedy discrimination by law. It is better to allow these ideas of discrimination which remain latent in public opinion to subside."

A. This is not true. Feelings of white superiority are not latent but taught in the schools, in the press, in the movies, in the churches. . . . The government could outlaw this crime tomorrow; it could make it illegal, along with all propaganda inciting such crimes. Instead it practices discrimination in every one of its departments, services and bureaus. It authorizes discrimination in the federal courts. It permits violations of constitutional laws which give Negroes equality of rights by authorizing each of the 48 states to make its own laws dealing with discrimination . . . . It is the crime of the government, not of the American people. . . .

Q. The USIS brochure says: "Education in the universities has made big steps . . . 128,000 Negroes are enrolled; more than 70 universities in the North have Negro professors; there are something like 68 Negro universities, of which the majority are situated in the South."

A. Racial segregation is practiced at the universities; there are Negro professors in only four or five universities—New York, Chicago, Harvard. Yes, there are 68 Negro universities in the South; the buildings are very old, the financial conditions very poor. This year, 1951, the Rockefeller, Morgan and Ford foundations have given $1,800,000 to these Negro universities and have distributed hundreds and hundreds of millions to white universities.

As regards primary education, conditions are appalling. There are schools where there are no washbasins, toilet facilities or drinking water. The white teachers receive double the salary of the Negro teachers in most of the states. The present governor of South Carolina, James F. Byrnes, former secretary of state, who was in on the formulation of plans for the U.N., has said that he prefers to see blood flow in the streets rather than permit Negro students to go to school with white children. . . .

Q. "American films" says the USIS brochure, "have reflected a striking change. Up to these last few years, the Negro was always shown as a comedian. In 1949 and 1950 Hollywood produced . . . half a dozen big pictures portraying the modern Negro, his problems and aspirations, with sincerity, dignity and a real perspicacity."

A. Before 1949, the caricatures which Hollywood presented were not without the tacit approval of the government . . . . Protests by Paul Robeson and other Negro artists forced Hollywood to change, but even today Hollywood takes care not to present the American

Negro as equal to others in American life. . . . They are careful not to
show his real contribution to music, to industry, to politics and to the
whole of American life. . . ."

Q. The USIS says: "Negroes attend army and navy officers' training
schools. Under orders of President Truman, all the military units
which were composed solely of Negroes have been rapidly broken up
and their members have been incorporated into mixed units—under
the same living conditions, the same recreation facilities, and may
apply for any grade for which they are qualified . . . there are actually
3,000 Negro officers commanding white troops as well as Negroes."

A. This is not so—there are Negro officers but they do not command
white troops and most of the larger military schools are in the South,
where racial segregation prevails. It also prevails in the camps, in one
of the largest military camps in the U.S.A., for instance, Fort Dix in
northern New Jersey. In the army Negroes eat and sleep in separate
quarters. I could go on with amply documented instances of the
grossest discrimination against Negro officers and men . . . and hor-
rendous stories of the status of Negroes in business, the press, the
government. Those who have elevated positions are the exceptions
and they too are subject to segregation in government restaurants,
canteens and other places. In spite of which, they are in fact
apologists for the government's racist crimes and in no way represent
the Negro masses. There are in the U.S. 15 million Negroes. And how
many Ralph Bunches are there? . . .

I felt that *Action* in publishing the interview had performed
a service not only to its French readers but to an international
audience as well. It had done something rarely done by the
American press.

As for the additional copies of the genocide petition, a cable
finally arrived from the London Post Office which informed
my friend that no package of any kind had come for a Mr.
William L. Patterson. I was not overwhelmed by surprise since
I was now certain that steps were being taken to thwart the
circulation of the petition and thus nullify its effect. Many
delegations had not received copies.

I began to see a definite change in the forms and methods of
racist ideology. For example, the brochure the USIS had
loosed in Europe on the status of the Negro in the United
States was something new. Not that there was any unqualified

condemnation of racism in the brochure; or any assertion that the government was determined to wipe out legal lynching or to attack and outlaw all aspects of racist propaganda. It was an apology for racism designed to leave our colonialist allies unshaken—the United States was not going to make the UN a forum for democracy and peace.

Naturally, now more than ever I wanted to reach those delegations in the UN who had not received copies of the petition. I wired friends in Hungary to whom the remaining 60 copies had been sent and word came back almost immediately: "Genocide received. Thought they were for distribution. Have given all out. Will collect some and forward." I had to laugh, but I wasn't beaten yet!

The American delegation was doing everything it could to keep the petition from coming before the Economic and Social Council or the Human Rights Commission—that much was clear. Friends suggested that I seek help from other delegations. Such a precedent had been set by the Rev. Michael Scott of South Africa in getting before the Human Rights Commission a petition exposing the savagery of the South African government toward the Herreros in Southwest Africa. I decided to fight it out along a similar line.

I considered the Indian delegation—India was at that moment approaching victory in her struggle for independence against the imperialists of Great Britain. The magnitude of that liberation fight was, however, such as to make it virtually impossible for India to antagonize the ruling circles in the United States.

The Indian delegation suggested that I reach Paul Robeson and ask him to get in touch with his friend Mr. Nehru, the Indian Prime Minister. Nehru could determine whether anything of a substantial character in support of the petition could be done by his UN delegation. I called and got Paul on the phone; he in turn reached Nehru, but India's commitments for the moment were too great for her to play a role in this struggle.

I turned to the Egyptian delegation; here again I found

conflicting interests that could not easily be reconciled. An open struggle had developed over the ownership of the Suez Canal; Egypt needed aid from U.S. imperialism which, for reasons of its own, might well support the Egyptians against France and England.

A meeting was organized for me with leaders of the Haitian, Dominican, Ethiopian and Liberian delegations. But all of these countries were soliciting aid from the United States under Point IV of the Marshall Plan and they were unwilling to do anything that would endanger their chances of receiving such help.

Clearly, the Negro question was inextricably bound up with the liberation struggles of all mankind, but the forces at work were complex. If I had not applied directly for aid to the socialist states, it was because it would have served no useful purpose. To have done so would have been to call forth an anti-Soviet barrage from the United States.

An ideological and moral victory had already been won; the moral bankruptcy of U.S. leaders even in the UN had been exposed. Every precaution had to be taken not to weaken the forces which were waging a consistent struggle in the UN against racism and for peace. If I had had the full support of American liberals and scholars, how much more might have been achieved!

One evening shortly after my meeting with the Haitians and other members of the UN, I was in my room pondering the next day's program when the doorbell rang. Guardedly I opened the door to face a man who could have been either British or American. "My name is Benjamin Welles," he said. "I'm with the *New York Times.* May I come in?" Welles was comparatively young; his eyes were eager and friendly. I let him in.

It turned out that he was a son of former assistant secretary of state, Sumner Welles. He was attached to the London Bureau of the *New York Times.* At the moment he was on special assignment at the U.S. military headquarters in Paris.

"I have seen the Genocide Petition," he said. "I regard it as a

powerful indictment of racism in our country. I would like to
interview you for an article in the magazine section of the
Times."

I could not conceal my amazement and I said bluntly:
"When you get an interview with me into the magazine section
of the *Times* on the genocidal policies of America's economic
overlords, it will be when the people themselves own the
paper. You don't mean to tell me that you have an assignment
from your New York office for such an interview?"

He shook his head and admitted he had undertaken the
interview on his own initiative. "I assume you know that Paul
Robeson has submitted copies of the petition to the UN
Secretariat in New York?" he asked.

I nodded. "But I'll bet the U.S. press hasn't given that
historic event any big play," I said.

He nodded assent, and the interview began.

"Are you a Communist?" he started.

"What has that to do with the petition?" I asked.

I told him of my faith in the progressive forces in the UN and
how I viewed the Negro people's struggle as part and parcel of
the world freedom movement. Than I added: "I did more than
edit the petition; I saw or thought I saw this form of attack on
racism as having a significant impact on millions at home and
abroad, so I formulated the main lines of the petition—with the
help of others. I wanted to raise the struggle against racism to
the international plane, and I knew that unimpeachable documentation of the charges could be found. It was found."

At this point my telephone rang. "This is the American
Embassy," said the voice at the other end.

"What can I do for you?" I asked and then I added jokingly.
"Am I invited to your Christmas dinner party?" The Embassy
had such parties during the Xmas holidays—but not for
Americans of my color.

"We have orders to cancel your passport and see that you go
home," the voice coldly informed me.

"Well, you go to hell," I said and abruptly hung up.

I told Welles what the Embassy spokesman had said. "I wouldn't be surprised if the French police showed up here at any moment," I added. "I'm sorry that I can't go on with our interview, but I'm moving."

Ever since I had acquired my "gray card" I had kept my bag packed. I had also placed an order for an air ticket without confirming any date.

Welles was so astounded at the rapid change in scene that for some moments he said nothing. Then he asked, "Where will you go?"

"To another hotel, I guess, until I can think over a future course of action," I said, as I hurriedly got my things together. We went downstairs and I checked out. At the entrance of the hotel he offered his hand. When I took it, he said simply, "I wish you good luck."

I believe he was sincere. I never saw him again, and I never saw an article in the *New York Times Magazine* about the Genocide Petition which had been presented at the UN.

I made a phone call to the air terminal and was told I would have a ticket on a plane leaving for Budapest via Zurich that night. Then I sat down at the terminal, where I had gone to find out the time of the flight, and began to think things over.

I had received a good European press. When I returned to the United States there would be a full analysis of the results of my trip in the Party press and elsewhere. The ruling class and the government had sustained an ideological and moral defeat, but I was by no means certain as to how the victory could be utilized. The Negro struggle had been lifted up to a new level; American reactionaries were afraid of the exposure of the cold, hard, murderous character of those who, since the time of Lincoln, had prescribed terror—not law and order, not constitutional government—as a policy toward one-tenth of the citizenry of the country.

The facts set forth in the petition had been confirmed five years earlier by the findings of President Truman's Civil Rights Commission in their report entitled *To Secure These*

Rights (Simon & Schuster, 1947). This report did not of course identify those responsible for the conditions it exposed; it did its best to conceal the real criminals. But no one could read it without seeing the complicity of the government in the persecutions extending over a century.

As for the guilty principle in matters of this kind, that had been laid down eloquently by Supreme Court Justice Robert Jackson when he opened the Nuremberg trials of the Nazi war criminals. His position had received world-wide acceptance.

"How a government treats its inhabitants generally," Justice Jackson had said, "is thought to be of no concern of other governments or of international society. Certainly few oppressions or cruelties would cause the interference of foreign powers. But the German mistreatment of Germans is now known to pass in magnitude and savagery the limits of what is tolerable by modern civilization. Other nations, by silence, would take a consenting part in such crimes. These Nazi persecutions, moreover, take on a character as international crimes because of the purpose for which they were undertaken."

Exactly the same words could be used in a trial of those who directed government-fostered crimes against Negro citizens. It was not too early to think about trials of American racists who were also warlords. I wondered why America's white liberals had never petitioned the UN against genocide, U.S.A.

In no way did I see in my departure from Paris a flight from the arena of battle. I was off to marshal new forces and map further steps in this far-reaching offensive.

Rumors of the State Department's restrictions on me had reached the U.S. press. The Paris edition of the *New York Herald Tribune,* in its issue of December 17, 1951, gave the following account:

"An official at the American Embassy in Paris said last night that there was 'no comment' for the time being regarding the report that the 'recall' of Mr. Patterson's passport had been asked. Mr. Patterson is alleged to have presented to the United

Nations General Assembly in Paris the same accusation of genocide that Paul Robeson and 15 other members of the Civil Rights Congress left at the U.N. headquarters in New York on December 17."

And on December 30, I learned on my return to the United States, that the notorious Walter Winchell included the following item in his always insidious Sunday evening broadcast:

"A few months ago, I revealed the name of the person now leading the Communist Party in Harlem, New York, the focal point for the American Reds to win over the Harlems from coast to coast. This man's name is William L. Patterson, one of the pets of the Civil Rights Congress, which was cited as subversive by the U.S. Attorney-General. Anyway, ladies and gentlemen, this is to make you feel good. Communist leader Patterson, now in France, has been given a swift kick in the seat by the Department of State. They have taken away his passport. When the State Department was asked the reason, a spokesman said, 'In the best interests of the United States.' Good riddance!"

When the plane reached Zurich, Switzerland, I remained in my seat. I had no desire to attract attention. I did not leave the plane until we landed at Prague. There, when I stepped on socialist ground, I felt the same thrill of freedom I had experienced as a lad when I first stepped onto Mexican soil. I was free now from lynching, mob violence, personal insult and arrest.

My pause in Prague was brief and in a relatively short time I was airborne again and coming into Ferihegy airport in Budapest. There I was met by warm friends, among them a young man named Hollai, who was to be my translator and guide. I was whisked through customs into a waiting car and off to that city of beauty on the banks of the Danube. A suite was ready for me at the lovely hotel on Margaret Island, in the middle of the Danube, and I was ready for it. I needed sleep.

Here are some excerpts from a letter I wrote my wife when I awoke:

Paul Robeson presents the Petition, *We Charge Genocide,* at the UN Secretariat in New York, December 1951.

"I am sitting here on the balcony of my room . . . and there is a serenity and calmness about the beautiful scene that might readily make one believe that the fascist beasts (the bullets from whose guns mar the walls of this hotel and whose bombs destroyed the magnificent bathhouse that flanked the hotel on the right) have gone forever. These people who have treated me as a fellow-human being will·see to that. But though thoughts of peace and harmony press in on me here, I recall that even as I write, my brothers and sisters are being jailed in the land from which I come, which is now the last refuge of Nazi warmakers and racist cannibals. Paul could not now be here for a moment's rest. Gene (Eugene Dennis) languishes in a hell hole, Ben (Benjamin J. Davis, Jr.), Winnie (Henry Winston) and the rest of the 11 face prison cells. . . . I cannot rest. . . .

"There are people of all nations here at this hotel. The Chinese have their legation here temporarily; a Polish friend is here to rest. Fifty-seven Hungarians from the Soviet Ukraine are here visiting Hungarian collective farms.Western Europe is absent and one Negro represents that America in which decency and humanism remain—a Negro overlooking the spot where princes and their mistresses cavorted and sneered at the people. . . .

"I shall be here a few days. I am terribly worried about the happenings in the States. I should like to write many things but if walls have ears in the U.S.A., paper has eyes and an eternal memory. So I close. I miss you very much."

While I was still writing, the telephone rang; I had no worries—I knew it was not the American Embassy on this occasion. I was asked if I was willing to speak over the radio. I was not ready to make independent personal engagements. The friends who knew of my coming would undoubtedly have a program worked out. I simply said, "Please call me later when I will be able to answer more definitely."

My friends did have a program. I was asked if I would speak to the English section of the editorial staff of the *Népszabad-ság*, the Party newspaper, then to a group of foreign correspondents, and then to the writers' club. Later I addressed members of the Foreign and Justice Ministries and members of the clergy. I found nothing in the program that I was not prepared to do.

My responsibility could not be met by a recital of the crimes against the Negro-American, regardless of their magnitude. These crimes had continued for a hundred years. What needed to be explained was the role of the government, the conspiracy of big business and government to rob Negroes.

We Charge Genocide: The Crime of Government Against the Negro People had been written in order to emphasize the depth of the problem by which Negroes were confronted and to demonstrate its international character. But most of all the petition had been written to arouse Negroes to think about the broad range of the necessary social and political changes to be made by the people. The government as it was constituted could not be the instrument for bringing about so fundamental a change. This the people had to learn before they could understand and assume their historic tasks.

I regarded as extremely important the talks I had with the members of the Hungarian Foreign and Justice Ministries. Presenting the petition to the UN was one thing; I was well aware, however, of the power the United States could wield within the UN to prevent the charge from getting an official airing. To be sure, the composition of the UN would change; new states would join the world organization—fresh victors in the struggle for national liberation. The charge must be repeated until the racists of the United States would have to abandon their diabolical practices, which could no longer be defended before an outraged world.

I quoted the then unrefuted statement of Milton R. Konvitz, Associate Professor of the School of Industrial and Labor Relations at Cornell University:

"Congress has refused to pass laws to declare the poll tax illegal, to make discrimination in private employment in interstate commerce a crime; to define and guarantee civil

rights in the District of Columbia. The Supreme Court has
failed to declare Jim Crowism in interstate commerce unconstitutional; to outlaw segregation in schools as a denial of due
process or equal protection of the law; to outlaw the restrictive
covenants in the sale or rental of property; to declare the poll
tax as an unconstitutional tax on a federally guaranteed right or
privilege. The Supreme Court has placed the Negro at the
mercy of the individual states; they alone have the power to
define and guarantee civil rights. . . ."

My statement in Budapest was broadcast to the world.

A few days later I went back to Prague, where a large press
conference was called. This was very helpful to our cause, for
there were American correspondents present, including one
whose name was William Oatis. Their feeble attempts to refute
what I had said were the best confirmation I could have had. In
Prague I repeated the Budapest performance, giving to lawyers
and clergy a special report on the essence of the genocide
petition.

In Paris, another account of the petition had appeared in the
press, this time in the civil-rights weekly *Droit et Liberté*. I
quote a portion of this report:

We Charge Genocide: that is the title of a document which Mr.
William Patterson, Secretary of the Civil Rights Congress in the
United States, recently presented to the United Nations.

Eighty-eight Americans, Negro and white, intellectuals and workers, artists and writers, have signed this volume of more than 200
pages, an irrefutable document, a vibrant call for justice in respect to
human rights.

Reading it, one can only be upset and angered by the violence of the
criminal racism which oppressed 15 million Negroes in the United
States. Racism, tolerated and encouraged by the authorities, weighing
hourly from birth to death upon the fates of "citizens of color."
Murderous racism, guilty of having exterminated in a century by
means of lynchings, "illegal" as well as "legal," more than 10,000
innocent people, not counting those who have died daily from the
ignoble sufferings of discrimination.

Quite unaccountably and rather obsurely, Mrs. Roosevelt

had changed her tune. On January 12 she gave an interview to
William A. Rutherford of the New York *Amsterdam News* and
the Associated Negro Press. Here is a part of what Rutherford
reported:

> Inan exclusive interview accorded to this correspondent, Mrs.
> Eleanor Roosevelt . . . stated her belief that the United Nations would
> be morally justified in taking action in favor of the American Negro
> people.
>
> (She) feels that the colored peoples of the world are finally coming
> into their own: They "have found strength in unity and can now make
> the big powers listen to their just demands. Their burdens of social
> and economic deprivation will be and are being overcome as they
> press their demands in the council of the world."
>
> When questioned about the petition charging the United States
> with genocide, which the Civil Rights Congress headed by William L.
> Patterson has been trying to present to the United Nations, Mrs.
> Roosevelt commented that it was "well done as a petition . . . (and
> was) based on sound and good documentation. (It) was not presented
> with spurious reasoning."
>
> She went on to add: "The charge of genocide against the colored
> people in America is ridiculous in terms of the United Nations
> definition." Her reasons were (1) although the Negro death rate is high
> in America, so is the birth rate; (2) although sickness and diseases
> carry off more colored people than in other groups, a real effort is
> being made to overcome this.
>
> Mrs. Roosevelt thought that in spite of these objections, the petition
> would do some good in focusing world attention on the bad situation
> in America. She also expressed the fear that the petition would play
> into the hands of some Southerners who would like nothing better
> than to institute genocide against the Negro people. . . .

When I returned to Paris the session of the General Assembly was over. I went to the post office once more to see if
the package of copies of petitions was there—it was. There was
no doubt that it had been willfully kept out of my hands. When
I returned to the United States, I was to learn that the
government had indeed held up the petitions in London as
well as in Paris.

I booked passage to London. Fearing that I might not be
permitted to leave the airport there, I sent a wire to D. N. Pritt,
King's Counsel, one of the world's great defenders of civil

rights, a truly great man, telling him I was on my way. I wanted
Mr. Pritt to prepare a protest demonstration if I were held up at
the airport.

It was fortunate that I did this. As it was, I was detained by
the authorities for 17 hours at the London airport. The CIA and
the CID (Criminal Investigation Department) of Scotland Yard
work together. When allowed to leave the airport through the
vigorous intervention of Pritt and others, I was granted a stay
of only five days in England. Pritt had a gathering at his home
in the Inns of Court, and I placed the indictment for genocide
and evidence of the government's guilt before a sympathetic
and yet objective audience.

On this occasion I was interviewed by the *Daily Worker,*
organ of the British Communist Party, and by the London
Daily Herald. I had the opportunity of talking with Johnny
Williamson, one of the outstanding leaders of the British
Communist Party. Johnny had spent most of the formative
years of his life in the United States. He had been a member of
the Young Communist League and had risen through the ranks
of the Party to be secretary of its labor commission. He had
been deported from his adopted home by the U.S. Department
of Justice. It was helpful to get Johnny's view as to the value of
the genocide petition. He felt that the petition had to be
popularized and sold far and wide, especially among Negro
Americans.

I agreed with him. Indeed, we sold a total of 45,000 in the
United States, while those sold in the Soviet Union, Czecho-
slovakia and Hungary went far beyond that figure.

I saw other friends in England, among them the magnificent
churchman, Hewlett Johnson, Dean of Canterbury, and Harry
Pollitt, head of the British Communist Party. I learned that
there, too, the petitions had been released from the post office
after the Paris session of the General Assembly had closed. I
paid another visit to Highgate Cemetery and placed a wreath
on the grave of Karl Marx. I observed that the grave was in
better condition than when I had visited it a few years before.

I was ready then to return to New York. In my notebook I

had written, "mission accomplished." By this I meant that the
struggle of American Black men for their rightful place in their
own nation was merging with the liberation struggles of the
people of Asia, Africa and Latin America, and that those who
fought sincerely for peace and fundamental freedoms here in
the United States would sooner or later see the inseparable
connection between their own struggles for justice and those of
the Negro people for their inalienable rights so long withheld.

At a press conference, July 30, 1964, with Henry Winston, Chairman,
and Gus Hall, General Secretary, Communist Party, USA.

CHAPTER 14

Homecoming

WHAT A happy sight met my eye as we landed at Idlewild! My wife and daughter, Paul Robeson, Angie Dickerson, whom I had left in charge of the Civil Rights Congress, other fellow-workers, along with a number of friends, had gathered to meet me. I waved to them and laughed joyfully as my daughter threw kisses. They seemed to be bubbling over with enthusiasm. I almost forgot that I must, before embracing them, have a meeting with customs.

I was about ready to place my baggage on the conveyor for examination when the blow fell. Gently, politely, without fanfare, an immigration inspector tapped me on the shoulder. I was to follow him. We walked the length of the hall to the far end, where he opened a door and we stepped into a small office. Three white men were chatting informally. They turned toward me, and as though to make me feel at ease, proceeded in the same informal manner to ask questions. In a conversational tone, they inquired as to the results of my trip. "Did you enjoy yourself?" I said "yes," no less affably.

Then the questions sharpened and took a curious turn. "What have you brought home?" "Nothing of any material value," I said. "Would you please open your bags?" The search was exhaustive, and I smiled inwardly. If I had left Europe with a bag of socialist gold, would I be fool enough to have it with me? On my person?

The next request was that I strip. I objected, but they were prepared to assist me. They had the power—I stripped. The search of my clothes was even more minute. I gave no evidence of my humiliation—these agents were not the main foe. They were hirelings of my Uncle Sam.

I was told to dress. The affair was over. Whether it had been directed from Washington, or whether these were ambitious men who hoped to further their own careers didn't matter much. The first act was over. I was pretty sure more was coming but evidently the authorities were not going to make a notorious incident out of my trip. They would get me quietly.

The inspector who had brought me in now courteously led me out, not through the hall but out of a rear door. My worried friends had been demanding that the authorities produce me. Newsmen were sniffing around trying to get a story. But this prelude was over; I was "free." I walked around to the front and there my friends pounced on me. Homecoming did have its compensations. The warm greetings dispelled the humiliation of the inquisition room. It was heartening to clasp the hand of Paul Robeson again; to return to a corps of freedom fighters, men and women who were dedicated to the struggle for the realization of a government by and for the people here in the United States.

Robeson and a group of white and Negro citizens had carried the genocide petition to the office of the Secretary General of the UN in New York on the same day I had presented copies to the various delegations in the Human Rights Committee at the Palais Chaillot in Paris. We did not talk long, although I was more than anxious to find out what had occurred in my absence. I was also eager to get to my apartment in Harlem and prepare a report of my trip. I had not gone to Paris in any individual capacity—I was but an emissary, a spokesman for the millions of Black Americans—and of white, too—for whom the weight of racism had become unbearable.

My wife and I were then living with our daughter on "Sugar Hill," in the northwest part of Harlem. We had moved several times since coming back to New York from Chicago. It was not too easy in either city for a Communist to get a place to live.

If I have forgotten the precise date of my homecoming from Paris, I do remember that I saw a huge poster announcing that a report-back-home meeting for William L. Patterson was scheduled for the coming Sunday in Rockland Palace, the largest meeting hall in Harlem. This was the work of Angie Dickerson, my wife Louise and a group of Negro women who called themselves "Sojourners for Truth and Justice." I saw that I would not have too much time to make ready for that event.

On the night of the meeting, the ballroom, nestling under the 155th Street viaduct on Eighth Avenue, was packed with about 2,500 people. This was a dramatic demonstration of the appreciation, interest and pride of the Harlem community in having had the Black man's appeal placed on the world's agenda. Their ghetto was no longer provincial, it was now a part of the turbulent political issues being discussed by the UN. Hope Stevens, the well-known Black attorney and businessman, presided over the meeting. Elizabeth Gurley Flynn, a life-long revolutionary and leader of the Communist Party, addressed the meeting as the Party's representative. The invitations sent to Republican and Democratic leaders to address the meeting were, as usual, ignored. They did not even observe the courtesy of sending regrets.

One of the occurrences that happened in the course of my speech comes back vividly. I had referred several times to the Negro and the tasks ahead when a woman stood up in the audience and cried out, "I'm not a Negro, and don't call me one!" I knew that Richard Moore, a great Negro orator, had been crusading against the word "Negro." He was writing a book condemning that term as an obnoxious legacy from the white oppressors and as an albatross around the necks of Black people. He had made this a matter of principle, offering as a substitute the term "Afro-American."

I could not see how changing the term by which Black

people were addressed, if it bore no inherent insult, would change the status of the people. We were not fighting a word, I thought. I remembered that the Supreme Court in *Davidson vs. New Orleans,* 96 US Reports 194, where a matter of capitalizing the term "Negro" arose, had quoted Dr. W. E. B. Du Bois: *"Negro* does not refer to color, simply, because there are black people who are not Negroes. *Negro* is the designation of a race of men just as Indian, Teutonic or Celt. Historically the word has always been capitalized, and the small letter was only used during the latter days of the slavery agitation when Negroes were classed with real estate."

It was not the time to debate this lady, but I could not let the challenge go unnoticed. I stopped and said: "My dear lady, substitute any term you want; if it is not insulting, it's agreeable to me. For myself, I like the term Black. I am a Black man, but if you like Afro-American, Negro-American, American, or what have you, it's all the same to me. A single word isn't the source of our distress. In deference to your wishes, I won't use the term Negro here today."

She sat down.

Throughout the meeting I sought to impress one fact upon my listeners: racism with all its accompanying evils was a policy condoned and exploited by *government* at the behest of American monopoly. Until the power of the monopolies was curbed, the status of the Black man would undergo no profound or fundamental change. With that knowledge and an appreciation of the political action it called for, the kind of program and tactics that would effect a cure could be worked out. This would require the unity in struggle of Black and white.

Every effort to get the Human Rights Commission of the UN to discuss the genocide charge had been blocked by the influence of American imperialism. The Latin American delegates were wholly in the U.S. grab bag. But a trail had been blazed. The potential of the UN in the fight for peace and against racism was almost limitless. The Socialist world would

Welcome at the airport after my return to New York. *Left to right,* Paul Robeson, Angie Dickerson, and my daughter, Mary Lou; *to my left,* Aubrey Grossman, Organizational Secretary, Civil Rights Congress.

keep alive those issues of peace and freedom upon which the very existence of the world depended. New nations, former victims of colonial, racist policies as carefully designed for maximum profits as were those of the United States, would gain their political independence and move into the arena on the side of universal freedom and human dignity. Historically, the days of imperialism were numbered, but we Americans had the major responsibility to shorten that period.

Only the united struggles of Negroes and whites could bring about the solution arising out of their common exploitation and oppression, resulting from the greed and rapacity of America's monopolists. The Civil Rights Congress could not expect broad popular support in the near future—nor even of a united Black community. But that would come. As sure as the UN had to entertain the issue of apartheid, it would have to deal with the question of racism in the United States. If the power of the United States now made the placing of U.S. racism on a par with apartheid in the UN impossible, eventually ways and means would be found for dealing with it.

The U.S. government had persistently ignored the resolutions and conventions against racism that her delegates voted for in the UN. The genocide petition proved this to the hilt.

If Black citizens became fully aware of this and white citizens joined with them, they would wage a struggle of decisive character against American imperialism.

Epilogue

TO BRING my story up to the present time, I have chosen from some of my recent articles and speeches passages that convey my thinking on what lies ahead in the Black liberation struggle, and some of the events that have led me to these conclusions.

The civil rights campaigns of the last three decades have taught us many political lessons. Victories have been won but the ghetto remains; the income of its residents is disgracefully below the national level; unemployment is many times higher than it is outside the ghetto walls; its death rate is double that of whites; there is chronic hunger in its slums, miseducation in its schools. Frustration has brought widespread drug addiction. The victories are partial only—they are token reforms.

The ideological offensive of imperialism is international in scope. In the United States it attains tremendous intensity around the national liberation struggles of Black Americans, Puerto Ricans, Chicanos and Indians. These struggles are becoming a greater danger to imperialism every day, and the danger is not confined to the domestic front. The freedom movement of Americans of color has taken its place among the foremost liberation struggles of the world.

A psychological assault is being waged by the military-industrial complex all along the front of racism. It is an attempt to bolster the morale of their armed white terrorists—the police—and to enlarge the ranks of what is known as the white backlash.

Reaction seeks to inaugurate a new reign of McCarthyism under the guise of enforcing "law and order" but the liberation movement nevertheless continues its unprecedented growth. In scope and depth the struggles waged by Black nationals have made an amazing impact on the American scene. They have become a leading force in affecting economic, political and technological changes in our country.

During the late 50's and 60's, new forms of battle and new leaders emerged. Again the limitless vitality of democratic demonstrative action was vindicated. As long ago as 1955, Rosa Parks refused to ride in the back of the bus in Montgomery, Alabama and set off a chain of events of historic consequences. When she was arrested, the Black community organized a bus boycott that was maintained in solid unity for over a year—indeed until the bus company and the city government had to capitulate. From this sharp struggle, Dr. Martin Luther King emerged as a new leader who rapidly attained world stature, preaching the doctrine of nonviolence. In August of 1963, a quarter of a million Blacks and whites participated in the great civil rights March on Washington led by Dr. King.

It did not take long for Dr. King to see the necessity for placing economic demands in the forefront of the civil rights program and for linking the movement to the peace issue. He saw the unspeakable destruction wrought by our war machine in Vietnam and eloquently opposed it, demanding that the squandered billions of our national treasure be expended on the crying economic and social needs of our own people. He was deeply concerned with justice for the working people and was in the process of bringing his organization to Memphis to help in the strike of the sanitation laborers when he met his death in an assassination that shook the world.

I touch only upon the highlights of the struggle, in which I remained vitally involved: the fight for desegregation in Little Rock; the battle of Blacks to enter the Universities of Alabama and Mississippi; the great pilgrimages of both Black and white freedom fighters to the South, braving hazards that resulted in beatings and jailings and the unspeakably cruel deaths of three young men—as well as other murders that exposed the implacable fanaticism of the enemies of liberation. To mention the immunity from punishment that most of these criminals were given by their fellow bigots is to add one more instance of the egregious state of justice in Southern courts, and in the United States generally.

Every president in recent administrations, at least from Truman on, has commissioned reports from official and private sources treating the scope and danger of racism and/or police brutality. During the Johnson administration, the famous Kerner report said, among other things: "It is time now to turn with all the purpose at our command to the major unfinished business of the nation. . . . It is time to make good the promises of American democracy to all citizens—urban and rural, white and Black, Spanish surname, American Indian and every minority group." Wasn't this the task, so far as the Blacks were concerned, for the Civil War and the era of Reconstruction? Obviously the time is indeed late—since racism has had 400 years to penetrate deeply into the fabric of American life. Recognizing that the preachment and practice of racism have created "two societies . . . separate and unequal," the Kerner Report suggests that the government "adopt strategies for action." This task, it seems to me, is an impossible one for the moribund, decadent bourgeoisie which is responsible for its existence. The task is for the people and it must be achieved under the leadership of a working class in which men and women of all colors participate.

From the bowels of the ghettos come cries, ever increasing in volume, to end police brutality. All over the nation minorities are demanding community control of the police, education and other public services, a decisive voice in their own destinies. The time calls for a new alignment of forces. The cheated

masses of the United States, so long hoaxed by a ruling class
ideology of "national security," are repudiating the wars in
Indochina. They become more and more apprehensive about
the pollution of their air and water for profit; they are burdened
by inflation and joblessness in the richest land on earth, and
they must and will awaken to the terrible havoc racism has
wrought. The struggle to reach their minds must be intensified
a thousand-fold.

It was as long ago as 1949 that the United Nations adopted a
convention on the punishment and prevention of the crime of
genocide. The centuries-long attacks upon the rights of Black
men, women and youth; the cold-blooded murder, indiscriminate arrest and imprisonment of Black citizens who are
seeking to end these injustices; the failure of government to
invoke the Constitution in behalf of its oppressed nationals
still spell out a conspiracy to commit genocide. The CRC
petition, *We Charge Genocide,* submitted to the UN in 1951
demonstrated, among other things, that the object of this
genocide was the perpetuation of economic and political
power by the few through throttling political protest by the
many. Its method is to demoralize and divide; its aim is to
increase the profits and prevent the people's challenge to the
control of a reactionary clique.

Now, nearly two decades later, the charges made then can be
materially enlarged. Characteristic of life in the United States
today are the murderous brutality visited upon Black citizens
in and out of the ghettos in which they are forced to live; the
use of state troopers to suppress their demonstrations, and the
use of Black nationals as armed gendarmes to force America's
brand of democracy upon foreign peoples.

And as I write, a new Genocide Petition is being readied for
submission to the United Nations. It calls for "economic and
political sanctions" against the U.S. Government until that
government abides by the UN Genocide Convention of 1949
and the Declaration of Human Rights. The goal is one million

signatures; leaders and organizations in the Black community
hope to fulfill this goal.

What is happening to the Black Panther Party and its
leadership symbolizes the profound changes in the kind of
"democracy" that now is being planned for the American
people. It threatens to destroy the fundamental rights of all,
regardless of color. We have only to consider the scene that
unfolded in the Chicago courtroom of Judge Julius Hoffman,
who presided in the case of the "Chicago Eight." Judge
Hoffman seems to have been assigned the task of instituting
the legal terror that was to become the pattern for other Panther
trials—long preliminary imprisonment, high bail, the placing
of insurmountable obstacles in the way of the defense. Here is
American fascism in its nascent form as it develops on the
judicial front.

Respect for the law is demanded by the courts but how can
the Black man, woman or child have respect for a system of
laws that has no respect for him or her? And how can a white
worker have respect for law that has no respect for the working
class? To an ever greater degree the law is being used as a
weapon against the national liberation movement. The law
takes no cognizance of the conspiracies against Black militants
that have been launched from coast to coast—except to participate in its own hypocritical way to implement the conspiracy.

A nationwide defense movement must be developed that
above all else will defend the constitutional rights of Black
activists. It should be a nonpartisan body that will promote a
multinational legal defense for antiwar and antiracist forces. It
should be a body that defends the G.I.'s, Black and white, who
are against the mass murder of aggressive war, that defends the
men of labor who also feel the full weight of government
security agencies when fighting for their just rights. In the new
decade that confronts us, only unity in struggle of Black,
Brown, Yellow and white working people can be of decisive

My daughter, Lola, 1961.

My daughter, Anna, 1966.

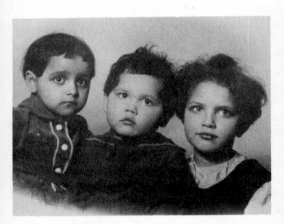

My grandchildren, Lena, Natasha and Tanya.

Mary Lou Patterson, 1961.

political consequence for all mankind. The alternative is submission to the iron grasp of the instruments of torture—surveillance, inquisition and all the brutal and refined cruelties of the police state.

No better example can be cited than the treatment of the Black Panthers. In a number of cities their headquarters have been cordoned off and shot into as one would shoot into a cage of wild beasts. An image of Black militants as rampaging terrorists is being created, and every branch of the government is involved in the process. Never, since the Reconstruction period, has this country witnessed such racist savagery as is now condoned and abetted by government.

The lessons of Watts, Chicago, New York, Atlanta, Cleveland and a score of other cities may have produced some fear-induced token efforts at concilation. But it is the political power of the Black people as they come into an era of new pride in their blackness, their heritage, their own inherent powers that is increasingly threatening the hitherto lily-white complexion of our elected officialdom. From Fayette to Newark, the formerly disenfranchised have elected Black mayors; throughout the country the articulate, highly developed representatives of the race lay claim to its identity as a people, to its history with roots deep in Africa but still conditioned by the United States and integrally a part of this country. They refuse to remain pariahs and exiles. A far more extensive opportunity for education has been fought for and partially won, and changes in the nature of this education are in process.

As a Black man naturally my heart has swelled with pride in the accomplishments of my people in the face of almost insuperable obstacles, and burned with indignation at the lengths to which its oppressors will go to prevent their attaining their full stature. If the potential contributions of the millions of Black citizens could be realized, how much they would enrich the life of the United States—now so threatened by the decadence of a racist, capitalist society, by the breakdown of its institutions of public health, safety, education and justice!

Dr. W. E. B. Du Bois said long ago in *Black Reconstruction in America:* "This the American Negro knows: his fight here is a fight to the finish. Either he dies or wins. If he wins, it will be no subterfuge or evasion of amalgamation. He will enter modern civilization in America as a black man on terms of perfect and unlimited equality with any white man or he will enter not at all. Either extermination root and branch or absolute equality. There can be no compromise."

At stake in the United States is the claim to being fully human and the preservation of any semblance of a democratic way of life. The fight against racism cannot be separated from the fight for a unified nation and for world peace. As the masses come to recognize that it is profit and the hunger for world markets at terrible cost to less powerful countries, the fight for justice in the United States will have to be linked with the fight for a socialist world.

If there are many dreadful portents on the horizon as the present Administration maneuvers its insidious way against its own and other peoples, there are also many signs of hope in the awakening of masses of people the world over. In the international arena, Soviet power and diplomacy constantly rear bulwarks against the incursions of imperialism, knowing full well the nature of the holocaust a third world war threatens. The revolutionary movement spreads all over Asia, Latin America, and Africa; and Cuba develops its valiant socialist revolution 90 miles from the world's most powerful aggressor.

And, perhaps above all, the youth of today, Black and white, repudiate with every breath the moral stench that arises from racism and imperialism. This revulsion knows no bounds, in the face of the lies and evasions of a government that demands that they lay down their lives in a criminal slaughter of Asians. The best of our youth, in ever greater number, reject the standards of a society whose prosperity is based upon the exploitation of working people, on racial discrimination, and on the immunities of the rich no matter what their depredations. They themselves are relentlessly attacked; threats against them grow apace; they, too, Black and white, have been subjected to unconscionable police brutality, to maiming and mass murders on the campuses. Kent, Jackson State and Orangeburg still cry out to high heaven, while the murderers go scot free. The youth see their institutions of learning as arms of the ruling class in the direct service of the Pentagon. They believe nothing that emanates from the White House these days. Truth and compassion and humanity are excess baggage in the frantic and desperate struggle of a dying system to hold on to its power.

In the meanwhile, the minorities in this land of minorities are heard on every hand—the Chicanos, the Indians and, more numerous than any of them, the Black people. Their patience is at an end; they will take no more degradation in "the promised land."

Most significantly, there is motion in labor's ranks, as rank-and-file movements and Black caucuses within the unions arise on every side, pressing for immediate needs and for the reallocation of resources from the dirty war in Indochina to the alleviation of urgent problems at home. There is no easy way to working-class unity regardless of skin color—the kind of unity in struggle that will replace Big Capital power with Worker power. It demands a sharp struggle to substitute a scientific world outlook for a racist mythology which has not only existed in the United States for hundreds of years but has constantly brought a premium to a small segment of the white workers. They must be made to understand the price they pay for their dehumanization. The closer we move toward a classless society the faster will the myth of a superiority of mind and body based upon color fade into oblivion.

And now, if this great ocean swell of militancy can be mobilized, unified, illuminated by an understanding of the class forces of which they are victims, there will be no turning back. No surveillance, persecution, jailing, murder of individuals can stop them. In the end, the people must prevail.

ON THE FAMILY

APOSTOLIC EXHORTATION
FAMILIARIS CONSORTIO

OF HIS HOLINESS
POPE JOHN PAUL II
TO THE EPISCOPATE
TO THE CLERGY AND TO THE FAITHFUL
OF THE WHOLE CATHOLIC CHURCH
REGARDING THE ROLE
OF THE CHRISTIAN FAMILY
IN THE MODERN WORLD

United States Catholic Conference
Washington, D.C.

Pub. No. 833-9
United States Catholic Conference
Washington, D.C.
ISBN 1-55586-833-9

Text and format from
LIBRERIA EDITRICE VATICANA
Vatican City

Published in the United States, February 1982
Eleventh Printing, November 1998

CONTENTS

INTRODUCTION

1. The Church at the Service of the Family

The family in the modern world, as much as and perhaps more than any other institution, has been beset by the many profound and rapid changes that have affected society and culture. Many families are living this situation in fidelity to those values that constitute the foundation of the institution of the family. Others have become uncertain and bewildered over their role or even doubtful and almost unaware of the ultimate meaning and truth of conjugal and family life. Finally, there are others who are hindered by various situations of injustice in the realization of their fundamental rights.

Knowing that marriage and the family constitute one of the most precious of human values, the church wishes to speak and offer her help to those who are already aware of the value of marriage and the family and seek to live it faithfully, to those who are uncertain and anxious and searching for the truth, and to those who are unjustly impeded from living freely their family lives. Supporting the first, illuminating the second and assisting the others, the church offers her services to every person who wonders about the destiny of marriage and the family.[1]

In a particular way the church addresses the young, who are beginning their journey toward marriage and family life, for the purpose of presenting them with new horizons, helping them to discover the beauty and grandeur of the vocation to love and the service of life.

2. The Synod of 1980 in Continuity with Preceding Synods

A sign of this profound interest of the church in the family was the last Synod of Bishops, held in Rome from Sept. 26 to Oct. 25, 1980. This was a natural continuation of the two preceding synods:[2] The Christian family, in fact, is the first community called to announce the Gospel to the human person during growth and to bring him or her, through a progressive education and catechesis, to full human and Christian maturity.

Furthermore, the recent synod is logically connected in some way as well with that on the ministerial priesthood and on justice in the modern world. In fact, as an educating community, the family must help man to discern his own vocation and to accept responsibility in the search for greater justice, educating him from the beginning in interpersonal relationships, rich in justice and in love.

At the close of their assembly, the synod fathers presented me with a long list of proposals in which they had gathered the fruits of their reflections, which had matured over intense days of work, and they asked me unanimously to be a spokesman before humanity of the church's lively care for the family and to give suitable indications for renewed pastoral effort in this fundamental sector of the life of man and of the church.

As I fulfill that mission with this exhortation, thus actuating in a particular matter the apostolic ministry with which I am entrusted, I wish to thank all the members of the synod for the very valuable contribution of teaching and experience that they made, especially through the *propositiones,* the text of which I am entrusting to the Pontifical Council for the Family with instructions to study it so as to bring out every aspect of its rich content.

3. The Precious Value of Marriage and of the Family

Illuminated by the faith that gives her an understanding of all the truth concerning the great value of marriage and the family and their deepest meaning, the church once again feels the pressing need to proclaim the Gospel, that is the "good news," to all people without exception, in particular to all those who are called to marriage and are preparing for it, to all married couples and parents in the world.

The church is deeply convinced that only by the acceptance of the Gospel are the hopes that man legitimately places in marriage and in the family capable of being fulfilled.

Willed by God in the very act of creation,[3] marriage and the family are interiorly ordained to fulfillment in Christ[4] and have need of his graces in order to be healed from the wounds of sin[5] and restored to their "beginning,"[6] that is, to full understanding and the full realization of God's plan.

At a moment of history in which the family is the object of numerous forces that seek to destroy it or in some way to deform it, and aware that the well-being of society and her own good are intimately tied to the good of the family,[7] the church perceives in a more urgent and compelling way her mission of proclaiming to all people the plan of God for marriage and the family, ensuring their full vitality and human and Christian development, and thus contributing to the renewal of society and of the people of God.

PART ONE
BRIGHT SPOTS AND SHADOWS
FOR THE FAMILY TODAY

4. The Need to Understand the Situation

Since God's plan for marriage and the family touches men and women in the concreteness of their daily existence in specific social and cultural situations, the church ought to apply herself to understanding the situations within which marriage and the family are lived today, in order to fulfill her task of serving.[8]

This understanding is therefore an inescapable requirement of the work of evangelization. It is, in fact, to the families of our times that the church must bring the unchangeable and ever new gospel of Jesus Christ, just as it is the families involved in the present conditions of the world that are called to accept and to live the plan of God that pertains to them. Moreover, the call and demands of the spirit resound in the very events of history, and so the church can also be guided to a more profound understanding of the inexhaustible mystery of marriage and the family by the circumstances, the questions and the anxieties and hopes of the young people, married couples and parents of today.[9]

To this ought to be added a further reflection of particular importance at the present time. Not infrequently ideas and solutions which are very appealing, but which obscure in varying degrees the truth and the dignity of the human person, are offered to the men and women of today in their sincere and deep search for a response to the important daily problems that affect their married and family life. These views are often supported by the powerful and pervasive organization of the means of social communication, which subtly endangers freedom and the capacity for objective judgment.

Many are already aware of this danger to the human person and are working for the truth. The church, with her evangelical discernment, joins with them, offering her own service to the truth, to freedom and to the dignity of every man and every woman.

5. Evangelical Discernment

The discernment effected by the church becomes the offering of an orientation in order that the entire truth and the full dignity of marriage and the family may be preserved and realized.

This discernment is accomplished through the sense of faith,[10] which is a gift that the Spirit gives to all the faithful,[11] and is therefore the

3

work of the whole church according to the diversity of the various gifts and charisms that, together with and according to the responsibility proper to each one, work together for a more profound understanding and activation of the word of God. The church, therefore, does not accomplish this discernment only through the pastors, who teach in the name and with the power of Christ, but also through the laity: Christ "made them his witnesses and gave them understanding of the faith and the grace of speech (cf. Acts 2:17–18; Rv. 19:10), so that the power of the Gospel might shine forth in their daily social and family life."[12] The laity, moreover, by reason of their particular vocation have the specific role of interpreting the history of the world in the light of Christ, inasmuch as they are called to illuminate and organize temporal realities according to the plan of God, creator and redeemer.

The "supernatural sense of faith,"[13] however, does not consist solely or necessarily in the consensus of the faithful. Following Christ, the church seeks the truth, which is not always the same as the majority opinion. She listens to conscience and not to power, and in this way she defends the poor and the downtrodden. The church values sociological and statistical research when it proves helpful in understanding the historical context in which pastoral action has to be developed and when it leads to a better understanding of the truth. Such research alone, however, is not to be considered in itself an expression of the sense of faith.

Because it is the task of the apostolic ministry to ensure that the church remains in the truth of Christ and to lead her ever more deeply into that truth, the pastors must promote the sense of faith in all the faithful, examine and authoritatively judge the genuineness of its expressions and educate the faithful in an ever more mature evangelical discernment.[14]

Christian spouses and parents can and should offer their unique and irreplaceable contribution to the elaboration of an authentic evangelical discernment in the various situations and cultures in which men and women live their marriage and their family life. They are qualified for this role by their charism or specific gift, the gift of the sacrament of matrimony.[15]

6. The Situation of the Family in the World Today

The situation in which the family finds itself presents positive and negative aspects: The first is a sign of the salvation of Christ operating in the world; the second, a sign of the refusal that man gives to the love of God.

On the one hand, in fact, there is a more lively awareness of personal freedom and greater attention to the quality of interpersonal relationships in marriage, in promoting the dignity of women, to responsible procreation, to the education of children. There is also an awareness of the need for the development of interfamily relationships, for reciprocal spiritual and material assistance, the rediscovery of the ecclesial mission proper to the family and its responsibility for the building of a more just society. On the other hand, however, signs are not lacking of a disturbing degradation of some fundamental values: a mistaken theoretical and practical concept of the independence of the spouses in relation to each other; serious misconceptions regarding the relationship of authority between parents and children; the concrete difficulties that the family itself experiences in the transmission of values; the growing number of divorces; the scourge of abortion; the ever more frequent recourse to sterilization; the appearance of a truly contraceptive mentality.

At the root of these negative phenomena there frequently lies a corruption of the idea and the experience of freedom, conceived not as a capacity for realizing the truth of God's plan for marriage and the family, but as an autonomous power of self-affirmation, often against others, for one's own selfish well-being.

Worthy of our attention also is the fact that in the countries of the so-called Third World, families often lack both the means necessary for survival, such as food, work, housing and medicine, and the most elementary freedoms. In the richer countries, on the contrary, excessive prosperity and the consumer mentality, paradoxically joined to a certain anguish and uncertainty about the future, deprive married couples of the generosity and courage needed for raising up new human life: Thus life is often perceived not as a blessing, but as a danger from which to defend oneself.

The historical situation in which the family lives therefore appears as an interplay of light and darkness.

This shows that history is not simply a fixed progression toward what is better, but rather an event of freedom, and even a struggle between freedoms that are in mutual conflict, that is, according to the well-known expression of St. Augustine, a conflict between two loves: the love of God to the point of disregarding self, and the love of self to the point of disregarding God.[16]

It follows that only an education for love rooted in faith can lead to the capacity of interpreting "the signs of the times," which are the historical expression of this twofold love.

7. The Influence of Circumstances on the Consciences of the Faithful

Living in such a world, under the pressures coming above all from the mass media, the faithful do not always remain immune from the obscuring of certain fundamental values, nor set themselves up as the critical conscience of family culture and as active agents in the building of an authentic family humanism.

Among the more troubling signs of this phenomenon, the synod fathers stressed the following, in particular: the spread of divorce and of recourse to a new union, even on the part of the faithful; the acceptance of purely civil marriage in contradiction to the vocation of the baptized to "be married in the Lord"; the celebration of the marriage sacrament without living faith, but for other motives; the rejection of the moral norms that guide and promote the human and Christian exercise of sexuality in marriage.

8. Our Age Needs Wisdom

The whole church is obliged to a deep reflection and commitment, so that the new culture now emerging may be evangelized in depth, true values acknowledged, the rights of men and women defended and justice promoted in the very structures of society. In this way the "new humanism" will not distract people from their relationship with God, but will lead them to it more fully.

Science and its technical applications offer new and immense possibilities in the construction of such a humanism. Still, as a consequence of political choices that decide the direction of research and its applications, science is often used against its original purpose, which is the advancement of the human person.

It becomes necessary, therefore, on the part of all to recover an awareness of the primacy of moral values, which are the values of the human person as such. The great task that has to be faced today for the renewal of society is that of recapturing the ultimate meaning of life and its fundamental values. Only an awareness of the primacy of these values enables man to use the immense possibilities given him by science

6

in such a way as to bring about the true advancement of the human person in his or her whole truth, in his or her freedom and dignity. Science is called to ally itself with wisdom.

The following words of the Second Vatican Council can therefore be applied to the problems of the family: "Our era needs such wisdom more than bygone ages if the discoveries made by man are to be further humanized. For the future of the world stands in peril unless wiser people are forthcoming." [17]

The education of the moral conscience, which makes every human being capable of judging and of discerning the proper ways to achieve self-realization according to his or her original truth, thus becomes a pressing requirement that cannot be renounced.

Modern culture must be led to a more profoundly restored covenant with divine wisdom. Every man is given a share of such wisdom through the creating action of God. And it is only in faithfulness to this covenant that the families of today will be in a position to influence positively the building of a more just and fraternal world.

9. Gradualness and Conversion

To the injustice originating from sin—which has profoundly penetrated the structures of today's world—and often hindering the family's full realization of itself and of its fundamental rights, we must all set ourselves in opposition through a conversion of mind and heart, following Christ crucified by denying our own selfishness: Such a conversion cannot fail to have a beneficial and renewing influence even on the structures of society.

What is needed is a continuous, permanent conversion which, while requiring an interior detachment from every evil and an adherence to good in its fullness, is brought about concretely in steps which lead us ever forward. Thus a dynamic process develops, one which advances gradually with the progressive integration of the gifts of God and the demands of his definitive and absolute love in the entire personal and social life of man. Therefore an educational growth process is necessary in order that individual believers, families and peoples, even civilization itself, by beginning from what they have already received of the mystery of Christ, may patiently be led forward, arriving at a richer understanding and a fuller integration of this mystery in their lives.

7

10. Inculturation

In conformity with her constant tradition, the church receives from the various cultures everything that is able to express better the unsearchable riches of Christ.[18] Only with the help of all the cultures will it be possible for these riches to be manifested ever more clearly and for the church to progress toward a daily, more complete and profound awareness of the truth, which has already been given to her in its entirety by the Lord.

Holding fast to the two principles of the compatibility with the Gospel of the various cultures to be taken up and of communion with the universal church, there must be further study, particularly by the episcopal conferences and the appropriate departments of the Roman Curia, and greater pastoral diligence so that this "inculturation" of the Christian faith may come about ever more extensively in the context of marriage and the family as well as in other fields.

It is by means of "inculturation" that one proceeds toward the full restoration of the covenant with the wisdom of God, which is Christ himself. The whole church will be enriched also by the cultures which, though lacking technology, abound in human wisdom and are enlivened by profound moral values.

So that the goal of this journey might be clear and consequently the way plainly indicated, the synod was right to begin by considering in depth the original design of God for marriage and the family: It "went back to the beginning," in deference to the teaching of Christ.[19]

PART TWO
THE PLAN OF GOD FOR MARRIAGE
AND THE FAMILY

11. Man, the Image of the God Who Is Love

God created man in his own image and likeness:[20] calling him to existence through love, he called him at the same time for love.

God is love[21] and in himself he lives a mystery of personal loving communion. Creating the human race in his own image and continually keeping it in being. God inscribed in the humanity of man and woman the vocation, and thus the capacity and responsibility, of love and communion.[22] Love is therefore the fundamental and innate vocation of every human being.

As an incarnate spirit, that is, a soul which expresses itself in a body and a body informed by an immortal spirit, man is called to love in his unified totality. Love includes the human body, and the body is made a sharer in spiritual love.

Christian revelation recognizes two specific ways of realizing the vocation of the human person, in its entirety, to love: marriage and virginity or celibacy. Either one is in its own proper form an actuation of the most profound truth of man, of his being "created in the image of God."

Consequently sexuality, by means of which man and woman give themselves to one another through the acts which are proper and exclusive to spouses, is by no means something purely biological, but concerns the innermost being of the human person as such. It is realized in a truly human way only if it is an integral part of the love by which a man and a woman commit themselves totally to one another until death. The total physical self-giving would be a lie if it were not the sign and fruit of a total personal self-giving, in which the whole person, including the temporal dimension, is present: If the person were to withhold something or reserve the possibility of deciding otherwise in the future, by this very fact he or she would not be giving totally.

This totality which is required by conjugal love also corresponds to the demands of responsible fertility. This fertility is directed to the generation of a human being, and so by its nature it surpasses the purely biological order and involves a whole series of personal values. For the harmonious growth of these values a persevering and unified contribution by both parents is necessary.

The only "place" in which this self-giving in its whole truth is made possible is marriage, the covenant of conjugal love freely and consciously chosen, whereby man and woman accept the intimate community of life and love willed by God himself,[23] which only in this light manifests its true meaning. The institution of marriage is not an undue interference by society or authority, nor the extrinsic imposition of a form. Rather, it is an interior requirement of the covenant of conjugal love which is publicly affirmed as unique and exclusive in order to live in complete fidelity to the plan of God, the creator. A person's freedom, far from being restricted by this fidelity, is secured against every form of subjectivism or relativism and is made a sharer in creative wisdom.

12. Marriage and Communion Between God and People

The communion of love between God and people, a fundamental part of the revelation and faith experience of Israel, finds a meaningful expression in the marriage covenant which is established between a man and a woman.

For this reason the central word of revelation, "God loves his people," is likewise proclaimed through the living and concrete word whereby a man and a woman express their conjugal love. Their bond of love becomes the image and the symbol of the covenant which unites god and his people.[24] And the same sin which can harm the conjugal covenant becomes an image of the infidelity of the people to their God: Idolatry is prostitution,[25] infidelity is adultery, disobedience to the law is abandonment of the spousal love of the Lord. But the infidelity of Israel does not destroy the eternal fidelity of the Lord, and therefore the ever faithful love of God is put forward as the model of the relations of faithful love which should exist between spouses.[26]

13. Jesus Christ, Bridegroom of the Church, and the Sacrament of Matrimony

The communion between God and his people finds its definitive fulfillment in Jesus Christ, the bridegroom who loves and gives himself as the savior of humanity, uniting it to himself as his body.

He reveals the original truth of marriage, the truth of the "beginning,"[27] and, freeing man from his hardness of heart, he makes man capable of realizing this truth in its entirety.

This revelation reaches its definitive fullness in the gift of love which the word of God makes to humanity in assuming a human nature, and

10

in the sacrifice which Jesus Christ makes of himself on the cross for his bride, the church. In this sacrifice there is entirely revealed that plan which God has imprinted on the humanity of man and woman since their creation,[28] the marriage of baptized persons thus becomes a real symbol of that new and eternal covenant sanctioned in the blood of Christ. The Spirit which the Lord pours forth gives a new heart, and renders man and woman capable of loving one another as Christ has loved us. Conjugal love reaches that fullness to which it is interiorly ordained, conjugal charity, which is the proper and specific way in which the spouses participate in and are called to live the very charity of Christ, who gave himself on the cross.

In a deservedly famous page, Tertullian has well expressed the greatness of this conjugal life in Christ and its beauty: "How can I ever express the happiness of the marriage that is joined together by the church, strengthened by an offering, sealed by a blessing, announced by angels and ratified by the Father? !!! How wonderful the bond between two believers, with a single hope, a single desire, a single observance, a single service! They are both brethren and both fellow servants; there is no separation between them in spirit or flesh. In fact they are truly two in one flesh, and where the flesh is one, one is the spirit.''[29]

Receiving and meditating faithfully on the word of God, the church has solemnly taught and continued to teach that the marriage of the baptized is one of the seven sacraments of the new covenant.[30]

Indeed by means of baptism, man and woman are definitively placed within the new and eternal covenant, in the spousal covenant of Christ with the church. And it is because of this indestructible insertion that the intimate community of conjugal life and love, founded by the creator,[31] is elevated and assumed into the spousal charity of Christ, sustained and enriched by his redeeming power.

By virtue of the sacramentality of their marriage, spouses are bound to one another in the most profoundly indissoluble manner. Their belonging to each other is the real representation, by means of the sacramental sign, of the very relationship of Christ with the church.

Spouses are therefore the permanent reminder to the church of what happened on the cross; they are for one another and for the children witnesses to the salvation in which the sacrament makes them sharers. Of this salvation event marriage, like every sacrament, is a memorial, actuation and prophecy:

"As a memorial, the sacrament gives them the grace and duty of commemorating the great works of God and of bearing witness to them before their children. As actuation, it gives them the grace and duty of putting into practice in the present, toward each other and their children, the demands of a love which forgives and redeems. As prophecy, it gives them the grace and duty of living and bearing witness to the hope of the future encounter with Christ." [32]

Like each of the seven sacraments, so also marriage is a real symbol of the event of salvation, but in its own way.

"The spouses participate in it as spouses, together, as a couple, so that the first and immediate effect of marriage (*res et sacramentum*) is not supernatural grace itself, but the Christian conjugal bond, a typically Christian communion of two persons because it represents the mystery of Christ's incarnation and the mystery of his covenant. The content of participation in Christ's life is also specific: Conjugal love involves a totality, in which all the elements of the person enter—appeal of the body and instinct, power of feeling and affectivity, aspiration of the spirit and of will. It aims at a deeply personal unity, the unity that, beyond union in one flesh, leads to forming one heart and soul; it demands indissolubility and faithfulness in definitive mutual giving; and it is open to fertility (cf. *Humanae Vitae,* 9). In a word, it is a question of the normal characteristics of all natural conjugal love, but with a new significance which not only purifies and strengthens them, but raises them to the extent of making them the expression of specifically Christian values." [33]

14. Children, the Precious Gift of Marriage

According to the plan of God, marriage is the foundation of the wider community of the family, since the very institution of marriage and conjugal love is ordained to the procreation and education of children, in whom it finds its crowning. [34]

In its most profound reality, love is essentially a gift; and conjugal love, while leading the spouses to the reciprocal "knowledge" which makes them "one flesh," [35] does not end with the couple, because it makes them capable of the greatest possible gift, the gift by which they become cooperators with God for giving life to a new human person. Thus the couple, while giving themselves to one another, give not just themselves but also the reality of children, who are a living reflection of their love, a permanent sign of conjugal unity and a living and inseparable synthesis of their being a father and a mother.

When they become parents, spouses receive from God the gift of a new responsibility. Their parental love is called to become for the children the visible sign of the very love of God, "from whom every family in heaven and on earth is named." [36]

It must not be forgotten however that, even when procreation is not possible, conjugal life does not for this reason lose its value. Physical sterility in fact, can be for spouses the occasion for other important services to the life of the human person, for example, adoption, various forms of educational work, and assistance to other families and to poor or handicapped children.

15. The Family, a Communion of Persons

In matrimony and in the family a complex of interpersonal relationships is set up—married life, fatherhood and motherhood, filiation and fraternity—through which each human person is introduced into the "human family" and into the "family of God," which is the church.

Christian marriage and the Christian family build up the church: for in the family the human person is not only brought into being and progressively introduced by means of education into the human community, but by means of the rebirth of baptism and education in the faith the child is also introduced into God's family, which is the church.

The human family, disunited by sin, is reconstituted in its unity by the redemptive power of the death and resurrection of Christ.[37] Christian marriage, by participating in the salvific efficacy of this event, constitutes the natural setting in which the human person is introduced into the great family of the church.

The commandment to grow and multiply, given to man and woman in the beginning, in this way reaches its whole truth and full realization.

The church thus finds in the family, born from the sacrament, the cradle and the setting in which she can enter the human generations and where these in their turn can enter the church.

16. Marriage and Virginity or Celibacy

Virginity or celibacy for the sake of the kingdom of God not only does not contradict the dignity of marriage but presupposes it and confirms it. Marriage and virginity or celibacy are two ways of expressing and living the one mystery of the covenant of God with his people.

When marriage is not esteemed, neither can consecrated virginity or celibacy exist; when human sexuality is not regarded as a great value given by the creator, the renunciation of it for the sake of the kingdom of heaven loses its meaning.

Rightly indeed does St. John Chrysostom say:

"Whoever denigrates marriage also diminishes the glory of virginity. Whoever praises it makes virginity more admirable and resplendent. What appears good only in comparison with evil would not be particularly good. It is something better than what is admitted to be good that is the most excellent good." [38]

In virginity or celibacy, the human being is awaiting, also in a bodily way, the eschatological marriage of Christ with the church, giving himself or herself completely to the church in the hope that Christ may give himself to the church in the full truth of eternal life. The celibate person thus anticipates in his or her flesh the new world of the future resurrection. [39]

By virtue of this witness, virginity or celibacy keeps alive in the church a consicousness of the mystery of marriage and defends it from any reduction and impoverishment.

Virginity or celibacy, by liberating the human heart in a unique way, [40] "so as to make it burn with greater love for God and all humanity," [41] bears witness that the kingdom of God and his justice is that pearl of great price which is preferred to every other value no matter how great, and hence must be sought as the only definitive value. It is for this reason that the church throughout her history has always defended the superiority of this charism to that of marriage, by reason of the wholly singular link which it has with the kingdom of God. [42]

In spite of having renounced physical fecundity, the celibate person becomes spiritually fruitful, the father and mother of many, cooperating in the realization of the family according to God's plan.

Christian couples therefore have the right to expect from celibate persons a good example and a witness of fidelity to their vocation until death. Just as fidelity at times becomes difficult for married people and requires sacrifice, mortification and self-denial, the same can happen to celibate persons, and their fidelity, even in the trials that may occur, should strengthen the fidelity of married couples. [43]

These reflections on virginity or celibacy can enlighten and help those who, for reasons independent of their own will, have been unable to marry and have then accepted their situation in a spirit of service.

14

PART THREE
THE ROLE OF THE CHRISTIAN FAMILY

17. Family, Become What You Are

The family finds in the plan of God the creator and redeemer not only its identity, what it is, but also its mission, what it can and should do. The role that God calls the family to perform in history derives from what the family is; its role represents the dynamic and existential development of what it is. Each family finds within itself a summons that cannot be ignored and that specifies both its dignity and its responsibility: Family, become what you are.

Accordingly, the family must go back to the "beginning" of God's creative act if it is to attain self-knowledge and self-realization in accordance with the inner truth not only of what it is, but also of what it does in history. And since in God's plan it has been established as an "intimate community of life and love," [44] the family has the mission to become more and more what it is, that is to say, a community of life and love in an effort that will find fulfillment, as will everything created and redeemed, in the kingdom of God. Looking at it in such a way as to reach its very roots, we must say that the essence and role of the family are in the final analysis specified by love. Hence the family has the mission to guard, reveal and communicate love, and this is a living reflection of and a real sharing in God's love for humanity and the love of Christ the Lord for the church, his bride.

Every particular task of the family is an expression and concrete actuation of that fundamental mission. We must therefore go deeper into the unique riches of the family's mission and probe its contents, which are both manifold and unified.

Thus, with love as its point of departure and making constant reference to it, the recent synod emphasized four general tasks for the family:

    I. Forming a community of persons;
    II. Serving life;
    III. Participating in the development of society;
    IV. Sharing in the life and mission of the church.

I. FORMING A COMMUNITY OF PERSONS

18. Love as the principle and power of communion

The family, which is founded and given life by love, is a community of persons: of husband and wife, of parents and children, of relatives. Its first task is to live with fidelity the reality of communion in a constant effort to develop an authentic community of persons.

The inner principle of that task, its permanent power and its final goal, is love: Without love the family is not a community of persons and, in the same way, without love the family cannot live, grow and perfect itself as a community of persons. What I wrote in the encyclical *Redemptor Hominis* applies primarily and especially within the family as such: "Man cannot live without love. He remains a being that is incomprehensible for himself, his life is senseless, if love is not revealed to him, if he does not encounter love, if he does not experience it and make it his own, if he does not participate intimately in it."[45]

The love between husband and wife and, in a derivatory and broader way, the love between members of the same family—between parents and children, brothers and sisters and relatives and members of the household—is given life and sustenance by an unceasing inner dynamism leading the family to ever deeper and more intense communion, which is the foundation and soul of the community of marriage and the family.

19. The indivisible unity of conjugal communion

The first communion is the one which is established and which develops between husband and wife: By virtue of the covenant of married life, the man and woman "are no longer two but one flesh"[46] and they are called to grow continually in their communion through day-to-day fidelity to their marriage promise of total mutual self-giving.

This conjugal communion sinks its roots in the natural complementarity that exists between man and woman and is nurtured through the personal willingness of the spouses to share their entire life project, what they have and what they are: For this reason such communion is the fruit and the sign of a profoundly human need. But in the Lord Christ God takes up this human need, confirms it, purifies it and elevates it, leading it to perfection through the sacrament of matrimony: the Holy Spirit who is poured out in the sacramental celebration offers Christian couples the gift of a new communion of love that is the living and real image of that unique unity which makes of the church the indivisible mystical body of the Lord Jesus.

The gift of the spirit is a commandment of life for Christian spouses and at the same time a stimulating impulse so that every day they may progress toward an ever richer union with each other on all levels—of the body, of the character, of the heart, of the intelligence and will, of the soul[47]—revealing in this way to the church and to the world the new communion of love, given by the grace of Christ.

Such a communion is radically contradicted by polygamy: This, in fact, directly negates the plan of God which was revealed from the beginning, because it is contrary to the equal personal dignity of men and women, who in matrimony give themselves with a love that is total and therefore unique and exclusive. As the Second Vatican Council writes: "Firmly established by the Lord, the unity of marriage will radiate from the equal personal dignity of husband and wife, a dignity acknowledged by mutual and total love."[48]

20. An indissoluble communion

Conjugal communion is characterized not only by its unity, but also by its indissolubility: "As a mutual gift of two persons, this intimate union, as well as the good of children, imposes total fidelity on the spouses and argues for an unbreakable oneness between them."[49]

It is a fundamental duty of the church to reaffirm strongly, as the synod fathers did, the doctrine of the indissolubility of marriage. To all those who in our times consider it too difficult or indeed impossible to be bound to one person for the whole of life, and to those caught up in a culture that rejects the indissolubility of marriage and openly mocks the commitment of spouses to fidelity, it is necessary to reconfirm the good news of the definitive nature of that conjugal love that has in Christ its foundation and strength.[50]

Being rooted in the personal and total self-giving of the couple and being required by the good of the children, the indissolubility of marriage finds its ultimate truth in the plan that God has manifested in his revelation: He wills and he communicates the indissolubility of marriage as a fruit, a sign and a requirement of the absolutely faithful love that God has for man and that the Lord Jesus has for the church.

Christ renews the first plan that the creator inscribed in the hearts of man and woman, and in the celebration of the sacrament of matrimony offers "a new heart": thus the couples are not only able to overcome "hardness of heart,"[51] but also, and above all, they are able to share the full and definitive love of Christ, the new and eternal covenant made flesh. Just as the Lord Jesus is the "faithful witness,"[52] the "yes" of the promises of God[53] and thus the supreme realization of the unconditional faithfulness with which God loves his people, so Christian couples are called to participate truly in the irrevocable indissolubility that binds Christ to the church, his bride, loved by him to the end.[54]

The gift of the sacrament is at the same time a vocation and commandment for the Christian spouses, that they may remain faithful to each other forever, beyond every trial and difficulty, in generous obedience to the holy will of the Lord: "What therefore God has joined together, let not man put asunder."[55]

To bear witness to the inestimable value of the indissolubility and fidelity of marriage is one of the most precious and most urgent tasks of Christian couples in our time. So, with all my brothers who participated in the Synod of Bishops, I praise and encourage those numerous couples who, though encountering no small difficulty, preserve and develop the value of indissolubility: Thus in a humble and courageous manner they perform the role committed to them of being in the world a "sign"—a small and precious sign, sometimes also subjected to temptation, but always renewed—of the unfailing fidelity with which God and Jesus Christ love each and every human being. But it is also proper to recognize the value of the witness of those spouses who, even when abandoned by their partner, with the strength of faith and of Christian hope have not entered a new union: These spouses too give an authentic witness to fidelity, of which the world today has a great need. For this reason they must be encouraged and helped by the pastors and the faithful of the church.

21. The broader communion of the family

Conjugal communion constitutes the foundation on which is built the broader communion of the family, of parents and children, of brothers and sisters with each other, of relatives and other members of the household.

This communion is rooted in the natural bonds of flesh and blood and grows to its specifically human perfection with the establishment and maturing of the still deeper and richer bonds of the spirit: The love that animates the interpersonal relationships of the different members of the family constitutes the interior strength that shapes and animates the family communion and community.

18

The Christian family is also called to experience a new and original communion which confirms and perfects natural and human communion. In fact the grace of Jesus Christ, "the firstborn among many brethren,"[56] is by its nature and interior dynamism "a grace of brotherhood," as St. Thomas Aquinas calls it.[57] The Holy Spirit, who is poured forth in the celebration of the sacraments, is the living source and inexhaustible sustenance of the supernatural communion that gathers believers and links them with Christ and with each other in the unity of the church of God. The Christian family constitutes a specific revelation and realization of ecclesial communion, and for this reason too it can and should be called "the domestic church."[58]

All members of the family, each according to his or her own gift, have the grace and responsibility of building day by day the communion of persons, making the family "a school of deeper humanity":[59] This happens where there is care and love for the little ones, the sick, the aged; where there is mutual service every day; when there is a sharing of goods, of joys and of sorrows.

A fundamental opportunity for building such a communion is constituted by the educational exchange between parents and children,[60] in which each gives and receives. By means of love, respect and obedience toward their parents, children offer their specific and irreplaceable contribution to the construction of an authentically human and Christian family.[61] They will be aided in this if parents exercise their unrenounceable authority as a true and proper "ministry," that is, as a service to the human and Christian well-being of their children and in particular as a service aimed at helping them acquire a truly responsible freedom, and if parents maintain a living awareness of the "gift" they continually receive from their children.

Family communion can only be preserved and perfected through a great spirit of sacrifice. It requires, in fact, a ready and generous openness of each and all to understanding, to forbearance, to pardon, to reconciliation. There is no family that does not know how selfishness, discord, tension and conflict violently attack and at times mortally wound its own communion: Hence there arise the many and varied forms of division in family life. But, at the same time, every family is called by the God of peace to have the joyous and renewing experience of "reconciliation," that is, communion re-established, unity restored. In particular, participation in the sacrament of reconciliation and in the banquet of the one body of Christ offers to the Christian family the

19

grace and the responsibility of overcoming every division and of moving toward the fullness of communion willed by God, responding in this way to the ardent desire of the Lord: "that they may be one." [62]

22. The rights and role of women

In that it is, and ought always to become, a communion and community of persons, the family finds in love the source and the constant impetus for welcoming, respecting and promoting each one of its members in his or her lofty dignity as a person, that is, as a living image of God. As the synod fathers rightly stated, the moral criterion for the authenticity of conjugal and family relationships consists in fostering the dignity and vocation of the individual persons, who achieve their fullness by sincere self-giving. [63]

In this perspective the synod devoted special attention to women, to their rights and role within the family and society. In the same perspective are also to be considered men as husbands and fathers, and likewise children and the elderly.

Above all it is important to underline the equal dignity and responsibility of women with men. This equality is realized in a unique manner in that reciprocal self-giving by each one to the other and by both to the children which is proper to marriage and the family. What human reason intuitively perceives and acknowledges is fully revealed by the word of God: The history of salvation, in fact, is a continuous and luminous testimony to the dignity of women.

In creating the human race "male and female," [64] God gives man and woman an equal personal dignity, endowing them with the inalienable rights and responsibilities proper to the human person. God then manifests the dignity of women in the highest form possible, by assuming human flesh from the Virgin Mary, whom the church honors as the mother of God, calling her the new Eve and presenting her as the model of redeemed woman. The sensitive respect of Jesus toward the women that he called to his following and his friendship, his appearing on Easter morning to a woman before the other disciples, the mission entrusted to women to carry the good news of the resurrection to the apostles—these are all signs that confirm the special esteem of the Lord Jesus for women. The apostle Paul will say: "In Christ Jesus you are all children of God through faith . . . There is neither slave nor free, there is neither male nor female; for you are all one in Christ Jesus." [65]

23. Women and society

Without intending to deal with all the various aspects of the vast and complex theme of the relationships between women and society and limiting these remarks to a few essential points, one cannot but observe that in the specific area of family life a widespread social and cultural tradition has considered women's role to be exclusively that of wife and mother, without adequate access to public functions, which have generally been reserved for men.

There is no doubt that the equal dignity and responsibility of men and women fully justifies women's access to public functions. On the other hand the true advancement of women requires that clear recognition be given to the value of their maternal and family role, by comparison with all other public roles and all other professions. Furthermore, these roles and professions should be harmoniously combined if we wish the evolution of society and culture to be truly and fully human.

This will come about more easily if, in accordance with the wishes expressed by the synod, a renewed "theology of work" can shed light upon and study in depth the meaning of work in the Christian life and determine the fundamental bond between work and the family, and therefore the original and irreplaceable meaning of work in the home be recognized and respected by all in its irreplaceable value.

This is of particular importance in education: For possible discrimination between the different types of work and professions is eliminated at its very root once it is clear that all people in every area are working with equal rights and equal responsibilities. The image of God in man and in woman will thus be seen with added luster.

While it must be recognized that women have the same right as men to perform various public functions, society must be structured in such a way that wives and mothers are not in practice compelled to work outside the home, and that their families can live and prosper in a dignified way even when they themselves devote their full time to their own family.

Furthermore, the mentality which honors women more for their work outside the home than for their work within the family must be overcome. This requires that men should truly esteem and love women with total respect for their personal dignity, and that society should create and develop conditions favoring work in the home.

With due respect to the different vocations of men and women, the church must in her own life promote as far as possible their equality of rights and dignity: and this for the good of all, the family, the church and society.

But clearly all of this does not mean for women a renunciation of their femininity or an imitation of the male role, but the fullness of true feminine humanity which should be expressed in their activity, whether in the family or outside of it, without disregarding the differences of customs and cultures in this sphere.

24. Offenses against women's dignity

Unfortunately the Christian message about the dignity of women is contradicted by that persistent mentality which considers the human being not as a person but as a thing, as an object of trade, at the service of selfish interest and mere pleasure: The first victims of this mentality are women.

This mentality produces very bitter fruits, such as contempt for men and for women, slavery, oppression of the weak, pornography, prostitution—especially in an organized form—and all those various forms of discrimination that exist in the fields of education, employment, wages, etc.

Besides, many forms of degrading discrimination still persist today in a great part of our society that affect and seriously harm particular categories of women, as for example childless wives, widows, separated or divorced women, and unmarried mothers.

The synod fathers deplored these and other forms of discrimination as strongly as possible. I therefore ask that vigorous and incisive pastoral action be taken by all to overcome them definitively so that the image of God that shines in all human beings without exception may be fully respected.

25. Men as husbands and fathers

Within the conjugal and family communion-community, the man is called upon to live his gift and role as husband and father.

In his wife he sees the fulfillment of God's intention: "It is not good that the man should be alone; I will make him a helper fit for him," [67] and he makes his own the cry of Adam, the first husband: "This at last is bone of my bones and flesh of my flesh." [68]

Authentic conjugal love presupposes and requires that a man have a profound respect for the equal dignity of his wife: "You are not her master," writes St. Ambrose, "but her husband; she was not given to you to be your slave, but your wife. ... Reciprocate her attentiveness to you and be grateful to her for her love."[69] With his wife a man should live "a very special form of personal friendship."[70] As for the Christian, he is called upon to develop a new attitude of love, manifesting toward his wife a charity that is both gentle and strong like that which Christ has for the church.[71]

Love for his wife as mother of their children and love for the children themselves are for the man the natural way of understanding and fulfilling his own fatherhood. Above all where social and cultural conditions so easily encourage a father to be less concerned with his family or at any rate less involved in the work of education, efforts must be made to restore socially the conviction that the place and task of the father in and for the family is of unique and irreplaceable importance.[72] As experience teaches, the absence of a father causes psychological and moral imbalance and notable difficulties in family relationships, as does, in contrary circumstances, the oppressive presence of a father, especially where there still prevails the phenomenon of "machismo," or a wrong superiority of male prerogatives which humiliates women and inhibits the development of healthy family relationships.

In revealing and in reliving on earth the very fatherhood of God,[73] a man is called upon to ensure the harmonious and united development of all the members of the family: He will perform this task by exercising generous responsibility for the life conceived under the heart of the mother, by a more solicitous commitment to education, a task he shares with his wife,[74] by work which is never a cause of division in the family but promotes its unity and stability, and by means of the witness he gives of an adult Christian life which effectively introduces the children into the living experience of Christ and the church.

26. The rights of children

In the family, which is a community of persons, special attention must be devoted to the children by developing a profound esteem for their personal dignity and a great respect and generous concern for their rights. This is true for every child, but it becomes all the more urgent the smaller the child is and the more it is in need of everything, when it is sick, suffering or handicapped.

By fostering and exercising a tender and strong concern for every child that comes into this world, the church fulfills a fundamental mission: for she is called upon to reveal and put forward anew in history the example and the commandment of Christ the Lord, who placed the child at the heart of the kingdom of God: "Let the children come to me, and do not hinder them, for to such belongs the kingdom of heaven." [75]

I repeat once again what I said to the General Assembly of the United Nations Oct. 2, 1979:

"I wish to express the joy that we all find in children, the springtime of life, the anticipation of the future history of each of our present earthly homelands. No country on earth, no political system can think of its own future otherwise than through the image of these new generations that will receive from their parents the manifold heritage of values, duties and aspirations of the nation to which they belong and of the whole human family. Concern for the child, even before birth, from the first moment of conception and then throughout the years of infancy and youth, is the primary and fundamental test of the relationship of one human being to another. And so, what better wish can I express for every nation and for the whole of mankind, and for all the children of the world than a better future in which respect for human rights will become a complete reality throughout the third millennium, which is drawing near." [76]

Acceptance, love, esteem, many-sided and united material, emotional, educational and spiritual concern for every child that comes into this world should always constitute a distinctive, essential characteristic of all Christians, in particular of the Christian family: Thus children, while they are able to grow "in wisdom and in stature, and in favor with God and man," [77] offer their own precious contribution to building up the family community and even to the sanctification of their parents. [78]

27. The elderly in the family

There are cultures which manifest a unique veneration and great love for the elderly: Far from being outcasts from the family or merely tolerated as a useless burden, they continue to be present and to take an active and responsible part in family life, though having to respect the autonomy of the new family, above all they carry out the important mission of being a witness to the past and a source of wisdom for the young and for the future.

24

Other cultures, however, especially in the wake of disordered industrial and urban development, have both in the past and in the present set the elderly aside in unacceptable ways. This causes acute suffering to them and spiritually impoverishes many families.

The pastoral activity of the church must help everyone to discover and to make good use of the role of the elderly within the civil and ecclesial community, in particular within the family. In fact, "the life of the aging helps to clarify a scale of human values; it shows the continuity of generations and marvelously demonstrates the interdependence of God's people. The elderly often have the charism to bridge generation gaps before they are made: How many children have found understanding and love in the eyes and words and caresses of the aging! And how many old people have willingly subscribed to the inspired word that the 'crown of the aged is their children's children' (Prv. 17:6)!" [79]

II. SERVING LIFE

A. *The transmission of life*

28. Cooperators in the love of God the creator

With the creation of man and woman in his own image and likeness, God crowns and brings to perfection the work of his hands: He calls them to a special sharing in his love and in his power as creator and Father through their free and responsible cooperation in transmitting the gift of human life: "God blessed them, and God said to them, 'be fruitful and multiply, and fill the earth and subdue it.'" [80]

Thus the fundamental task of the family is to serve life, to actualize in history the original blessing of the creator—that of transmitting by procreation the divine image from person to person. [81]

Fecundity is the fruit and the sign of conjugal love, the living testimony of the full reciprocal self-giving of the spouses: "While not making the other purposes of matrimony of less account, the true practice of conjugal love, and the whole meaning of the family life which results from it, have this aim: that the couple be ready with stout hearts to cooperate with the love of the creator and the savior, who through them will enlarge and enrich his own family day by day." [82]

However, the fruitfulness of conjugal love is not restricted solely to the procreation of children, even understood in its specifically human dimension: It is enlarged and enriched by all those fruits of moral, spiritual and supernatural life which the father and mother are called to hand on to their children, and through the children to the church and to the world.

29. The church's teaching and norm, always old yet always new

Precisely because the love of husband and wife is a unique participation in the mystery of life and of the love of God himself, the church knows that she has received the special mission of guarding and protecting the lofty dignity of marriage and the most serious responsibility of the transmission of human life.

Thus, in continuity with the living tradition of the ecclesial community throughout history, the recent Second Vatican Council and the magisterium of my predecessor Paul VI, expressed above all in the encyclical *Humanae Vitae,* have handed on to our times a truly prophetic proclamation, which reaffirms and reproposes with clarity the church's teaching and norm, always old yet always new, regarding marriage and regarding the transmission of human life.

For this reason the synod fathers made the following declaration at their last assembly:

"This sacred synod, gathered together with the successor of Peter in the unity of faith, firmly holds what has been set forth in the Second Vatican Council (cf. *Gaudium et Spes,* 50) and afterward in the encyclical *Humanae Vitae,* particularly that love between husband and wife must be fully human, exclusive and open to new life (*Humanae Vitae,* 11: cf. 9, 12)."[83]

30. The church stands for life

The teaching of the church in our day is placed in a social and cultural context which renders it more difficult to understand and yet more urgent and irreplaceable for promoting the true good of men and women.

Scientific and technological progress, which contemporary man is continually expanding in his dominion over nature, not only offers the hope of creating a new and better humanity, but also causes ever greater anxiety regarding the future. Some ask themselves if it is a good thing to be alive or if it would be better never to have been born; they doubt therefore if it is right to bring others into life when perhaps they will curse their existence in a cruel world with unforeseeable terrors. Others consider themselves to be the only ones for whom the advantages of technology are intended and they exclude others by imposing on them contraceptives or even worse means. Still others imprisoned in a consumer mentality and whose sole concern is to bring about a continual growth of material goods, finish by ceasing to understand, and thus by refusing, the spiritual riches of a new human life. The ultimate reason for these mentalities is the absence in people's hearts of God, whose love alone is stronger than all the world's fears and can conquer them.

Thus an anti-life mentality is born, as can be seen in many current issues: One thinks, for example of a certain panic deriving from the studies of ecologists and futurologists on population growth, which sometimes exaggerate the danger of demographic increase to the quality of life.

But the church firmly believes that human life, even if weak and suffering, is always a splendid gift of God's goodness. Against the pessimism and selfishness which cast a shadow over the world, the church stands for life: In each human life she sees the splendor of that "yes," that "amen," who is Christ himself.[84] To the "no" which assails and afflicts the world, she replies with this living "yes," thus defending the human person and the world from all who plot against and harm life.

The church is called upon to manifest anew to everyone, with clear and stronger conviction, her will to promote human life by every means and to defend it against all attacks in whatever condition or state of development it is found.

Thus the church condemns as a grave offense against human dignity and justice all those activities of governments or other public authorities which attempt to limit in any way the freedom of couples in deciding about children. Consequently any violence applied by such authorities in favor of contraception or, still worse, of sterilization and procured abortion must be altogether condemned and forcefully rejected. Likewise to be denounced as gravely unjust are cases where in international relations economic help given for the advancement of peoples is made conditional on programs of contraception, sterilization and procured abortion.[85]

31. That God's design may be ever more completely fulfilled

The church is certainly aware of the many complex problems which couples in many countries face today in their task of transmitting life in a responsible way. She also recognizes the serious problem of population growth in the form it has taken in many parts of the world and its moral implications.

However, she holds that consideration in depth of all the aspects of these problems offers a new and stronger confirmation of the importance of the authentic teaching on birth regulation reproposed in the Second Vatican Council and in the encyclical *Humanae Vitae.*

For this reason, together with the synod fathers I feel it is my duty to extend a pressing invitation to theologians, asking them to unite their efforts in order to collaborate with the hierarchical magisterium and to commit themselves to the task of illustrating ever more clearly the biblical foundations, the ethical grounds and the personalistic reasons behind this doctrine. Thus it will be possible, in the context of an organic exposition, to render the teaching of the church on this fundamental question truly accessible to all people of good will, fostering a daily more enlightened and profound understanding of it. In this way God's plan will be ever more completely fulfilled for the salvation of humanity and for the glory of the Creator.

A united effort by theologians in this regard, inspired by a convinced adherence to the magisterium, which is the one authentic guide for the people of God, is particularly urgent for reasons that include the close link between Catholic teaching on this matter and the view of the human person that the church proposes: Doubt or error in the field of marriage or the family involves obscuring to a serious extent the integral truth about the human person in a cultural situation that is already so often confused and contradictory. In fulfillment of their specific role theologians are called upon to provide enlightenment and a deeper understanding, and their contribution is of incomparable value and represents a unique and highly meritorious service to the family and humanity.

32. In an integral vision of the human person and of his or her vocation

In the context of a culture which seriously distorts or entirely misinterprets the true meaning of human sexuality because it separates it from its essential reference to the person, the church more urgently feels how irreplaceable is her mission of presenting sexuality as a value and task of the whole person, created male and female in the image of God.

In this perspective the Second Vatican Council clearly affirmed that "when there is a question of harmonizing conjugal love with the responsible transmission of life, the moral aspect of any procedure does not depend solely on sincere intentions or on an evaluation of motives. It must be determined by objective standards. These, based on the nature of the human person and his or her acts, preserve the full sense of mutual self-giving and human procreation in the context of true love. Such a goal cannot be achieved unless the virtue of conjugal chastity is sincerely practiced."[86]

It is precisely by moving from "an integral vision of man and of his vocation, not only his natural and earthly, but also his supernatural and eternal vocation,"[87] that Paul VI affirmed that the teaching of the church "is founded upon the inseparable connection wiled by God and unable to be broken by man on his own initiative between the two meanings of the conjugal act: the unitive meaning and the procreative meaning."[88] And he concluded by re-emphasizing that there must be excluded as intrinsically immoral "every action which, either in anticipation of the conjugal act, or in its accomplishment, or in the development of its natural consequences, proposes, whether as an end or as a means, to render procreation impossible."[89]

When couples, by means of recourse to contraception, separate these two meanings that God the creator has inscribed in the being of man and woman and in the dynamism of their sexual communion, they act as "arbiters" of the divine plan and they "manipulate" and degrade human sexuality and with it themselves and their married partner by altering its value of "total" self-giving. Thus the innate language that expresses the total reciprocal self-giving of husband and wife is overlaid, through contraception, by an objectively contradictory language, namely, that of not giving oneself totally to the other. This leads not only to a positive refusal to be open to life, but also to a falsification of the inner truth of conjugal love, which is called upon to give itself in personal totality.

When, instead, by means of recourse to periods of infertility, the couple respect the inseparable connection between the unitive and procreative meanings of human sexuality, they are acting as "ministers" of God's plan and they "benefit from" their sexuality according to the original dynamism of "total" self-giving, without manipulation or alteration.[90]

In the light of the experience of many couples and of the data provided by the different human sciences, theological reflection is able to perceive and is called to study further the difference, both anthropological and moral, between contraception and recourse to the rhythm of the cycle: It is a difference which is much wider and deeper than is usually thought, one which involves in the final analysis two irreconcilable concepts of the human person and of human sexuality. The choice of the natural rhythms involves accepting the cycle of the person, that is, the woman, and thereby accepting dialogue, reciprocal respect, shared responsibility and self-control. To accept the cycle and to enter into dialogue means to recognize both the spiritual and corporal character of conjugal communion and to live personal love with its requirement of fidelity. In this context the couple comes to experience how conjugal communion is enriched with those values of tenderness and affection which constitute the inner soul of human sexuality in its physical dimension also. In this way sexuality is respected and promoted in its truly and fully human dimension and is never "used" as an "object" that, by breaking the personal unity of soul and body, strikes at God's creation itself at the level of the deepest interaction of nature and person.

33. The church as teacher and mother for couples in difficulty

In the field of conjugal morality the church is teacher and mother and acts as such.

As teacher, she never tires of proclaiming the moral norm that must guide the responsible transmission of life. The church is in no way the author or the arbiter of this norm. In obedience to the truth which is Christ, whose image is reflected in the nature and dignity of the human person, the church interprets the moral norm and proposes it to all people of good will without concealing its demands of radicalness and perfection.

As mother, the church is close to the many married couples who find themselves in difficulty over this important point of the moral life: She knows well their situation, which is often very arduous and at times truly tormented by difficulties of every kind, not only individual difficulties but social ones as well; she knows that many couples encounter difficulties not only in the concrete fulfillment of the moral norm but even in understanding its inherent values.

But it is one and the same church that is both teacher and mother. And so the church never ceases to exhort and encourage all to resolve whatever conjugal difficulties may arise without ever falsifying or compromising the truth: She is convinced that there can be no true contradiction between the divine law on transmitting life and that on fostering authentic married love.[91] Accordingly, the concrete pedagogy of the church must always remain linked with her doctrine and never be separated from it. With the same conviction as my predecessor, I therefore repeat: "To diminish in no way the saving teaching of Christ constitutes an eminent form of charity for souls."[92]

On the other hand, authentic ecclesial pedagogy displays its realism and wisdom only by making a tenacious and courageous effort to create and uphold all the human conditions—psychological, moral and spiritual—indispensable for understanding and living the moral value and norm.

There is no doubt that these conditions must include persistence and patience, humility and strength of mind, filial trust in God and in his grace, and frequent recourse to prayer and to the sacraments of the eucharist and of reconciliation.[93] Thus strengthened, Christian husbands and wives will be able to keep alive their awareness of the unique influence that the grace of the sacrament of marriage has on every aspect of married life including, therefore, their sexuality: The gift of the Spirit, accepted and responded to by husband and wife, helps them to live their human sexuality in accordance with God's plan and as a sign of the unitive and fruitful love of Christ for his church.

But the necessary conditions also include knowledge of the bodily aspect and the body's rhythms of fertility. Accordingly, every effort must be made to render such knowledge accessible to all married people and also to young adults before marriage through clear, timely and serious instruction and education given by married couples, doctors and experts. Knowledge must then lead to education in self-control: Hence the absolute necessity for the virtue of chastity and for permanent education in it. In the Christian view, chastity by no means signifies rejection of human sexuality or lack of esteem for it: Rather it signifies spiritual energy capable of defending love from the perils of selfishness and aggressiveness, and able to advance it toward its full realization.

With deeply wise and loving intuition, Paul VI was only voicing the experience of many married couples when he wrote in his encyclical:

"To dominate instinct by means of one's reason and free will undoubtedly requires ascetical practices, so that the affective manifestations of conjugal life may observe the correct order, in particular with regard to the observance of periodic continence. Yet this discipline which is proper to the purity of married couples, far from harming conjugal love, rather confers on it a higher human value. It demands continual effort, yet thanks to its beneficent influence husband and wife fully develop their personalities, being enriched with spiritual values. Such discipline bestows upon family life fruits of serenity and peace, and facilitates the solution of other problems; it favors attention for one's partner, helps both parties to drive out selfishness, the enemy of true love, and deepens their sense of responsibility. By its means, parents acquire the capacity of having a deeper and more efficacious influence on the education of their offspring." [94]

34. The moral progress of married people

It is always very important to have a right notion of the moral order, its values and its norms; and the importance is all the greater when the difficulties in the way or respecting them become more numerous and serious.

Since the moral order reveals and sets forth the plan of God the creator, for this very reason it cannot be something that harms man, something impersonal. On the contrary, by responding to the deepest demands of the human being created by God, it places itself at the service of that person's full humanity with the delicate and binding love whereby God himself inspires, sustains and guides every creature toward its happiness.

But man, who has been called to live God's wise and loving design in a responsible manner, is an historical being who day by day builds himself up through his many free decisions; and so he knows, loves and accomplishes moral good by stages of growth.

Married people too are called upon to progress unceasingly in their moral life with the support of a sincere and active desire to gain ever better knowledge of the values enshrined in and fostered by the law of God. They must also be supported by an upright and generous willingness to embody these values in their concrete decisions. They cannot, however, look on the law as merely an ideal to be achieved in the future: They must consider it as a command of Christ the Lord to overcome difficulties with constancy. "And so what is known as 'the law of gradualness' or step-by-step advance cannot be identified with 'gradualness of the law,' as if there were different degrees or forms of precept in God's law for different individuals and situations. In God's plan, all husbands and wives are called in marriage to holiness, and this lofty vocation is fulfilled to the extent that the human person is able to respond to God's command with serene confidence in God's grace and in his or her own will.'' [95] On the same lines, it is part of the church's pedagogy that husbands and wives should first of all recognize clearly the teaching of *Humanae Vitae* as indicating the norm for the exercise of their sexuality, and that they should endeavor to establish the conditions necessary for observing that norm. As the synod noted, this pedagogy embraces the whole of married life. Accordingly, the function of transmitting life must be integrated into the overall mission of Christian life as a whole which, without the cross, cannot reach the resurrection. In such a context it is understandable that sacrifice cannot be removed from family life, but must in fact be wholeheartedly accepted if the love between husband and wife is to be deepened and become a source of intimate joy.

This shared progress demands reflection, instruction and suitable education on the part of the priests, religious and lay people engaged in family pastoral work: they will all be able to assist married people in their human and spiritual progress, a progress that demands awareness of sin, a sincere commitment to observe the moral law and the ministry of reconciliation. It must also be kept in mind that conjugal intimacy involves the wills of two persons, who are thereby called to harmonize their mentality and behavior, requiring much patience, understanding and time. Uniquely important in this field is unity of moral and pastoral judgment by priests—a unity that must be carefully sought and ensured in order that the faithful may not have to suffer anxiety of conscience. [96]

It will be easier for married people to make progress if, with respect for the church's teaching and with trust in the grace of Christ, and with the help and support of the pastors of souls and the entire ecclesial community, they are able to discover and experience the liberating and inspiring value of the authentic love that is offered by the Gospel and set before us by the Lord's commandment.

33

35. Instilling conviction and offering practical help

With regard to the question of lawful birth regulation, the ecclesial community at the present time must take on the task of instilling conviction and offering practical help to those who wish to live out their parenthood in a truly responsible way.

In this matter, while the church notes with satisfaction the results achieved by scientific research aimed at a more precise knowledge of the rhythms of women's fertility, and while it encourages a more decisive and wide-ranging extension of that research, it cannot fail to call with renewed vigor on the responsibility of all—doctors, experts, marriage counselors, teachers and married couples—who can actually help married people to live their love with respect for the structure and finalities of the conjugal act which expresses that love. This implies a broader, more decisive and more systematic effort to make the natural methods of regulating fertility known, respected and applied.[97]

A very valuable witness can and should be given by those husbands and wives who, through the joint exercise of periodic continence, have reached a more mature personal responsibility with regard to love and life. As Paul VI wrote: "To them the Lord entrusts the task of making visible to people the holiness and sweetness of the law which unites the mutual love of husband and wife with their cooperation with the love of God the author of human life."[98]

B. Education

36. The right and duty of parents regarding education

The task of giving education is rooted in the primary vocation of married couples to participate in God's creative activity: By begetting in love and for love a new person who has within himself or herself the vocation for growth and development, parents by that very fact take the task of helping that person effectively to live a fully human life. As the Second Vatican Council recalled, "Since parents have conferred life on their children, they have a most solemn obligation to educate their offspring. Hence, parents must be acknowledged as the first and foremost educators of their children. Their role as educators is so decisive that scarcely anything can compensate for their failure in it. For it devolves on parents to create a family atmosphere so animated with love and reverence for God and others that a well-rounded personal and social development will be fostered among the children.

Hence, the family is the first school of those social virtues which every society needs." [99]

The right and duty of parents to give education is essential, since it is connected with the transmission of human life; it is original and primary with regard to the educational role of others on account of the uniqueness of the loving relationship between parents and children; and it is irreplaceable and inalienable and therefore incapable of being entirely delegated to others or usurped by others.

In addition to those characteristics, it cannot be forgotten that the most basic element, so basic that it qualifies the educational role of parents, is parental love, which finds fulfillment in the task of education as it completes and perfects its service of life. As well as being a source, the parents' love is also the animating principle and therefore the norm inspiring and guiding all concrete educational activity, enriching it with the values of kindness, constancy, goodness, service, disinterestedness and self-sacrifice that are the most precious fruit of love.

37. Educating in the essential values of human life

Even amid the difficulties of the work of education, difficulties which are often greater today, parents must trustingly and courageously train their children in the essential values of human life. Children must grow up with a correct attitude of freedom with regard to material goods, by adopting a simple and austere lifestyle and being fully convinced that "man is more precious for what he is than for what he has." [100]

In a society shaken and split by tensions and conflicts caused by the violent clash of various kinds of individualism and selfishness, children must be enriched not only with a sense of true justice, which alone leads to respect for the personal dignity of each individual, but also and more powerfully by a sense of true love, understood as sincere solicitude and disinterested service with regard to others, especially the poorest and those in most need. The family is the first and fundamental school of social living: As a community of love, it finds in self-giving the law that guides it and makes it grow. The self-giving that inspires the love of husband and wife for each other is the model and norm for the self-giving that must be practiced in the relationships between brothers and sisters and the different generations living together in the family. And the communion and sharing that are part of everday life in the home at times of joy and at times of difficulty are the most concrete and effective pedagogy for the active, responsible and fruitful inclusion of the children in the wider horizon of society.

Education in love as self-giving is also the indispensable premise for parents called to give their children a clear and delicate sex education. Faced with a culture that largely reduces human sexuality to the level of something commonplace, since it interprets and lives it in a reductive and impoverished way by linking it solely with the body and with selfish pleasure, the educational service of parents must aim firmly at a training in the area of sex that is truly and fully personal: for sexuality is an enrichment of the whole person—body, emotions and soul—and it manifests its inmost meaning in leading the person to the gift of self in love.

Sex education, which is a basic right and duty of parents, must always be carried out under their attentive guidance whether at home or in educational centers chosen and controlled by them. In this regard, the church reaffirms the law of subsidiarity, which the school is bound to observe when it cooperates in sex education, by entering into the same spirit that animates the parents.

In this context education for chastity is absolutely essential, for it is a virtue that develops a person's authentic maturity and makes him or her capable of respecting and fostering the "nuptial meaning" of the body. Indeed Christian parents, discerning the signs of God's call, will devote special attention and care to education in virginity or celibacy as the supreme form of that self-giving that constitutes the very meaning of human sexuality.

In view of the close links between the sexual dimension of the person and his or her ethical values, education must bring the children to a knowledge of and respect for the moral norms as the necessary and highly valuable guarantee for responsible personal growth in human sexuality.

For this reason the church is firmly opposed to an often widespread form of imparting sex information dissociated from moral principles. That would merely be an introduction to the experience of pleasure and a stimulus leading to the loss of serenity—while still in the years of innocence—by opening the way to vice.

36

38. The mission to educate and the sacrament of marriage

For Christian parents the mission to educate, a mission rooted as we have said in their participation in God's creating activity, has a new specific source in the sacrament of marriage, which consecrates them for the strictly Christian education of their children: that is to say, it calls upon them to share in the very authority and love of God the Father and Christ the shepherd, and in the motherly love of the church, and it enriches them with wisdom, counsel, fortitude and all the other gifts of the Holy Spirit in order to help the children in their growth as human beings and as Christians.

The sacrament of marriage gives to the educational role the dignity and vocation of being really and truly a "ministry" of the church at the service of the building up of her members. So great and splendid is the educational ministry of Christian parents that St. Thomas has no hesitation in comparing it with the ministry of priests: "Some only propagate and guard spiritual life by a spiritual ministry: This is the role of the sacrament of orders, others do this for both corporal and spiritual life, and this is brought about by the sacrament of marriage, by which a man and a woman join in order to beget offspring and bring them up to worship God." [101]

A vivid and attentive awareness of the mission that they have received with the sacrament of marriage will help Christian parents to place themselves at the service of their children's education with great serenity and trustfulness, and also with a sense of responsibility before God, who calls them and gives them the mission of building up the church in their children. Thus in the case of baptized people, the family, called together by word and sacrament as the church of the home, is both teacher and mother, the same as the worldwide church.

39. First experience of the church

The mission to educate demands that Christian parents should present to their children all the topics that are necessary for the gradual maturing of their personality from a Christian and ecclesial point of view. They will therefore follow the educational lines mentioned above, taking care to show their children the depths of significance to which the faith and love of Jesus Christ can lead. Furthermore, their awareness that the Lord is entrusting to them the growth of a child of God, a brother or sister of Christ, a temple of the Holy Spirit, a member of the church, will support Christian parents in their task of strengthening the gift of divine grace in their children's souls.

The Second Vatican Council describes the content of Christian education as follows: "Such an education does not merely strive to foster maturity...in the human person. Rather, its principal aims are these: that as baptized persons are gradually introduced into a knowledge of the mystery of salvation, they may daily grow more conscious of the gift of faith which they have received; that they may learn to adore God the Father in spirit and in truth (cf. Jn. 4:23), especially through liturgical worship; that they may be trained to conduct their personal life in true righteousness and holiness, according to their new nature (Eph. 4:22-24), and thus grow to maturity, to the stature of the fullness of Christ (cf. Eph. 4:13), and devote themselves to the up-building of the mystical body. Moreover, aware of their calling, they should grow accustomed to giving witness to the hope that is in them (cf. 1 Pt. 3:15), and to promoting the Christian transformation of the world." [102]

The synod too, taking up and developing the indications of the council, presented the educational mission of the Christian family as a true ministry through which the Gospel is transmitted and radiated, so that family life itself becomes an itinerary of faith and in some way a Christian initiation and a school of following Christ. Within a family that is aware of this gift, as Paul VI wrote, "all the members evangelize and are evangelized." [103]

By virtue of their ministry of educating, parents are through the witness of their lives the first heralds of the Gospel for their children. Furthermore, by praying with their children, by reading the word of God with them and by introducing them deeply through Christian initiation into the body of Christ—both the eucharistic and the ecclesial body—they become fully parents, in that they are begetters not only of bodily life but also of the life that through the Spirit's renewal flows from the cross and resurrection of Christ.

In order that Christian parents may worthily carry out their ministry of education, the synod fathers expressed the hope that a suitable catechism for families would be prepared, one that would be clear, brief and easily assimilated by all. The episcopal conferences were warmly invited to contribute to producing this catechism.

40. Relations with other educating agents

The family is the primary but not the only and exclusive educating community. Man's community aspect itself—both civil and ecclesial—demands and leads to a broader and more articulated activity resulting from well-ordered collaboration between the various agents of education. All these agents are necessary, even though each can and should play its part in accordance with the special competence and contribution proper to itself.[104]

The educational role of the Christian family therefore has a very important place in organic pastoral work. This involves a new form of cooperation between parents and Christian communities and between the various educational groups and pastors. In this sense, the renewal of the Catholic school must give special attention both to the parents of the pupils and to the formation of a perfect educating community.

The right of parents to choose an education in conformity with their religious faith must be absolutely guaranteed.

The state and the church have the obligation to give families all possible aid to enable them to perform their educational role properly. Therefore both the church and the state must create and foster the institutions and activities that families justly demand, and the aid must be in proportion to the families' needs. However, those in society who are in charge of schools must never forget that the parents have been appointed by God himself as the first and principal educators of their children and that their right is completely inalienable.

But corresponding to their right, parents have a serious duty to commit themselves totally to a cordial and active relationship with the teachers and school authorities.

If ideologies opposed to the Christian faith are taught in the schools, the family must join with other families, if possible through family associations, and with all its strength and with wisdom help the young not to depart from the faith. In this case the family needs special assistance from pastors of souls, who must never forget that parents have the inviolable right to entrust their children to the ecclesial community.

41. Manifold service to life

Fruitful married love expresses itself in serving life in many ways. Of these ways, begetting and educating children are the most immediate, specific and irreplaceable. In fact, every act of true love toward a human being bears witness to and perfects the spiritual fecundity of the family, since it is an act of obedience to the deep inner dynamism of love as self-giving to others.

For everyone this perspective is full of value and commitment, and it can be an inspiration in particular for couples who experience physical sterility.

Christian families, recognizing with faith all human beings as children of the same heavenly Father, will respond generously to the children of other families, giving them support and love not as outsiders but as members of the one family of God's children. Christian parents will thus be able to spread their love beyond the bonds of flesh and blood, nourishing the links that are rooted in the spirit and that develop through concrete service to the children of other families, who are often without even the barest necessities.

Christian families will be able to show greater readiness to adopt and foster children who have lost their parents or have been abandoned by them. Rediscovering the warmth of affection of a family, these children will be able to experience God's loving and provident fatherhood witnessed to by Christian parents, and they will thus be able to grow up with serenity and confidence in life. At the same time the whole family will be enriched with the spiritual values of a wider fraternity.

Family fecundity must have an unceasing "creativity," a marvelous fruit of the Spirit of God, who opens the eyes of the heart to discover the new needs and sufferings of our society and gives courage for accepting them and responding to them. A vast field of activity lies open to families: Today even more preoccupying than child abandonment is the phenomenon of social and cultural exclusion, which seriously affects the elderly, the sick, the disabled, drug addicts, ex-prisoners, etc.

This broadens enormously the horizons of the parenthood of Christian families: These and many other urgent needs of our time are a challenge to their spiritually fruitful love. With families and through them, the Lord Jesus continues to "have compassion" on the multitudes.

III. PARTICIPATING IN THE DEVELOPMENT OF SOCIETY

42. The family as the first and vital cell of society

"Since the Creator of all things has established the conjugal partnership as the beginning and basis of human society," the family is "the first and vital cell of society."[105]

The family has vital and organic links with society since it is its foundation and nourishes it continually through its role of service to life: It is from the family that citizens come to birth and it is within the family that they find the first school of the social virtues that are the animating principle of the existence and development of society itself.

Thus, far from being closed in on itself, the family is by nature and vocation open to other families and to society and undertakes its social role.

43. Family life as an experience of communion and sharing

The very experience of communion and sharing that should characterize the family's daily life represents its first and fundamental contribution to society.

The relationships between the members of the family community are inspired and guided by the law of "free giving." By respecting and fostering personal dignity in each and every one as the only basis for value, this free giving takes the form of heartfelt acceptance, encounter and dialogue, disinterested availability, generous service and deep solidarity.

Thus the fostering of authentic and mature communion between persons within the family is the first and irreplaceable school of social life, an example and stimulus for the broader community of relationships marked by respect, justice, dialogue and love.

The family is thus, as the synod fathers recalled, the place of origin and the most effective means for humanizing and personalizing society: It makes an original contribution in depth in building up the world, by making possible a life that is, properly speaking, human, in particular by guarding and transmitting virtues and "values." As the Second Vatican Council states, in the family "the various generations come together and help one another to grow wiser and to harmonize personal rights with the other requirements of social living."[106]

Consequently, faced with a society that is running the risk of becoming more and more depersonalized and standardized and therefore inhuman and dehumanizing, with the negative results of many forms of escapism—such as alcoholism, drugs and even terrorism—the family possesses and continues still to release formidable energies capable of taking man out of his anonymity, keeping him conscious of his personal dignity, enriching him with deep humanity and actively placing him, in his uniqueness and unrepeatability, within the fabric of society.

44. The social and political role

The social role of the family certainly cannot stop short at procreation and education even if this constitutes its primary and irreplaceable form of expression.

Families therefore, either singly or in association, can and should devote themselves to manifold social service activities, especially in favor of the poor or at any rate for the benefit of all people and situations that cannot be reached by the public authorities' welfare organization.

The social contribution of the family has an original character of its own, one that should be given greater recognition and more decisive encouragement, especially as the children grow up, and actually involving all its members as much as possible.[107]

In particular, note must be taken of the ever greater importance in our society of hospitality in all its forms, from opening the door of one's home, and still more of one's heart, to the pleas of one's brothers and sisters, to concrete efforts to ensure that every family has its own home as the natural environment that preserves it and makes it grow. In a special way the Christian family is called upon to listen to the apostle's recommendation. "Practice hospitality,"[108] and therefore, imitating Christ's example and sharing in his love, welcome the brother or sister in need: "Whoever gives to one of these little ones even a cup of cold water because he is a disciple, truly, I say to you, he shall not lose his reward."[109]

The social role of families is called upon to find expression also in the form of political intervention: Families should be the first to take steps to see that the laws and institutions of the state not only do not offend, but support and positively defend the rights and duties of the family. Along these lines families should grow in awareness of being "protagonists" of what is known as "family politics" and assume responsibility for transforming society; otherwise families will be the first victims of the evils that they have done no more than note with indifference. The Second Vatican Council's appeal to go beyond an individualistic ethic therefore also holds good for the family as such.[110]

42

45. Society at the service of the family

Just as the intimate connection between the family and society demands that the family be open to and participate in society and its development, so also it requires that society should never fail in its fundamental task of respecting and fostering the family.

The family and society have complementary functions in defending and fostering the good of each and every human being. But society—more specifically the state—must recognize that "the family is a society in its own original right," [111] and so society is under a grave obligation in its relations with the family to adhere to the principle of subsidiarity.

from families the functions that they can just as well perform on their own or in free associations; instead it must positively favor and encourage as far as possible responsible initiative by families. In the conviction that the good of the family is an indispensable and essential value of the civil community, the public authorities must do everything possible to ensure that families have all those aids—economic, social, educational, political and cultural assistance—that they need in order to face all their responsibilities in a human way.

46. The charter of family rights

The ideal of mutual support and development between the family and society is often very seriously in conflict with the reality of their separation and even opposition.

In fact, as was repeatedly denounced by the synod, the situation experienced by many families in various countries is highly problematical if not entirely negative: Institutions and laws unjustly ignore the inviolable rights of the family and of the human person; and society, far from putting itself at the service of the family, attacks it violently in its values and fundamental requirements. Thus the family, which in God's plan is the basic cell of society and a subject of rights and duties before the state or any other community, finds itself the victim of society, of the delays and slowness with which it acts, and even of its blatant injustice.

For this reason the church openly and strongly defends the rights of the family against the intolerable usurpations of society and the state. In particular the synod fathers mentioned the following rights of the family:

—The right to exist and progress as a family, that is to say, the right of every human being, even if he or she is poor, to found a family and to have adequate means to support it;

—The right to exercise its responsibility regarding the transmission of life and to educate children;

—The right to the intimacy of conjugal and family life;

—The right to the stability of the bond and of the institution of marriage;

—The right to believe in and profess one's faith and to propagate it;

—The right to bring up children in accordance with the family's own traditions and religious and cultural values, with the necessary instruments, means and institutions;

—The right, especially of the poor and the sick, to obtain physical, social, political and economic security;

—The right to housing suitable for living family life in a proper way;

—The right to expression and to representation, either directly or through associations, before the economic, social and cultural public authorities and lower authorities;

—The right to form associations with other families and institutions in order to fulfill the family's role suitably and expeditiously;

—The right to protect minors by adequate institutions and legislation from harmful drugs, pornography, alcoholism, etc.;

—The right to wholesome recreation of a kind that also fosters family values;

—The right of the elderly to a worthy life and a worthy death;

—The right to emigrate as a family in search of a better life.[112]

Acceding to the synod's explicit request, the Holy See will give prompt attention to studying these suggestions in depth and to the preparation of a charter of rights of the family to be presented to the quarters and authorities concerned.

47. The Christian family's grace and responsibility

The social role that belongs to every family pertains by a new and original right to the Christian family, which is based on the sacrament of marriage. By taking up the human reality of the love between husband and wife in all its implications, the sacrament gives to Christian couples and parents a power and a commitment to live their vocation as lay people and therefore to "seek the kingdom of God by engaging in temporal affairs and by ordering them according to the plan of God."[113]

The social and political role is included in the kingly mission of service in which Christian couples share by virtue of the sacrament of marriage, and they receive both a command which they cannot ignore and a grace which sustains and stimulates them.

The Christian family is thus called upon to offer everyone a witness of generous and disinterested dedication to social matters through a "preferential option" for the poor and disadvantaged. Therefore, advancing in its following of the Lord by special love for all the poor, it must have special concern for the hungry, the poor, the old, the sick, drug victims and those who have no family.

48. For a new international order

In view of the worldwide dimension of various social questions nowadays, the family has seen its role with regard to the development of society extended in a completely new way: It now also involves cooperating for a new international order, since it is only in worldwide solidarity that the enormous and dramatic issues of world justice, the freedom of peoples and the peace of humanity can be dealt with and solved.

The spiritual communion between Christian families, rooted in a common faith and hope and given life by love, constitutes an inner energy that generates, spreads and develops justice, reconciliation, fraternity and peace among human beings. Insofar as it is a "small-scale church," the Christian family is called upon, like the "large-scale church," to be a sign of unity for the world and in this way to exercise its prophetic role by bearing witness to the kingdom and peace of Christ, toward which the whole world is journeying.

Christian families can do this through their educational activity—that is to say, by presenting to their children a model of life based on the values of truth, freedom, justice and love—both through active and responsible involvement in the authentically human growth of society and its institutions, and supporting in various ways the associations specifically devoted to international issues.

IV. SHARING IN THE LIFE AND MISSION OF THE CHURCH

49. The family within the mystery of the church

Among the fundamental tasks of the Christian family is its ecclesial task: The family is placed at the service of the building up of the kingdom of God in history by participating in the life and mission of the church.

In order to understand better the foundations, the contents and the characteristics of this participation, we must examine the many profound bonds linking the church and the Christian family and establishing the family as a "church in miniature" (*ecclesia domestica*),[114] in such a way that in its own way the family is a living image and historical representation of the mystery of the church.

It is, above all, the church as mother that gives birth to, educates and builds up the Christian family by putting into effect in its regard the saving mission which she has received from her Lord. By proclaiming the word of God the church reveals to the Christian family its true identity, what it is and should be according to the Lord's plan; by celebrating the sacraments the church enriches and strengthens the Christian family with the grace of Christ for its sanctification to the glory of the Father; by the continuous proclamation of the new commandment of love the church encourages and guides the Christian family to the service of love so that it may imitate and relive the same self-giving and sacrificial love that the Lord Jesus has for the entire human race.

In turn, the Christian family is grafted into the mystery of the church to such a degree as to become a sharer, in its own way, in the saving mission proper to the church: By virtue of the sacrament Christian married couples and parents "in their state and way of life have their own special gift among the people of God."[115] For this reason they not only receive the love of Christ and become a saved community, but they are also called upon to communicate Christ's love to their brethren thus becoming a saving community. In this way, while the Christian family is a fruit and sign of the supernatural fecundity of the church, it stands also as a symbol, witness and participant of the church's motherhood.[114]

50. A specific and original ecclesial role

The Christian family is called upon to take part actively and responsibly in the mission of the church in a way that is original and specific by placing itself in what it is and what it does as an "intimate community of life and love" at the service of the church and of society.

Since the Christian family is a community in which the relationships are renewed by Christ through faith and the sacraments, the family's sharing in the church's mission should follow a community pattern: The spouses together as a couple, the parents and children as a family, must live their service to the church and to the world. They must be "of one heart and soul"[117] in faith, through the shared apostolic zeal that animates them and through their shared commitment to works of service in the ecclesial and civil communities.

The Christian family also builds up the kingdom of God in history through the everyday realities that concern and distinguish its state of life. It is thus in the love between husband and wife and between the members of the family—a love lived out in all its extraordinary richness of values and demands: totality, oneness, fidelity and fruitful ness[118]—that the Christian family's participation in the prophetic, priestly and kingly mission of Jesus Christ and of his church finds expression and realization. Therefore, love and life constitute the nucleus of the saving mission of the Christian family in the church and for the church.

The Second Vatican Council recalls this fact when it writes: "Families will share their spiritual riches generously with other families too. Thus the Christian family, which springs from marriage as a reflection of the loving covenant uniting Christ with the church, and as a participation in that covenant will manifest to all people the savior's living presence in the world, and the genuine nature of the church. This the family will do by the mutual love of the spouses, by their generous fruitfulness, their solidarity and faithfulness, and by the loving way in which all the members of the family work together."[119]

Having laid the foundation of the participation of the christian family in the church's mission, it is now time to illustrate its substance in reference to Jesus Christ as prophet, priest and king—three aspects of a single reality—by presenting the Christian family as 1) a believing and evangelizing community, 2) a community in dialogue with God, and 3) a community at the service of man.

A. The Christian family as a believing and evangelizing community

51. Faith as the discovery and admiring awareness of God's plan for the family

As a sharer in the life and mission of the church, which listens to the word of God with reverence and proclaims it confidently,[120] the Christian family fulfills its prophetic role by welcoming and announcing the word of God: It thus becomes more and more each day a believing and evangelizing community.

Christian spouses and parents are required to offer "the obedience of faith."[121] They are called upon to welcome the word of the Lord, which reveals to them the marvelous news—the good news—of their conjugal and family life sanctified and made a source of sanctity by Christ himself. Only in faith can they discover and admire with joyful gratitude the dignity to which God has deigned to raise marriage and the family, making them a sign and meeting place of the loving covenant between God and man, between Jesus Christ and his bride, the church.

The very preparation for Christian marriage is itself a journey of faith. It is a special opportunity for the engaged to rediscover and deepen the faith received in baptism and nourished by their Christian upbringing. In this way they come to recognize and freely accept their vocation to follow Christ and to serve the kingdom of God in the married state.

The celebration of the sacrament of marriage is the basic moment of the faith of the couple. This sacrament, in essence, is the proclamation in the church of the good news concerning married love. It is the word of God that "reveals" and "fulfills" the wise and loving plan of God for the married couple, giving them a mysterious and real share in the very love with which God himself loves humanity. Since the sacramental celebration of marriage is itself a proclamation of the word of God, it must also be a "profession of faith" within and with the church, as a community of believers, on the part of all those who in different ways participate in its celebration.

This profession of faith demands that it be prolonged in the life of the married couple and of the family. God, who called the couple to marriage, continues to call them in marriage.[122] In and through the events, problems, difficulties and circumstances of everyday life, God comes to them, revealing and presenting the concrete "demands" of their sharing in the love of Christ for his church in the particular family, social and ecclesial situation in which they find themselves.

The discovery of and obedience to the plan of God on the part of the conjugal and family community must take place in "togetherness," through the human experience of love between husband and wife, between parents and children, lived in the spirit of Christ.

Thus the little domestic church, like the greater church, needs to be constantly and intensely evangelized: hence its duty regarding permanent education in the faith.

52. The Christian family's ministry of evangelization

To the extent in which the Christian family accepts the Gospel and matures in faith, it becomes an evangelizing community. Let us listen again to Paul VI: "The family, like the church, ought to be a place where the Gospel is transmitted and from which the Gospel radiates. In a family which is conscious of this mission, all the members evangelize and are evangelized. The parents not only communicate the Gospel to their children, but from their children they can themselves receive the same Gospel as deeply lived by them. And such a family becomes the evangelizer of many other families and of the neighborhood of which it forms part."[123]

As the synod repeated, taking up the appeal which I launched at Puebla, the future of evangelization depends in great part on the church of the home.[124] This apostolic mission of the family is rooted in baptism and receives from the grace of the sacrament of marriage new strength to transmit the faith, to sanctify and transform our present society according to God's plan.

Particularly today the Christian family has a special vocation to witness to the paschal covenant of Christ by constantly radiating the joy of love and the certainty of the hope for which it must give account: "The Christian family loudly proclaims both the present virtues of the kingdom of God and the hope of a blessed life to come."[125]

The absolute need for family catechesis emerges with particular force in certain situations that the church unfortunately experiences in some places: "In places where anti-religious legislation endeavors even to prevent education in the faith, and in places where widespread unbelief or invasive secularism makes real religious growth practically impossible, 'the church of the home' remains the one place where children and young people can receive an authentic catechesis."[126]

53. Ecclesial service

The ministry of evangelization carried out by Christian parents is original and irreplaceable. It assumes the characteristics typical of family life itself, which should be interwoven with love, simplicity, practicality and daily witness.[127]

The family must educate the children for life in such a way that each one may fully perform his or her role according to the vocation received from God. Indeed the family that is open to transcendent values, that serves its brothers and sisters with joy, that fulfills its duties with generous fidelity and is aware of its daily sharing in the mystery of the glorious cross of Christ, becomes the primary and most excellent seedbed of vocations to a life of consecration to the kingdom of God.

The parents' ministry of evangelization and catechesis ought to play a part in their children's lives also during adolescence and youth, when the children, as often happens, challenge or even reject the Christian faith received in earlier years. Just as in the church the work of evangelization can never be separated from the sufferings of the apostle, so in the Christian family parents must face with courage and great interior serenity the difficulties that their ministry of evangelization sometimes encounters in their own children.

It should not be forgotten that the service rendered by Christian spouses and parents to the Gospel is essentially an ecclesial service. It has its place within the context of the whole church as an evangelized and evangelizing community. Insofar as the ministry of evangelization and catechesis of the church of the home is rooted in and derives from the one mission of the church and is ordained to the upbuilding of the one body of Christ,[126] it must remain in intimate communion and collaborate responsibly with all the other evangelizing and catechetical activities present and at work in the ecclesial community at the diocesan and parochial levels.

54. To preach the Gospel to the whole creation

Evangelization, urged on within by irrepressible missionary zeal, is characterized by a universality without boundaries. It is the response to Christ's explicit and unequivocal command: "Go into all the world and preach the Gospel to the whole creation."[129]

The Christian family's faith and evangelizing mission also possesses this Catholic missionary inspiration. The sacrament of marriage takes up and reproposes the task of defending and spreading the faith, a task that has its roots in baptism and confirmation,[130] and makes Christian married couples and parents witnesses of Christ "to the end of the earth,"[131] missionaries, in the true and proper sense, of love and life.

A form of missionary activity can be exercised even within the family. This happens when some member of the family does not have the faith or does not practice it with consistency. In such a case the other members must give him or her a living witness of their own faith in order to encourage and support him or her along the path toward full acceptance of Christ the savior.[132]

Animated in its own inner life by missionary zeal, the church of the home is also called to be a luminous sign of the presence of Christ and of his love for those who are "far away," for families who do not yet believe and for those Christian families who no longer live in accordance with the faith that they once received. The Christian family is called to enlighten "by its example and its witness those who seek the truth."[133]

Just as at the dawn of Christianity Aquila and Priscilla were presented as a missionary couple,[134] so today the church shows forth her perennial newness and fruitfulness by the presence of Christian couples and families who dedicate at least a part of their lives to working in missionary territories, proclaiming the Gospel and doing service to their fellow man in the love of Jesus Christ.

Christian families offer a special contribution to the missionary cause of the church by fostering missionary vocations among their sons and daughters[135] and, more generally, "by training their children from childhood to recognize God's love for all people."[136]

B. The Christian family as a community in dialogue with God

55. The church's sanctuary in the home

The proclamation of the Gospel and its acceptance in faith reach their fullness in the celebration of the sacraments. The church which is a believing and evangelizing community is also a priestly people invested with the dignity and sharing in the power of Christ the high priest of the new and eternal covenant.[137]

The Christian family too is part of this priestly people which is the church. By means of the sacrament of marriage, in which it is rooted and from which it draws its nourishment, the Christian family is continuously vivified by the Lord Jesus and called and engaged by him in a dialogue with God through the sacraments, through the offering of one's life and through prayer.

This is the priestly role which the Christian family can and ought to exercise in intimate communion with the whole church through the daily realities of married and family life. In this way the Christian family is called to be sanctified and to sanctify the ecclesial community and the world.

56. Marriage as a sacrament of mutual sanctification and an act of worship

The sacrament of marriage is the specific source and original means of sanctification for Christian married couples and families. It takes up again and makes specific the sanctifying grace of baptism. By virtue of the mystery of the death and resurrection of Christ, of which the spouses are made part in a new way by marriage, conjugal love is purified and made holy: "This love the Lord has judged worthy of special gifts, healing, perfecting and exalting gifts of grace and of charity." [138]

The gift of Jesus Christ is not exhausted in the actual celebration of the sacrament of marriage, but rather accompanies the married couple throughout their lives. This fact is explicitly recalled by the Second Vatican Council when it says that Jesus Christ "abides with them so that just as he loved the church and handed himself over on her behalf, the spouses may love each other with perpetual fidelity through mutual self-bestowal. . . For this reason, Christian spouses have a special sacrament by which they are fortified and receive a kind of consecration in the duties and dignity of their state. By virtue of this sacrament, as spouses fulfill their conjugal and family obligations they are penetrated with the spirit of Christ, who fills their whole lives with faith, hope and charity. Thus they increasingly advance toward their own perfection as well as toward their mutual sanctification, and hence contribute jointly to the glory of God." [139]

Christian spouses and parents are included in the universal call to sanctity. For them this call is specified by the sacrament they have celebrated and is carried out concretely in the realities proper to their conjugal and family life. [140] This gives rise to the grace and requirement of an authentic and profound conjugal and family spirituality that draws its inspiration from the themes of creation, covenant, cross, resurrection and sign, which were stressed more than once by the synod.

Christian marriage, like the other sacraments, "whose purpose is to sanctify people, to build up the body of Christ, and finally, to give worship to God,"[141] is in itself a liturgical action glorifying God in Jesus Christ and in the church. By celebrating it, Christian spouses profess their gratitude to God for the sublime gift bestowed on them of being able to live in their married and family lives the very love of God for people and that of the Lord Jesus for the church, his bride.

Just as husbands and wives receive from the sacrament the gift and responsibility of translating into daily living the sanctification bestowed on them, so the same sacrament confers on them the grace and moral obligation of transforming their whole lives into a "spiritual sacrifice."[142] What the council says of the laity applies also to Christian spouses and parents, especially with regard to the earthly and temporal realities that characterize their lives: "As worshippers leading holy lives in every place, the laity consecrate the world itself to God."[143]

57. Marriage and the eucharist

The Christian family's sanctifying role is grounded in baptism and has its highest expression in the eucharist, to which Christian marriage is intimately connected. The Second Vatican Council drew attention to the unique relationship between the eucharist and marriage by requesting that "marriage normally be celebrated within the Mass."[144] To understand better and live more intensely the graces and responsibilities of Christian marriage and family life, it is altogether necessary to rediscover and strengthen this relationship.

The eucharist is the very source of Christian marriage. The eucharistic sacrifice in fact represents Christ's covenant of love with the church, sealed with his blood on the cross.[145] In this sacrifice of the new and eternal covenant, Christian spouses encounter the source from which their own marriage covenant flows, is interiorly structured and continuously renewed. As a representation of Christ's sacrifice of love for the church, the eucharist is a fountain of charity. In the eucharistic gift of charity the Christian family finds the foundation and soul of its "communion" and its "mission": By partaking in the eucharistic bread, the different members of the Christian family become one body, which reveals and shares in the wider unity of the church. Their sharing in the body of Christ that is "given up" and in his blood that is "shed" becomes a never-ending source of missionary and apostolic dynamism for the Christian family.

58. The sacrament of conversion and reconciliation

An essential and permanent part of the Christian family's sanctifying role consists in accepting the call to conversion that the Gospel addresses to all Christians, who do not always remain faithful to the "newness" of the baptism that constitutes them "saints." The Christian family too is sometimes unfaithful to the law of baptismal grace and holiness proclaimed anew in the sacrament of marriage.

Repentance and mutual pardon within the bosom of the Christian family, so much a part of daily life, receive their specific sacramental expression in Christian penance. In the encyclical *Humanae Vitae*, Paul VI wrote of married couples: "And if sin should still keep its hold over them, let them not be discouraged, but rather have recourse with humble perseverance to the mercy of God, which is abundantly poured forth in the sacrament of penance." [146]

The celebration of this sacrament acquires special significance for family life. While they discover in faith that sin contradicts not only the covenant with God, but also the covenant between husband and wife and the communion of the family, the married couple and the other members of the family are led to an encounter with God, who is "rich in mercy," [147] who bestows on them his love which is more powerful than sin, [148] and who reconstructs and brings to perfection the marriage covenant and the family communion.

59. Family prayer

The church prays for the Christian family and educates the family to live in generous accord with the priestly gift and role received from Christ the high priest. In effect, the baptismal priesthood of the faithful exercised in the sacrament of marriage constitutes the basis of a priestly vocation and mission for the spouses and family by which their daily lives are transformed into "spiritual sacrifices acceptable to God through Jesus Christ." [149] This transformation is achieved not only by celebrating the eucharist and the other sacraments and through offering themselves to the glory of God, but also through a life of prayer, through prayerful dialogue with the Father, through Jesus Christ, in the Holy Spirit.

54

Family prayer has its own characteristic qualities. It is prayer offered in common, husband and wife together, parents and children together. Communion in prayer is both a consequence of and a requirement for the communion bestowed by the sacraments of baptism and matrimony. The words with which the Lord Jesus promises his presence can be applied to the members of the Christian family in a special way: "Again I say to you, if two of you agree on earth about anything they ask it will be done for them by my Father in heaven. For where two or three are gathered in my name, there am I in the midst of them."[150]

Family prayer has for its very own object family life itself, which in all its varying circumstances is seen as a call from God and lived as a filial response to his call. Joys and sorrows, hopes and disappointments, births and birthday celebrations, wedding anniversaries of the parents, departures, separations and homecomings, important and far-reaching decisions, the death of those who are dear, etc.—all of these mark God's loving intervention in the family's history. They should be seen as suitable moments for thanksgiving, for petition, for trusting abandonment of the family into the hands of their common Father in heaven. The dignity and responsibility of the Christian family as the domestic church can be achieved only with God's unceasing aid, which will surely be granted if it is humbly and trustingly petitioned in prayer.

60. Educators in prayer

By reason of their dignity and mission, Christian parents have the specific responsibility of educating their children in prayer, introducing them to gradual discovery of the mystery of God and to personal dialogue with him: "It is particularly in the Christian family, enriched by the grace and the office of the sacrament of matrimony, that from the earliest years children should be taught, according to the faith received in baptism, to have a knowledge of God, to worship him and to love their neighbor."[151]

The concrete example and living witness of parents is fundamental and irreplaceable in educating their children to pray. Only by praying together with their children can a father and mother—exercising their royal priesthood—penetrate the innermost depths of their children's hearts and leave an impression that the future events in their lives will not be able to efface.

Let us again listen to the appeal made by Paul VI to parents: "Mothers, do you teach your children the Christian prayers? Do you prepare them, in conjunction with the priests, for the sacraments that they receive when they are young: confession, communion and confirmation? Do you encourage them when they are sick to think of Christ suffering, to invoke the aid of the Blessed Virgin and the saints? Do you say the family rosary together? And you, fathers, do you pray with your children, with the whole domestic community, at least sometimes? Your example of honesty in thought and action, joined to some common prayer, is a lesson for life, an act of worship of singular value. In this way you bring peace to your homes: *Pax huic domui.* Remember, it is thus that you build up the church."[152]

61. Liturgical prayer and private prayer

There exists a deep and vital bond between the prayer of the church and the prayer of the individual faithful as has been clearly reaffirmed by the Second Vatican Council.[153] An important purpose of the prayer of the domestic church is to serve as the natural introduction for the children to the liturgical prayer of the whole church, both in the sense of preparing for it and of extending it into personal, family and social life. Hence the need for gradual participation by all the members of the Christian family in the celebration of the eucharist, especially on Sundays and feast days, and of the other sacraments, particularly the sacraments of Christian initiation of the children. The directives of the council opened up a new possibility for the Christian family when it listed the family among those groups to whom it recommends the recitation of the Divine Office in common.[154] Likewise, the Christian family will strive to celebrate at home and in a way suited to the members the times and feasts of the liturgical year.

As preparation for the worship celebrated in church and as its prolongation in the home, the Christian family makes use of private prayer, which presents a great variety of forms. While this variety testifies to the extraordinary richness with which the spirit vivifies Christian prayer, it serves also to meet the various needs and life situations of those who turn to the Lord in prayer. Apart from morning and evening prayers, certain forms of prayer are to be expressly encouraged, following the indications of the synod fathers, such as reading and meditating on the word of God, preparation for the reception of the sacraments, devotion and consecration to the Sacred Heart of Jesus, the various forms of veneration of the Blessed Virgin Mary, grace before and after meals and observance of popular devotions.

While respecting the freedom of the children of God, the church has always proposed certain practices of piety to the faithful with particular solicitude and insistence. Among these should be mentioned the recitation of the rosary: "We now desire, as a continuation of the thought of our predecessors, to recommend strongly the recitation of the family rosary...There is no doubt that...the rosary should be considered as one of the best and most efficacious prayers in common that the Christian family is invited to recite. We like to think and sincerely hope that when the family gathering becomes a time of prayer the rosary is a frequent and favored manner of praying."[155] In this way authentic devotion to Mary, which finds expression in sincere love and generous imitation of the Blessed Virgin's interior spiritual attitude, constitutes a special instrument for nourishing loving communion in the family and for developing conjugal and family spirituality. For she who is the mother of Christ and of the church is in a special way the mother of Christian families, of domestic churches.

62. Prayer and life

It should never be forgotten that prayer constitutes an essential part of Christian life, understood in its fullness and centrality. Indeed, prayer is an important part of our very humanity: It is "the first expression of man's inner truth, the first condition for authentic freedom of spirit."[156]

Far from being a form of escapism from everyday commitments, prayer constitutes the strongest incentive for the Christian family to assume and comply fully with all its responsibilities as the primary and fundamental cell of human society. Thus the Christian family's actual participation in the church's life and mission is in direct proportion to the fidelity and intensity of the prayer with which it is united with the fruitful vine that is Christ the Lord.[157]

The fruitfulness of the Christian family in its specific service to human advancement, which of itself cannot but lead to the transformation of the world, derives from its living union with Christ, nourished by the liturgy, by self-oblation and by prayer.[158]

C. The Christian family as a community at the service of man

63. The new commandment of love

The church, a prophetic, priestly and kingly people, is endowed with the mission of bringing all human beings to accept the word of God in faith, to celebrate and profess it in the sacraments and in prayer, and to give expression to it in the concrete realities of life in accordance with the gift and new commandment of love.

The law of Christian life is to be found not in a written code, but in the personal action of the Holy Spirit who inspires and guides the Christian. It is the "law of the Spirit of life in Christ Jesus":[159] "God's love has been poured into our hearts through the Holy Spirit who has been given to us."[160]

This is true also for the Christian couple and family. Their guide and rule of life is the Spirit of Jesus poured into their hearts in the celebration of the sacrament of matrimony. In continuity with baptism in water and the Spirit, marriage sets forth anew the evangelical law of love, and with the gift of the Spirit engraves it more profoundly on the hearts of Christian husbands and wives. Their love, purified and saved, is a fruit of the Spirit acting in the hearts of believers and constituting, at the same time, the fundamental commandment of their moral life to be lived in responsible freedom.

Thus the Christian family is inspired and guided by the new law of the Spirit and, in intimate communion with the church, the kingly people, it is called to exercise its "service" of love toward God and toward its fellow human beings.

Just as Christ exercises his royal power by serving us,[161] so also the Christian finds the authentic meaning of his participation in the kingship of his Lord in sharing his spirit and practice of service to man. "Christ has communicated this power to his disciples that they might be established in royal freedom and that by self-denial and a holy life they might conquer the reign of sin in themselves (cf. Rom. 6:12). Further, he has shared this power so that by serving him in their fellow human beings they might through humility and patience lead their brothers and sisters to that King whom to serve is to reign. For the Lord wishes to spread his kingdom by means of the laity also, a kingdom of truth and life, a kingdom of holiness and grace, a kingdom of justice, love and peace. In this kingdom, creation itself will be delivered out of its slavery to corruption and into the freedom of the glory of the children of God (cf. Rom. 8:21)'' [162]

64. To discover the image of God in each brother and sister

Inspired and sustained by the new commandment of love, the Christian family welcomes, respects and serves every human being, considering each one in his or her dignity as a person and as a child of God.

It should be so especially between husband and wife and within the family, through a daily effort to promote a truly personal community, initiated and fostered by an inner communion of love. This way of life should then be extended to the wider circle of the ecclesial community of which the Christian family is a part.

Thanks to love within the family, the church can and ought to take on a more homelike or family dimension, developing a more human and fraternal style of relationships.

Love, too, goes beyond our brothers and sisters of the same faith since "everybody is my brother or sister." In each individual, especially in the poor, the weak and those who suffer or are unjustly treated, love knows how to discover the face of Christ, and discover a fellow human being to be loved and served.

In order that the family may serve man in a truly evangelical way, the instructions of the Second Vatican Council must be carefully put into practice: "That the exercise of such charity may rise above any deficiencies in fact and even in appearance, certain fundamentals must be observed. Thus attention is to be paid to the image of God in which our neighbor has been created, and also to Christ the Lord to whom is really offered whatever is given to a needy person." [163]

While building up the church in love, the Christian family places itself at the service of the human person and the world, really bringing about the "human advancement" whose substance was given in summary form in the synod's message to families: "Another task for the family is to form persons in love and also to practice love in all its relationships, so that it does not live closed in on itself, but remains open to the community, moved by a sense of justice and concern for others, as well as by a consciousness of its responsibility toward the whole of society." [164]

PART FOUR
PASTORAL CARE OF THE FAMILY

I. STAGES OF PASTORAL CARE OF THE FAMILY

65. The church accompanies the Christian family on its journey through life

Like every other living reality, the family too is called upon to develop and grow. After the preparation of engagement and the sacramental celebration of marriage, the couple begin their daily journey toward the progressive actuation of the values and duties of marriage itself.

In the light of faith and by virtue of hope, the Christian family, too, shares in communion with the church and in the experience of the earthly pilgrimage toward the full revelation and manifestation of the kingdom of God.

Therefore, it must be emphasized once more that the pastoral intervention of the church in support of the family is a matter of urgency. Every effort should be made to strengthen and develop pastoral care for the family, which should be treated as a real matter of priority, in the certainty that future evangelization depends largely on the domestic church.[165]

The church's pastoral concern will not be limited only to the Christian families closest at hand; it will extend its horizons in harmony with the heart of Christ and will show itself to be even more lively for families in general and for those families in particular which are in difficult or irregular situations. For all of them the church will have a word of truth, goodness, understanding, hope and deep sympathy with their sometimes tragic difficulties. To all of them she will offer her disinterested help so that they can come closer to that model of a family which the creator intended from "the beginning" and which Christ has renewed with his redeeming grace.

The church's pastoral action must be progressive also in the sense that it must follow the family, accompanying it step by step in the different stages of its formation and development.

66. Preparation for marriage

More than ever necessary in our times is preparation of young people for marriage and family life. In some countries it is still the families themselves that, according to ancient customs, ensure the passing on to young people of the values concerning married and family life, and they do this through a gradual process of education or initiation. But the changes that have taken place within almost all modern societies demand that not only the family but also society and the church should be involved in the effort of properly preparing young people for their future responsibilities.

Many negative phenomena which are today noted with regret in family life derive from the fact that in the new situations young people not only lose sight of the correct hierarchy of values but, since they no longer have certain criteria of behavior, they do not know how to face and deal with the new difficulties. But experience teaches that young people who have been well prepared for family life generally succeed better than others.

This is even more applicable to Christian marriage, which influences the holiness of large numbers of men and women. The church must therefore promote better and more intensive programs of marriage preparation in order to eliminate as far as possible the difficulties that many married couples find themselves in, and even more in order to favor positively the establishing and maturing of successful marriages.

Marriage preparation has to be seen and put into practice as a gradual and continuous process. It includes three main stages: remote, proximate and immediate preparation.

Remote preparation begins in early childhood in that wise family training which leads children to discover themselves as beings endowed with a rich and complex psychology and with a particular personality with its own strengths and weaknesses. It is the period when esteem for all authentic human values is instilled, both in interpersonal and in social relationships, with all that this signifies for the formation of character, for the control and right use of one's inclinations, for the manner of regarding and meeting people of the opposite sex, and so on. Also necessary, especially for Christians, is solid spiritual and catechetical formation that will show that marriage is a true vocation and mission, without excluding the possibility of the total gift of self to God in the vocation to the priestly or religious life.

Upon this basis there will subsequently and gradually be built up the proximate preparation, which—from the suitable age and with adequate catechesis, as in a catechumenal process—involves a more specific preparation for the sacraments, as it were, a rediscovery of them. This renewed catechesis of young people and others preparing for Christian marriage is absolutely necessary in order that the sacrament may be celebrated and lived with the right moral and spiritual dispositions. The religious formation of young people should be integrated, at the right moment and in accordance with the various concrete requirements, with a preparation for life as a couple. This preparation will present marriage as an interpersonal relationship of a man and a woman that has to be continually developed, and it will encourage those concerned to study the nature of conjugal sexuality and responsible parenthood, with the essential medical and biological knowledge connected with it. It will also acquaint those concerned with correct methods for the education of children and will assist them in gaining the basic requisites for well-ordered family life, such as stable work, sufficient financial resources, sensible administration, notions of housekeeping.

Finally, one must not overlook preparation for the family apostolate, for fraternal solidarity and collaboration with other families, for active membership in groups, associations, movements and undertakings set up for the human and Christian benefit of the family.

The immediate preparation for the celebration of the sacrament of matrimony should take place in the months and weeks immediately preceding the wedding so as to give a new meaning, content and form to the so-called premarital inquiry required by canon law. This preparation is not only necessary in every case, but is also more urgently needed for engaged couples that still manifest shortcomings or difficulties in Christian doctrine and practice.

Among the elements to be instilled in this journey of faith, which is similar to the catechumenate, there must also be a deeper knowledge of the mystery of Christ and the church, of the meaning of grace and of the responsibility of Christian marriage, as well as preparation for taking an active and conscious part in the rites of the marriage liturgy.

The Christian family and the whole of the ecclesial community should feel involved in the different phases of the preparation for marriage which have been described only in their broad outlines. It is to be hoped that the episcopal conferences, just as they are concerned with appropriate initiatives to help engaged couples to be more aware of the seriousness of their choice and also to help pastors of souls to make sure of the couples' proper dispositions, so they will also take steps to see that there is issued a directory for the pastoral care of the family. In this they should lay down in the first place, the minimum content, duration and method of the "preparation courses," balancing the different aspects—doctrinal, pedagogical, legal and medical—concerning marriage and structuring them in such a way that those preparing for marriage will not only receive an intellectual training, but will also feel a desire to enter actively into the ecclesial community.

Although one must not underestimate the necessity and obligation of the immediate preparation for marriage—which would happen if dispensations from it were easily given—nevertheless such preparation must always be set forth and put into practice in such a way that omitting it is not an impediment to the celebration of marriage.

67. The celebration

Christian marriage normally requires a liturgical celebration expressing in social and community form the essentially ecclesial and sacramental nature of the conjugal covenant between baptized persons.

Inasmuch as it is a sacramental action of sanctification, the celebration of marriage—inserted into the liturgy, which is the summit of the church's action and the source of her sanctifying power[166]—must be *per se* valid, worthy and fruitful. This opens a wide field for pastoral solicitude, in order that the needs deriving from the nature of the conjugal covenant, elevated into a sacrament, may be fully met and also in order that the church's discipline regarding free consent, impediments, the canonical form and the actual rite of the celebration may be faithfully observed. The celebration should be simple and dignified, according to the norms of the competent authorities of the church. It is also for them—in accordance with concrete circumstances of time and place and in conformity with the norms issued by the Apostolic See[167]—to include in the liturgical celebration such elements proper to each culture which serve to express more clearly the profound human and religious significance of the marriage contract, provided that such elements contain nothing that is not in harmony with Christian faith and morality.

Inasmuch as it is a sign, the liturgical celebration should be conducted in such a way as to constitute, also in its external reality, a proclamation of the word of God and a profession of faith on the part of the community of believers, Pastoral commitment will be expressed here through the intelligent and careful preparation of the liturgy of the

64

word and through the education to faith of those participating in the celebration and in the first place the couple being married.

Inasmuch as it is a sacramental action of the church, the liturgical celebration of marriage should involve the Christian community, with the full, active and responsible participation of all those present, according to the place and task of each individual: the bride and bridegroom, the priest, the witnesses, the relatives, the friends, the other members of the faithful, all of them members of an assembly that manifests and lives the mystery of Christ and His church. For the celebration of Christian marriage in the sphere of ancestral cultures or traditions, the principles laid down above should be followed.

68. Celebration of marriage and evangelization of non-believing baptized persons

Precisely because in the celebration of the sacrament very special attention must be devoted to the moral and spiritual dispositions of those being married, in particular to their faith, we must here deal with a not infrequent difficulty in which the pastors of the church can find themselves in the context of our secularized society.

In fact, the faith of the person asking the church for marriage can exist in different degrees, and it is the primary duty of pastors to bring about a rediscovery of this faith and to nourish it and bring it to maturity. But pastors must also understand the reasons that lead the church also to admit to the celebration of marriage those who are imperfectly disposed.

The sacrament of matrimony has this specific element that distinguishes it from all the other sacraments: It is the sacrament of something that was part of the very economy of creation; it is the very conjugal covenant instituted by the Creator "in the beginning." Therefore the decision of a man and a woman to marry in accordance with this divine plan, that is to say, the decision to commit by their irrevocable conjugal consent their whole lives in indissoluble love and unconditional fidelity, really involves, even if not in a fully conscious way, an attitude of profound obedience to the will of God, an attitude which cannot exist without God's grace. They have thus already begun what is in a true and proper sense a journey toward salvation, a journey which the celebration of the sacrament and the immediate preparation for it can complement and bring to completion, given the uprightness of their intention.

On the other hand it is true that in some places engaged couples ask to be married in church for motives which are social rather than genuinely religious. This is not surprising. Marriage, in fact, is not an event that concerns only the persons actually getting married. By its very nature it is also a social matter, committing the couple being married in the eyes of society. And its celebration has always been an occasion of rejoicing that brings together families and friends. It therefore goes without saying that social as well as personal motives enter into the request to be married in church.

Nevertheless, it must not be forgotten that these engaged couples by virtue of their baptism are already really sharers in Christ's marriage covenant with the church, and that, by their right intention, they have accepted God's plan regarding marriage and therefore, at least implicitly, consent to what the church intends to do when she celebrates marriage. Thus the fact that motives of a social nature also enter into the request is not enough to justify refusal on the part of pastors. Moreover, as the Second Vatican Council teaches, the sacraments by words and ritual elements nourish and strengthen faith:[168] that faith toward which the married couple are already journeying by reason of the uprightness of their intention, which Christ's grace certainly does not fail to favor and support.

As for wishing to lay down further criteria for admission to the ecclesial celebration of marriage, criteria that would concern the level of faith of those to be married, this would above all involve grave risks. In the first place, the risk of making unfounded and discriminatory judgments; second, the risk of causing doubts about the validity of marriages already celebrated, with grave harm to Christian communities and new and unjustified anxieties to the consciences of married couples; one would also fall into the danger of calling into question the sacramental nature of many marriages of brethren separated from full communion with the Catholic Church, thus contradicting ecclesial tradition.

However, when in spite of all efforts engaged couples show that they reject explicitly and formally what the church intends to do when the marriage of baptized persons is celebrated, the pastor of souls cannot admit them to the celebration of marriage. In spite of his reluctance to do so, he has the duty to take note of the situation and to make it clear to those concerned that in these circumstances it is not the church that is placing an obstacle in the way of the celebration that they are asking for, but themselves.

Once more there appears in all its urgency the need for evangelization and catechesis before and after marriage, effected by the whole Christian community, so that every man and woman that gets married celebrates the sacrament of matrimony not only validly but also fruitfully.

69. Pastoral care after marriage

The pastoral care of the regularly established family signifies, in practice, the commitment of all the members of the local ecclesial community to helping the couple to discover and live their new vocation and mission. In order that the family may be ever more a true community of love, it is necessary that all its members should be helped and trained in their responsibilities as they face the new problems that arise, in mutual service and in active sharing in family life.

This holds true especially for young families, which, finding themselves in a context of new values and responsibilities, are more vulnerable, especially in the first years of marriage, to possible difficulties such as those created by adaptation to life together or by the birth of children. Young married couples should learn to accept willingly and make good use of the discreet, tactful and generous help offered by other couples that already have more experience of married and family life. Thus within the ecclesial community—the great family made up of Christian families—there will take place a mutual exchange of presence and help among all the families, each one putting at the service of the others its own experience of life, as well as the gifts of faith and grace. Animated by a true apostolic spirit, this assistance from family to family will constitute one of the simplest, most effective and most accessible means for transmitting from one to another those Christian values which are both the starting point and goal of all pastoral care. Thus young families will not limit themselves merely to receiving, but in their turn, having been helped in this way, will become a source of enrichment for other longer established families through their witness of life and practical contribution.

In her pastoral care of young families the church must also pay special attention to helping them to live married love responsibly in relationship with its demands of communion and service to life. She must likewise help them to harmonize the intimacy of home life with the generous shared work of building up the church and society. When children are born and the married couple becomes a family in the full and specific sense, the church will still remain close to the parents in order that they may accept their children and love them as a gift received from the Lord of life and joyfully accept the task of serving them in their human and Christian growth.

II. STRUCTURES OF FAMILY PASTORAL CARE

Pastoral activity is always the dynamic expression of the reality of the church, committed to her mission of salvation. Family pastoral care too—which is a particular and specific form of pastoral activity—has as its operative principle and responsible agent the church herself, through her structures and workers.

70. The ecclesial community and in particular the parish

The church, which is at the same time a saved and a saving community, has to be considered here under two aspects: as universal and particular. The second aspect is expressed and actuated in the diocesan community, which is pastorally divided up into lesser communities of which the parish is of special importance.

Communion with the universal church does not hinder, but rather guarantees and promotes the substance and originality of the various particular churches. These latter remain the more immediate and more effective subjects of operation for putting the pastoral care of the family into practice. In this sense every local church and, in more particular terms, every parochial community must become more vividly aware of the grace and responsibility that it receives from the Lord in order that it may promote the pastoral care of the family. No plan ofr organized pastoral work at any level must ever fail to take into consideration the pastoral area of the family.

Also to be seen in the light of this responsibility is the importance of the proper preparation of all those who will be more specifically engaged in this kind of apostolate. Priests and men and women religious from the time of their formation should be oriented and trained progressively and thoroughly for the various tasks. Among the various initiatives I am pleased to emphasize the recent establishment in Rome, at the Pontifical Lateran University, of a higher institute for the study of the problems of the family. Institutes of this kind have also been set up in some dioceses. Bishops should see to it that as many priests as possible attend specialized courses there before taking on parish responsibilities. Elsewhere, formation courses are periodically held at higher institutes of theological and pastoral studies. Such initiatives should be encouraged, sustained, increased in number, and of course are also open to lay people who intend to use their professional skills (medical, legal, psychological, social or educational) to help the family.

71. The family

But it is especially necessary to recognize the unique place that in this field belongs to the mission of married couples and Christian families by virtue of the grace received in the sacrament. This mission must be placed at the service of the building up of the church, the establishing of the kingdom of God in history. This is demanded as an act of docile obedience to Christ the Lord. For it is he who, by virtue of the fact that marriage of baptized persons has been raised to a sacrament, confers upon Christian married couples a special mission as apostles, sending them as workers into his vineyard and in a very special way into this field of the family.

In this activity married couples act in communion and collaboration with the other members of the church, who also work for the family, contributing their own gifts and ministries. This apostolate will be exercised in the first place within the families of those concerned, through the witness of a life lived in conformity with the divine law in all its aspects, through the Christian formation of the children, through helping them to mature in faith, through education to chastity, through preparation for life, through vigilance in protecting them from the ideological and moral dangers with which they are often threatened, through their gradual and responsible inclusion in the ecclesial community and the civil community, through help and advice in choosing a vocation, through mutual help among family members for human and Christian growth together, and so on. The apostolate of the family will also become wider through works of spiritual and material charity toward other families, especially those most in need of help and support, toward the poor, the sick, the old, the handicapped, orphans, widows, spouses that have been abandoned, unmarried mothers and mothers-to-be in difficult situations who are tempted to have recourse to abortion, and so on.

72. Associations of families for families

Still within the church, which is the subject responsible for the pastoral care of the family, mention should be made of the various groupings of members of the faithful in which the mystery of Christ's church is in some measure manifested and lived. One should therefore recognize and make good use of—each one in relationship to its own characteristics, purposes, effectiveness and methods—the different ecclesial communities, the various groups and the numerous movements engaged in various ways, for different reasons and at different levels, in the pastoral care of the family.

For this reason the synod expressly recognized the useful contribution made by such associations of spirituality, formation and apostolate. It will be their task to foster among the faithful a lively sense of solidarity, to favor a manner of living inspired by the Gospel and by the faith of the church, to form consciences according to Christian values and not according to the standards of public opinion; to stimulate people to perform works of charity for one another and for others with a spirit of openness which will make Christian families into a true source of light and a wholesome leaven for other families.

It is similarly desirable that, with a lively sense of the common good, Christian families should become actively engaged at every level in other non-ecclesial associations as well. Some of these associations work for the preservation, transmission and protection of the wholesome ethical and cultural values of each people, the development of the human person, the medical, juridical and social protection of mothers and young children, the just advancement of women and the struggle against all that is detrimental to their dignity, the increase of mutual solidarity, knowledge of the problems connected with the responsible regulation of fertility in accordance with natural methods that are in conformity with human dignity and the teaching of the church.

Other associations work for the building of a more just and human world; for the promotion of just laws favoring the right social order with full respect for the dignity and every legitimate freedom of the individual and the family on both the national and the international level; for collaboration with the school and with the other institutions that complete the education of children, and so forth.

III. AGENTS OF THE PASTORAL CARE OF THE FAMILY

As well as the family, which is the object but above all the subject of pastoral care of the family, one must also mention the other main agents in this particular sector.

73. Bishops and priests

The person principally responsible in the diocese for the pastoral care of the family is the bishop. As father and pastor, he must exercise particular solicitude in this clearly priority sector of pastoral care. He must devote to it personal interest, care, time, personnel and resources, but above all personal support for the families and for all those who, in the various diocesan structures, assist him in the pastoral care of the family.

It will be his particular care to make the diocese ever more truly a "diocesan family," a model and source of hope for the many families that belong to it. The setting up of the Pontifical Council for the family is to be seen in this light to be a sign of the importance that I attribute to pastoral care for the family in the world, and at the same time to be an effective instrument for aiding and promoting it at every level.

The bishops avail themselves especially of the priests, whose task—as the synod expressly emphasized—constitutes an essential part of the church's ministry regarding marriage and the family. The same is true of deacons to whose care this sector of pastoral work may be entrusted.

Their responsibility extends not only to moral and liturgical matters, but to personal and social matters as well. They must support the family in its difficulties and sufferings, caring for its members and helping them to see their lives in the light of the Gospel. It is not superfluous to note that from this mission, if it is exercised with due discernment and with a truly apostolic spirit, the minister of the church draws fresh encouragement and spiritual energy for his own vocation, too, and for the exercise of his ministry.

Priests and deacons, when they have received timely and serious preparation for this apostolate, must unceasingly act toward families as fathers, brothers, pastors and teachers, assisting them with the means of grace and enlightening them with the light of truth. Their teaching and advice must therefore always be in full harmony with the authentic magisterium of the church, in such a way as to help the people of God to gain a correct sense of the faith to be subsequently applied to practical life. Such fidelity to the magisterium will also enable priests to make every effort to be united in their judgments in order to avoid troubling the consciences of the faithful.

In the church, the pastors and the laity share in the prophetic mission of Christ: The laity do so by witnessing to the faith by their words and by their Christian lives; the pastors do so by distinguishing in that witness what is the expression of genuine faith from what is less in harmony with the light of faith; the family, as a Christian community, does so through its special sharing and witness of faith.

Thus there begins a dialogue also between pastors and families. Theologians and experts in family matters can be of great help in this dialogue. By explaining exactly the content of the church's magisterium and the content of the experience of family life. In this way the teaching of the magisterium becomes better understood and the way is opened to its progressive development.

But it is useful to recall that the proximate and obligatory norm in the teaching of the faith—also concerning family matters—belongs to the hierarchical magisterium. Clearly defined relationships between theologians, experts in family matters and the magisterium are of no little assistance for the correct understanding of the faith and for promoting—within the boundaries of the faith—legitimate pluralism.

74. Men and women religious

The contribution that can be made to the apostolate of the family by men and women religious and consecrated persons in general finds its primary, fundamental and original expression precisely in their consecration to God. By reason of this consecration, "for all Christ's faithful religious recall that wonderful marriage made by God, which will be fully manifested in the future age, and in which the church has Christ for her only spouse,"[169] and they are witnesses to that universal charity which, through chastity embraced for the kingdom of heaven, makes them every more available to dedicate themselves generously to the service of God and to the works of the apostolate.

Hence the possibility for men and women religious and members of secular institutes and other institutes of perfection, either individually or in groups, to develop their service to families, with particular solicitude for children, especially if they are abandoned, unwanted, orphaned, poor or handicapped. They can also visit families and look after the sick; they can foster relationships of respect and charity toward one-parent families or families that are in difficulties or are separated; they can offer their own work of teaching and counseling in the preparation of young people for marriage and in helping couples toward truly responsible parenthood; they can open their own houses for simple and cordial hospitality so that families can find there the sense of God's presence and gain a taste for prayer and recollection and see the practical examples of lives lived in charity and fraternal joy as members of the larger family of God.

I would like to add a most pressing exhortation to the heads of institutes of consecrated life to consider—always with substantial respect for the proper and original charism of each one—the apostolate of the family as one of the priority tasks rendered even more urgent by the present state of the world.

75. Lay specialists

Considerable help can be given to families by lay specialists (doctors, lawyers, psychologists, social workers, consultants, etc.) who either as individuals or as members of various associations and undertakings offer their contribution of enlightenment, advice, orientation and support. To these people one can well apply the exhortations that I had the occasion to address to the Confederation of Family Advisory Bureaus of Christian Inspiration:

"Yours is a commitment that well deserves the title of mission, so noble are the aims that it pursues, and so determining, for the good of society and the Christian community itself, are the results that derive from it...All that you succeed in doing to support the family is destined to have an effectiveness that goes beyond its own sphere and reaches other people too, and has an effect on society. The future of the world and of the church passes through the family." [170]

76. Recipients and agents of social communications

This very important category in modern life deserves a word of its own. It is well known that the means of social communication "affect, and often profoundly, the minds of those who use them, under the affective and intellectual aspect and also under the moral and religious aspect," especially in the case of young people. [171] They can thus exercise a beneficial influence on the life and habits of the family and on the education of children, but at the same time they also conceal "snares and dangers that cannot be ignored." [172] They could also become a vehicle—sometimes cleverly and systematically manipulated, as unfortunately happens in various countries of the world—for divisive ideologies and distorted ways of looking at life, the family, religion and morality, attitudes that lack respect for man's true dignity and destiny.

This danger is all the more real inasmuch as "the modern lifestyle—especially in the more industrialized nations—all too often causes families to abandon their responsibility to educate their children. Evasion of this duty is made easy for them by the presence of television and certain publications in the home, and in this way they keep their children's time and energies occupied." [173] Hence "the duty...to protect the young from the forms of aggression they are subjected to by the mass media," and to ensure that the use of the media in the family is carefully regulated. Families should also take care to seek for their children other forms of entertainment that are more wholesome, useful and physically, morally and spiritually formative, "to develop and use to advantage the free time of the young and direct their energies." [174]

Furthermore, because the means of social communication, like the school and the environment, often have a notable influence on the formation of children, parents as recipients must actively ensure the moderate, critical, watchful and prudent use of the media by discovering what effect they have on their children and by controlling the use of media in such a way as to "train the conscience of their children to express calm and objective judgments, which will then guide them in the choice or rejection of programs available." [175]

With equal commitment parents will endeavor to influence the selection and the preparation of the programs themselves by keeping in contact—through suitable initiatives—with those in charge of the various phases of production and transmission. In this way they will ensure that the fundamental human values that form part of the true good of society are not ignored or deliberately attacked. Rather they will ensure the broadcasting of programs that present in the right light family problems and their proper solution. In this regard my venerated predecessor Paul VI wrote:

"Producers must know and respect the needs of the family, and this sometimes presupposes in them true courage, and always a high sense of responsibility. In fact they are expected to avoid anything that could harm the family in its existence, its stability, its balance and its happiness. Every attack on the fundamental value of the family—meaning eroticism or violence, the defense of divorce or of anti-social attitudes among young people—is an attack on the true good of man."[176]

I myself, on a similar occasion, pointed out that families "to a considerable extent need to be able to count on the good will, integrity and sense of responsiblity of the media professionals—publishers, writers, producers, directors, playwrights, newsmen, commentators and actors."[177] It is therefore also the duty of the church to continue to devote every care to these categories, at the same time encouraging and supporting Catholics who feel the call and have the necessary talents to take up this sensitive type of work.

IV. PASTORAL CARE OF THE FAMILY IN DIFFICULT CASES

77. Particular circumstances

An even more generous, intelligent and prudent pastoral commitment, modeled on the Good Shepherd, is called for in the case of families which, often independently of their own wishes and through pressures of various other kinds, find themselves faced by situations which are objectively difficult.

In this regard it is necessary to call special attention to certain particular groups which are more in need not only of assistance but also of more incisive action upon public opinion and especially upon cultural, economic and juridical structures, in order that the profound causes of their needs may be eliminated as far as possible.

Such, for example, are the families of migrant workers; the families of those obliged to be away for long periods, such as members of the armed forces, sailors and all kinds of itinerant people; the families of those in prison, of refugees and exiles; the families in big cities living, practically speaking, as outcasts; families with no home; incomplete or single-parent families; families with children that are handicapped or addicted to drugs; the families of alcoholics; families that have been uprooted from their cultural and social environment or are in danger of losing it; families discriminated against for political or other reasons; families that are ideologically divided; families that are unable to make ready contact with the parish; families experiencing violence or unjust treatment because of their faith; teen-age married couples; the elderly, who are often obliged to live alone with inadequate means of subsistence.

The families of migrants, especially in the case of manual workers and farm workers, should be able to find a homeland everywhere in the church. This is a task stemming from the nature of the church, as being the sign of unity in diversity. As far as possible these people should be looked after by priests of their own rite, culture and language. It is also the church's task to appeal to the public conscience and to all those in authority in social, economic and political life, in order that workers may find employment in their own regions and homelands, that they may receive just wages, that their families may be reunited as soon as possible, be respected in their cultural identity and treated on an equal footing with others, and that their children may be given the chance to learn a trade and exercise it, as also the chance to own the land needed for working and living.

A difficult problem is that of the family which is ideologically divided. In these cases particular pastoral care is needed. In the first place it is necessary to maintain tactful personal contact with such families. The believing members must be strengthened in their faith and supported in their Christian lives. Although the party faithful to Catholicism cannot give way, dialogue with the other party must always be kept alive. Love and respect must be freely shown in the firm hope that unity will be maintained. Much also depends on the relationship between parents and children. Moreover, ideologies which are alien to the faith can stimulate the believing members of the family to grow in faith and in the witness of love.

Other difficult circumstances in which the family needs the help of the ecclesial community and its pastors are: the children's adolescence, which can be disturbed, rebellious and sometimes stormy; the children's marriage, which takes them away from their family; lack of understanding or lack of love on the part of those held most dear; abandonment by one of the spouses or his or her death, which brings the painful experience of widowhood, or the death of a family member, which breaks up and deeply transforms the original family nucleus.

Similarly, the church cannot ignore the time of old age with all its positive and negative aspects. In old age married love, which has been increasingly purified and ennobled by long and unbroken fidelity, can be deepened. There is the opportunity of offering to others in a new form the kindness and the wisdom gathered over the years and what energies remain. But there is also the burden of loneliness, more often psychological and emotional rather than physical, which results from abandonment or neglect on the part of children and relations. There is also suffering caused by ill-health, by the gradual loss of strength, by the humiliation of having to depend on others, by the sorrow of feeling that one is perhaps a burden to one's loved ones, and by the approach of the end of life. These are the circumstances in which, as the synod fathers suggested, it is easier to help people understand and live the lofty aspects of the spirituality of marriage and the family, aspects which take their inspiration from the value of Christ's cross and resurrection, the source of sanctification and profound happiness in daily life, in the light of the great eschatological realities of eternal life.

In all these different situations let prayer, the source of light and strength and the nourishment of Christian hope, never be neglected.

78. Mixed Marriages

The growing number of mixed marriages between Catholics and other baptized persons also calls for special pastoral attention in the light of the directives and norms contained in the most recent documents of the Holy See and in those drawn up by the episcopal conferences, in order to permit their practical application to the various situations.

Couples living in a mixed marriage have special needs, which can be put under three main headings.

In the first place, attention must be paid to the obligations that faith imposes on the Catholic party with regard to the free exercise of the faith and the consequent obligation to ensure, as far as is possible, the baptism and upbringing of the children in the Catholic faith.[178]

There must be borne in mind the particular difficulties inherent in the relationships between husband and wife with regard to respect for religious freedom: This freedom could be violated either by undue pressure to make the partner change his or her beliefs or by placing obstacles in the way of the free manifestation of these beliefs by religious practice.

With regard to the liturgical and canonical form of marriage, ordinaries can make wide use of their faculties to meet various necessities.

In dealing with these special needs, the following points should be kept in mind:

—In the appropriate preparation for this type of marriage every reasonable effort must be made to ensure a proper understanding of

Catholic teaching on the qualities and obligations of marriage and also to ensure that the pressures and obstacles mentioned above will not occur.

—It is of the greatest importance that through the support of the community the Catholic party should be strengthened in faith and positively helped to mature in understanding and practicing that faith so as to become a credible witness within the family through his or her own life and through the quality of love shown to the other spouse and the children.

Marriages between Catholics and other baptized persons have their particular nature, but they contain numerous elements that could well be made good use of and developed, both for their intrinsic value and for the contribution that they can make to the ecumenical movement. This is particularly true when both parties are faithful to their religious duties. Their common baptism and the dynamism of grace provide the spouses in these marriages with the basis and motivation for expressing their unity in the sphere of moral and spiritual values.

For this purpose and also in order to highlight the ecumenical importance of mixed marriages which are fully lived in the faith of the two Christian spouses an effort should be made to establish cordial cooperation between the Catholic and the non-Catholic ministers from the time that preparations begin for the marriage and the wedding ceremony even though this does not always prove easy.

With regard to the sharing of the non-Catholic party in eucharistic communion, the norms issued by the Secretariat for Promoting Christian Unity should be followed.[179]

Today in many parts of the world marriages between Catholics and non-baptized persons are growing in numbers. In many such marriages the non-baptized partner professes another religion and his beliefs are to be treated with respect in accordance with the principles set out in the Second Vatican Council's declaration *Nostra Aetate* on relations with non-Christian religions. But in many other such marriages, particularly in secularized societies, the non-baptized person professes no religion at all. In these marriages there is a need for episcopal conferences and for individual bishops to ensure that there are proper pastoral safeguards for the faith of the Catholic partner and for the free exercise of his faith, above all in regard to his duty to do all in his power to ensure the Catholic baptism and education of the children of the marriage. Likewise the Catholic must be assisted in every possible way to offer within his family a genuine witness to the Catholic faith and to Catholic life.

79. Pastoral action in certain irregular situations

In its solicitude to protect the family in all its dimensions, not only the religious one, the Synod of Bishops did not fail to take into careful consideration certain situations which are irregular in a religious sense and often in the civil sense too. Such situations, as a result of today's rapid cultural changes, are unfortunately becoming widespread also among Catholics with no little damage to the very institution of the family and to society, of which the family constitutes the basic cell.

80. a. *Trial marriages*

A first example of an irregular situation is provided by what are called "trial marriages," which many people today would like to justify by attributing a certain value to them. But human reason leads one to see that they are unacceptable, by showing the unconvincing nature of carrying out an "experiment" with human beings, whose dignity demands that they should be always and solely the term of a self-giving love without limitations of time or of any other circumstance.

The church, for her part, cannot admit such a kind of union for further and original reasons which derive from faith. For, in the first place, the gift of the body in the sexual relationship is a real symbol of the giving of the whole person: Such a giving, moreover, in the present state of things cannot take place with full truth without the concourse of the love of charity, given by Christ. In the second place, marriage between two baptized persons is a real symbol of the union of Christ and the church, which is not a temporary or "trial" union, but one which is eternally faithful. Therefore between two baptized persons there can exist only an indissoluble marriage.

Such a situation cannot usually be overcome unless the human person from childhood, with the help of Christ's grace and without fear, has been trained to dominate concupiscence from the beginning and to establish relationships of genuine love with other people. This cannot be secured without a true education in genuine love and in the right use of sexuality, such as to introduce the human person in every aspect, and therefore the bodily aspect too, into the fullness of the mystery of Christ.

It will be very useful to investigate the causes of this phenomenon, including its psychological and sociological aspect, in order to find the proper remedy.

81. *b. De facto free unions*

This means unions without any publicly recognized institutional bond, either civil or religious. This phenomenon, which is becoming ever more frequent, cannot fail to concern pastors of souls, also because it may be based on widely varying factors, the consequences of which may perhaps be containable by suitable action.

Some people consider themselves almost forced into a free union by difficult economic, cultural or religious situations, on the grounds that if they would be exposed to some form of harm, would lose economic advantages, would be discriminated against, etc. In other cases, however, one encounters people who scorn, rebel against or reject society, the institution of the family and the social and political order, or who are solely seeking pleasure. Then there are those who are driven to such situations by extreme ignorance or poverty, sometimes by a conditioning due to situations of real injustice or by a certain psychological immaturity that makes them uncertain or afraid to enter into a stable and definitive union. In some countries traditional customs presume that the true and proper marriage will take place only after a period of cohabitation and the birth of the first child.

Each of these elements presents the church with arduous pastoral problems, by reason of the serious consequences deriving from them, both religious and moral (the loss of the religious sense of marriage seen in the light of the covenant of God with his people; deprivation of the grace of the sacrament; grave scandal) and also social consequences (the destruction of the concept of the family; the weakening of the sense of fidelity, also toward society; possible psychological damage to the children; the strengthening of selfishness).

The pastors and the ecclesial community should take care to become acquainted with such situations and their actual causes, case by case. They should make tactful and respectful contact with the couples concerned and enlighten them patiently, correct them charitably and show them the witness of Christian family life in such a way as to smooth the path for them to regularize their situation. But above all there must be a campaign of prevention, by fostering the sense of fidelity in the whole moral and religious training of the young, instructing them concerning

80

the conditions and structures that favor such fidelity, without which there is no true freedom; they must be helped to reach spiritual maturity and enabled to understand the rich human and supernatural reality of marriage as a sacrament.

82. c. *Catholics in civil marriages*

There are increasing cases of Catholics who for ideological or practical reasons prefer to contract a merely civil marrage and who reject or at least defer religious marriage. Their situation cannot, of course, be likened to that of people simply living together without any bond at all, because in the present case there is at least a certain commitment to a properly defined and probably stable state of life even though the possiblility of a future divorce is often present in the minds of those entering a civil marriage. By seeking public recognition of their bond on the part of the state, such couples show that they are ready to accept not only its advantages but also its obligations. Nevertheless, not even this situation is acceptable to the church.

The aim of pastoral action will be to make these people understand the need for consistency between their choice of life and the faith that they profess, and to try to do everything possible to induce them to regularize their situation in the light of Christian principles. While treating them with great charity and bringing them into the life of the respective communities, the pastors of the church will regrettably not be able to admit them to the sacraments.

83. d. *Separated or divorced persons who have not remarried*

Various reasons can unfortunately lead to the often irreparable breakdown of valid marriages. These include mutual lack of understanding and the inability to enter into interpersonal relationships. Obviously, separation must be considered as a last resort, after all other reasonable attempts at reconciliation have proved vain.

Loneliness and other difficulties are often the lot of separated spouses especially when they are the innocent parties. The ecclesial community must support such people more than ever. It must give them much respect, solidarity, understanding and practical help, so that they can preserve their fidelity even in their difficult situation; and it must help them to cultivate the need to forgive which is inherent in Christian love and to be ready perhaps to return to their former married life.

The situation is similar for people who have undergone divorce, but, being well aware that the valid marriage bond is indissoluble, refrain from becoming involved in a new union and devote themselves solely to carrying out their family duties and the responsibilities of Christian life. In such cases their example of fidelity and Christian consistency takes on particular value as a witness before the world and the church. Here it is even more necessary for the church to offer continual love and assistance without there being any obstacle to admission to the sacraments.

84. e. *Divorced persons who have remarried*

Daily experience unfortunately shows that people who have obtained a divorce usually intend to enter into a new union, obviously not with a Catholic religious ceremony. Since this is an evil that like the others is affecting more and more Catholics as well, the problem must be faced with resolution and without delay. The synod fathers studied it expressly. The church, which was set up to lead to salvation all people and especially the baptized, cannot abandon to their own devices those who have been previously bound by sacramental marriage and who have attempted a second marriage. The church will therefore make untiring efforts to put at their disposal her means of salvation.

Pastors must know that for the sake of truth they are obliged to exercise careful discernment of situations. There is, in fact, a difference between those who have sincerely tried to save their first marriage and have been unjustly abandoned and those who, through their own grave fault, have destroyed a canonically valid marriage.

Finally, there are those who have entered into a second union for the sake of the children's upbringing and who are sometimes subjectively certain in conscience that their previous and irreparably destroyed marriage had never been valid.

Together with the synod, I earnestly call upon pastors and the whole community of the faithful to help the divorced and with solicitous care to make sure that they do not consider themselves as separated from the church, for as baptized persons they can and indeed must share in her life. They should be encouraged to listen to the word of God, to attend the sacrifice of the Mass, to persevere in prayer, to contribute to works of charity and to community efforts in favor of justice, to bring up their children in the Christian faith, to cultivate the spirit and practice of penance and thus implore, day by day, God's grace. Let the church pray for them, encourage them and show herself a merciful mother and thus sustain them in faith and hope.

However, the church reaffirms her practice, which is based upon sacred scripture, of not admitting to eucharistic communion divorced persons who have remarried. They are unable to be admitted thereto from the fact that their state and condition of life objectively contradict that union of love between Christ and the church which is signified and effected by the eucharist. Besides this there is another special pastoral reason: If these people were admitted to the eucharist the faithful would be led into error and confusion regarding the church's teaching about the indissolubility of marriage.

Reconciliation in the sacrament of penance, which would open the way to the eucharist, can only be granted to those who, repenting of having broken the sign of the convenant and of fidelity to Christ, are sincerely ready to undertake a way of life that is no longer in contradiction to the indissolubility of marriage.

This means, in practice, that when, for serious reasons such as, for example, the children's upbringing, a man and a woman cannot satisfy the obligation to separate, they "take on themselves the duty to live in complete continence, that is, by abstinence from the acts proper to married couples." [180]

Similarly, the respect due to the sacrament of matrimony, to the couples themselves and their families, and also to the community of the faithful forbids any pastor for whatever reason or pretext, even of a pastoral nature, to perform ceremonies of any kind for divorced people who remarry. Such ceremonies would give the impression of the celebration of a new, sacramentally valid marriage and would thus lead people into error concerning the indissolubility of a validly contracted marriage.

By acting in this way the church professes her own fidelity to Christ and to his truth. At the same time she shows motherly concern for these children of hers, especially those who, through no fault of their own, have been abandoned by their legitimate partner.

With firm confidence she believes that those who have rejected the Lord's command and are still living in this state will be able to obtain from God the grace of conversion and salvation, provided that they have persevered in prayer, penance and charity.

85. Those without a family

I wish to add a further word for a category of people whom, as a result of the actual circumstances in which they are living, and this often not through their own deliberate wish, I consider particularly close to the heart of Christ and deserving of the affection and active solicitude of the church and of pastors.

There exist in the world countless people who unfortunately cannot in any sense claim membership in what could be called, in the proper sense, a family. Large sections of humanity live in conditions of extreme poverty in which promiscuity, lack of housing, the irregular nature and instability of relationships and the extreme lack of education make it impossible in practice to speak of a true family. There are others who for various reasons have been left alone in the world. And yet for all of these people there exists a "good news of the family."

On behalf of those living in extreme poverty I have already spoken of the urgent need to work courageously in order to find solutions also at the political level, which will make it possible to help them and to overcome this inhuman condition of degradation.

It is a special task that faces the whole of society, but in a special way the authorities, by reason of their position and the responsibilities flowing therefrom, and also families, which must show great understanding and willingness to help.

For those who have no natural family the doors of the great family which is the church—the church which finds concrete expression in the diocesan and the parish family, in ecclesial basic communities and in movements of the apostolate—must be opened even wider. No one is without a family in this world: The church is a home and family for everyone, especially those who "labor and are heavy laden."[181]

86. CONCLUSION

At the end of this apostolic exhortation my thoughts turn with earnest solicitude:

To you, married couples, to you, fathers and mothers of families;

To you, young men and women, the future and the hope of the church and the world, destined to be the dynamic central nucleus of the family in the approaching third millennium;

To you, venerable and dear brothers in the episcopate and in the priesthood, beloved sons and daughters in the religious life, souls consecrated to the Lord, who bear witness before married couples to the ultimate reality of the love of God;

To you, upright men and women, who for any reason whatever give thought to the fate of the family.

The future of humanity passes by way of the family.

It is therefore indispensable and urgent that every person of good will should endeavor to save and foster the values and requirements of the family.

I feel that I must ask for a particular effort in this field from the sons and daughters of the church. Faith gives them full knowledge of God's wonderful plan: They therefore have an extra reason for caring for the reality that is the family in this time of trial and of grace.

They must show the family special love. This is an injunction that calls for concrete action.

Loving the family means being able to appreciate its values and capabilities, fostering them always. Loving the family means identifying the dangers and the evils that menace it in order to overcome them. Loving the family means endeavoring to create for it an environment favorable for its development. The modern Christian family is often tempted to be discouraged and is distressed at the growth of its difficulties; it is an eminent form of love to give it back its reasons for confidence in itself, in the riches that it possesses by nature and grace, and in the mission that God has entrusted to it. "Yes, indeed, the families of today must be called back to their original position. They must follow Christ." [182]

Christians also have the mission of proclaiming with joy and conviction the good news about the family, for the family absolutely needs to hear ever anew and to understand ever more deeply the authentic words that reveal its identity, its inner resources and the importance of its mission in the city of God and in that of man.

The church knows the path by which the family can reach the heart of the deepest truth about itself. The church has learned this path at the school of Christ and the school of history interpreted in the light of the Spirit. She does not impose it, but she feels an urgent need to propose it to everyone without fear and indeed with great confidence and hope, although she knows that the good news includes the subject of the cross. But it is through the cross that the family can attain the fullness of its being and the perfection of its love.

Finally, I wish to call on all Christians to collaborate cordially and courageously with all people of good will who are serving the family in accordance with their responsibilities. The individuals and groups, movements and associations in the church which devote themselves to the family's welfare, acting in the Church's name and under her inspiration, often find themselves side by side with other individuals and institutions working for the same ideal. With faithfulness to the values of the Gospel and of the human person and with respect for lawful pluralism in initiatives, this collaboration can favor a more rapid and integral advancement of the family.

And now, at the end of my pastoral message, which is intended to draw everyone's attention to the demanding yet fascinating roles of the Christian family, I wish to invoke the protection of the Holy Family of Nazareth.

Through God's mysterious design, it was in that family that the Son of God spent long years of a hidden life. It is therefore the prototype and example for all Christian families. It was unique in the world. Its life was passed in anonymity and silence in a little town in Palestine. It underwent trials of poverty, persecution and exile. It glorified God in an incomparably exalted and pure way. And it will not fail to help Christian families—indeed all the families in the world—to be faithful to their day-to-day duties, to bear the cares and tribulations of life, to be open and generous to the needs of others and to fulfill with joy the plan of God in their regard.

St. Joseph was "a just man," a tireless worker, the upright guardian of those entrusted to his care. May he always guard, protect and enlighten families.

May the Virgin Mary, who is the mother of the church, also be the mother of "the church of the home." Thanks to her motherly aid, may each Christian family really become a "little church" in which the mystery of the church of Christ is mirrored and given new life. May she, the handmaid of the Lord, be an example of humble and generous acceptance of the will of God. May she, the sorrowful mother at the foot of the cross, comfort the sufferings and dry the tears of those in distress because of the difficulties of their families.

May Christ the Lord, the universal king, the king of families, be present in every Christian home as he was at Cana, bestowing light, joy, serenity and strength. On the solemn day dedicated to his kingship I beg of him that every family may generously make its own contribution to the coming of his kingdom in the world—"a kingdom of truth and life, a kingdom of holiness and grace, a kingdom of justice, love and peace,"[183] toward which history is journeying.

I entrust each family to him, to Mary and to Joseph. To their hands and their hearts I offer this exhortation: May it be they who present it to you, venerable brothers and beloved sons and daughters, and may it be they who open your hearts to the light that the Gospel sheds on every family.

I assure you all of my constant prayers and I cordially impart the apostolic blessing to each and every one of you, in the name of the Father, and of the Son and of the Holy Spirit.

Given in Rome, at St. Peter's, Nov. 22, 1981, the solemnity of our Lord Jesus Christ, universal king, the fourth of the pontificate.

NOTES

[1] Cf. Second Vatican Council, *Gaudium et Spes*, 52.

[2] Cf. John Paul II, Homily for the Opening of the Sixth Synod of Bishops (Sept. 26, 1980), 2: AAS 72 (1980), 1008.

[3] Cf. Gn. 1–2.

[4] Cf. Eph. 5.

[5] Cf. Second Vatican Council, GS, 47; Pope John Paul II, Letter *Appropinquat Iam* (Aug. 15, 1980), 1: AAS 72 (1980), 791.

[6] Cf. Mt. 19:4.

[7] Cf. Second Vatican Council, GS, 47.

[8] Cf. John Paul II, Address to Council of the General Secretariat of the Synod of Bishops (Feb. 23, 1980): *Insegnamenti di Giovanni Paolo II,*) III, 1 (1980), 472–476.

[9] Cf. Second Vatican Council, GS, 4.

[10] Cf. Second Vatican Council, *Lumen Gentium,* 12.

[11] Cf. 1 Jn. 2:20.

[12] Second Vatican Council, LG, 35.

[13] Cf. Second Vatican Council, LG, 12; Congregation for the Doctrine of the Faith, Declaration *Mysterium Ecclesiae,* 2: AAS 65 (1973), 398–400.

[14] Cf. Second Vatican Council, LG, 12; *Dei Verbum,* 10.

[15] Cf. John Paul II, Homily for the Opening of the Sixth Synod of Bishops, 3.

[16] Cf. St. Augustine, *De Civitate Dei,* XIV, 28; CSEL 40, II, 56–57.

[17] GS, 15.

[18] Cf. Eph. 3:8; Second Vatican Council, GS, 44; *Ad Gentes,* 15,22.

[19] Cf. Mt. 19:4–6.

[20] Cf. Gn. 1:26–27.

[21] 1 Jn. 4:8.

[22] Cf. Second Vatican Council, GS, 12.

[23] Cf. *Ibid.,* 48.

[24] Cf. e.g., Hos. 2:21; Jer. 3:6–13; Is. 54.

[25] Ez. 16:25.

[26] Cf. Hos. 3.

[27] Cf. Gn. 2:24; Mt. 19:5.

[28] Cf. Eph. 5:32–33.

[29] Tertullian, *Ad Uxorem,* II, VIII, 6–8: CCL, I, 393.

[30] Cf. Council of Trent, Session XXIV, Canon 1: I.D. Mansi, *Sacrorum Conciliorum Nova et Amplissima Collectio,* 33, 149–150.

[31] Cf. Second Vatican Council, GS, 48.

[32] John Paul II, Address to the delegates of the *Centre de Liaison des Equipes de Recherche* (Nov. 3, 1979), 3: *Insegnamenti* II, 2 (1979), 1038.

[33] *Ibid.,* 4; *loc. cit.,* 1032.

[34] Cf. Second Vatican Council, GS, 50.

[35] Cf. Gn. 2:24.

[36] Eph. 3:15.

[37] Cf. Second Vatican Council, GS, 78.

[38] St. John Chrysostom, *Virginity,* X: PG 48:540.

[39] Cf. Mt. 22:30.

[40] Cf. 1 Cor. 7:32–35.

[41] Second Vatican Council, *Perfectae Caritatis,* 12.

[42] Cf. Pius XII, Encyclical *Sacra Virginitas,* II: AAS 46 (1954), 174ff.

[43] Cf. John Paul II, Letter *Novo Incipiente* (April 8, 1979), 9: AAS 71 (1979), 410–411.

[44] Second Vatican Council, GS, 48.

[45] Encyclical *Redemptor Hominis,* 10: AAS 71 (1979), 274.

[46] Mt. 19:6; cf. Gn. 2:24.

[47] Cf. John Paul II, Address to Married Peopel at Kinshasa (May 3, 1980) 4: AAS 72 (1980), 426–427.

[48] GS, 49; cf. John Paul II, Address at Kinshasa 4: *loc. cit.*

[49] Second Vatican Council, GS, 48.

[50] Cf. Eph. 5:25.

[51] Mt. 19:8.

[52] Rv. 3:14.

[53] Cf. 2 Cor. 1:20.

[54] Cf. Jn. 13:1.

[55] Mt. 19:6.

[56] Rom. 8:29.

[57] St. Thomas Aquinas, *Summa Theologiae,* II–II, q. 14, art. 2, ad 4.

[58] Second Vatican Council, LG, 11; cf. *Apostolicam Actuositatem,* 11.

[59] Second Vatican Council, GS, 52.

[60] Cf. Eph. 6:1–4; Col. 3:20–21.

[61] Cf. Second Vatican Council, GS, 48.

[62] Jn. 17:21.

[63] Cf. Second Vatican Council, GS, 24.

[64] Gn. 1:27.

[65] Gal. 3:26, 28.

[66] Cf. John Paul II, Encyclical *Laborem Exercens,* 19: AAS 73 (1981), 625.

[67] Gn. 2:18.

[68] Gn. 2:23.

[69] St. Ambrose, *Exameron,* V 7, 19: CSEL 32, I, 154.

[70] Paul VI, Encyclical *Humanae Vitae,* 9: AAS 60 (1968), 486.

[71] Cf. Eph. 5:25.

[72] Cf. John Paul II, Homily to the Faithful of Terni (March 19, 1981), 3-5: AAS 73 (1981), 268-271.

[73] Cf. Eph. 3:15.

[74] Cf. Second Vatican Council, GS, 52.

[75] Lk. 18:16; cf. Mt. 19:14; Mk. 18:16.

[76] John Paul II, Address to the General Assembly of the United Nations (Oct. 2, 1979), 21: AAS 71 (1979), 1159.

[77] Lk. 2:52.

[78] Cf. Second Vatican Council, GS, 48.

[79] John Paul II, Address to the Participants in the International Forum on Active Aging (Sept. 5, 1980), 5: *Insegnamenti*, III, 2 (1980), 539.

[80] Gn. 1:28.

[81] Cf. Gn. 5:1-3.

[82] Second Vatican Council, GS, 50.

[83] *Propositio* 21. Section 11 of the encyclical *Humanae Vitae* ends with the statement: "The church, calling people back to the observance of the norms of the natural law, as interpreted by her constant doctrine, teaches that each and every marriage act must remain open to the transmission of life (*ut quilibet matrimonii usus ad vitam humanam procreandam per se destinatus permaneat*)": AAS 60 (1968), 488.

[84] Cf. 2 Cor. 1:19; Rv. 3:14.

[85] Cf. The sixth Synod of Bishops' Message to Christian Families in the Modern World (Oct. 24, 1980), 5.

[86] GS, 51.

[87] Encyclical *Humanae Vitae,* 7: AAS 60 (1968), 485.

[88] *Ibid.,* 12: *loc. cit.,* 488-489.

[89] *Ibid.,* 14: *loc. cit.,* 490.

[90] *Ibid.,* 13: *loc. cit.,m* 489.

[91] Cf. Second Vatican Council, GS, 51.

[92] Encyclical *Humanae Vitae,* 29: AAS 60 (1968), 501.

[93] Cf. *Ibid.,* 25: *loc. cit.,* 498-499.

[94] *Ibid.,* 21: *loc. cit.,* 496.

[95] John Paul II, Homily at the Close of the Sixth Synod of Bishops (Oct. 25, 1980), 8: AAS 72 (1980), 1083.

[96] Cf. Paúl VI, Encyclical *Humanae Vitae,* 28: AAS 60 (1968), 501.

[97] Cf. John Paul II, Address to the Delegates of the *Centre de Liaison des Equipes de Recherche* (Nov. 3, 1979), 9: *Insegnamenti*, II, 2 (1979), 1035; and cf. Address to the Participants in the First Congress for the Family of Africa and Europe (Jan. 15, 1981): L'Osservatore Romano, Jan. 16, 1981.

[98] Encyclical *Humanae Vitae,* 25: AAS 60 (1968), 499.

[99] *Gravissimum Educationis,* 3.

[100] Second Vatican Council, GS, 35.

[101] St. Thomas Aquinas, *Summa Contra Gentiles,* IV, 58.

[102] GE, 2.

[103] Apostolic exhortation *Evangelii Nuntiandi,* 71: AAS 68 (1976), 60–61.

[104] Cf. Second Vatican Council, GE, 3.

[105] Second Vatican Council, AA, 11.

[106] GS, 52.

[107] Cf. Second Vatican Council, AA, 11.

[108] Rom. 12:13.

[109] Mt. 10:42.

[110] Cf. GS, 30.

[111] Second Vatican Council, *Dignitatis Humanae,* 5.

[112] Cf. *Propositio* 42.

[113] Second Vatican Council, LG, 31.

[114] Cf. Second Vatican Council, LG, 11; AA, II; Pope John Paul II, Homily for the Opening of the Sixth Synod of Bishops (Sept. 26, 1980), 3: AAS 72 (1980) 1008.

[115] Second Vatican Council, LG, 11.

[116] Cf. *Ibid.,* 41.

[117] Acts 4:32.

[118] Cf. Paul VI, *Humanae Vitae,* 9.

[119] GS, 48.

[120] Cf. Second Vatican Council, DV, 1.

[121] Rom. 16:26.

[122] Cf. Paul VI, *Humanae Vitae,* 25.

[123] *Evangelii Nuntiandi,* 71.

[124] Cf. Address to the Third General Assembly of the Bishops of Latin America (Jan. 28, 1979), IV A: AAS 71 (1979), 204.

[125] Second Vatican Council, LG, 35.

[126] John Paul II, Apostolic Exhortation *Catechesi Tradendae,* 68: AAS 71 (1979), 1334.

[127] Cf. *Ibid.,* 36: *loc. cit.,* 1308.

[128] Cf. 1 Cor. 12:4–6; Eph. 4:12–13.

[129] Mk. 16:15.

[130] Cf. Second Vatican Council, LG, 11.

[131] Acts 1:8.

[132] Cf. 1 Pt. 3:1–2.

[133] Second Vatican Council, LG, 35; cf. AA, 11.

[134] Cf. Acts 18; Rom. 16:3–4.

[135] Cf. Second Vatican Council, AG, 39.

[136] Second Vatican Council, AA, 30.

[137] Cf. Second Vatican Council, LG, 10.

[138] Second Vatican Council, GS, 49.

[139] *Ibid.,* 48.

[140] Cf. Second Vatican Council, LG, 41.

[141] Second Vatican Council, *Sacrosanctum Concilium,* 59.

[142] Cf. 1 Pt. 2:5; Second Vatican Council, LG, 34.

[143] Second Vatican Council, LG, 34.

[144] SC, 78.

[145] Cf. Jn. 19:34.

[146] Section 25: AAS 60 (1968), 499.

[147] Eph. 2:4.

[148] Cf. John Paul II, Encyclical *Dives in Misericordia,* 13: AAS 72 (1980) 1218–1219.

[149] 1 Pt. 2:5.

[150] Mt. 18:19–20.

[151] Second Vatican Council, GE, 3; cf. Pope John Paul II, *Catechesi Tradendae,* 36: AAS 71 (1979), 1308.

[152] General Audience Address, Aug. 11, 1976: *Insegnamenti di Paolo VI,* XIV (1976), 640.

[153] Cf. SC, 12.

[154] Cf. *Institutio Generalis de Liturgia Horarum,* 27.

[155] Paul VI, Apostolic Exhortation *Marialis Cultus,* 52, 54: AAS 66 (1974), 160–161.

[156] John Paul II, Address at the Mentorella Shrine (Oct. 29, 1978): *Insegnamenti,* I (1978), 78–79.

[157] Cf. Second Vatican Council, AA, 4.

[158] Cf. John Paul I, Address to the Bishops of the 12th Pastoral Region of the United States (Sept. 21, 1978): AAS, 70 (1978), 767.

[159] Rom. 8:2.

[160] Rom. 5:5.

[161] Cf. Mk. 10:45.

[162] Second Vatican Council, LG, 36.

[163] AA, 8.

[164] Cf. Synod of Bishops' Message to Christian Families (Oct. 24, 1980), 12.

[165] Cf. John Paul II, Address to the Third General Assembly of the Bishops of Latin America (Jan. 28, 1979), IV A: AAS 71 (1979), 204.

[166] Cf. Second Vatican Council, SC, 10.

[167] Cf. *Ordo Celebrandi Matrimonium,* 17.

[168] Cf. Second Vatican Council, SC, 59.

[169] Second Vatican Council, PC, 12.

[170] John Paul II, Address to the Confederation of Family Advisory Bureaus of Christian Inspiration (Nov. 29, 1980), 3–4: *Insegnamenti* III, 2 (1980), 1453–1454.

[171] Paul VI, Message for the Third Social Communications Day (April 7,

1969): AAS 61 (1969), 455.

[172] John Paul II, Message for the 1980 World Social Communications Day (May 1, 1980): *Insegnamenti* III, 1 (1980), 1042.

[173] John Paul II, Message for the 1981 World Social Communications Day (May 10, 1981), 5: L'Osservatore Romano, May 22, 1981.

[174] *Ibid.*

[175] Paul VI, Message for the Third Social Communications Day: AAS 61 (1969), 456.

[176] *Ibid.*

[177] John Paul II, Message for the 1980 World Social Communications Day, *loc. sit.,* 1044.

[178] Cf. Paul VI, Motu Proprio *Matrimonia Mixta,* 4–5: AAS 62 (1970), 257–259; John Paul II, Address to the Participants in the Plenary Meeting of the Secretariat for Promoting Christian Unity (Nov. 13, 1981): L'Osservatore Romano, Nov. 14, 1981.

[179] Instruction *In Quibus Rerum Circumstantiis* (June 15, 1972): AAS 64 (1972), 518–525; Note of Oct. 17, 1973; AAS 65 (1973), 616–619.

[180] John Paul II, Homily at the Close of the Sixth Synod of Bishops, 7 (Oct. 25, 1980): AAS 72 (1980), 1082.

[181] Mt. 11:28.

[182] John Paul II, Letter *Appropinquat Iam* (Aug. 15, 1980), 1: AAS 72 (1980), 791.

[183] The Roman Missal, Preface of Christ the King.